Children's Literature: Resource for the Classroom

Children's Literature: Resource for the Classroom

Masha Kabakow Rudman
Editor

Christopher-Gordon Publishers, Inc.
Norwood, MA

Credit Lines

Christopher-Gordon Publishers, Inc.
480 Washington Street
Norwood, MA 02062

Printed in the United States of America
10 9 8 7 6 5 4 3 2   98 97 96 95 94

ISBN 0-926842-31-5

Dedication

To my daughters, Rachel, Reva, and Deborah for helping me to see different perspectives and for the joy I've experienced in bringing them up.

Table of Contents

Part II: Perspectives on Evaluation and Selection in Children's Literature

Chapter 6: Multicultural Children's Literature: The Search for Universals 113

Chapter 7: Selection as a Means of Diffusing Censorship 147

Part III: Literature In and Beyond the Classroom

Chapter 8: Children's Literature in the Reading Program 171

Chapter 9: Poetry — Practically 201
Lee Bennett Hopkins

Chapter 10: Global Education and Children's Literature 211
Jennifer Ladd

Preface

Children's Literature: Resource for the Classroom is designed for teachers who wish to make the best use of children's literature in the classroom. General background information, specific ideas and suggestions for evaluating, selecting, and using a variety of books with children are provided. Topics were identified through surveys and informal conversations with elementary classroom teachers and reading specialists, and, once determined, an acknowledged authority in each field was asked to contribute to the volume.

The book is divided into three parts. Part I: Context and Background for Using Children's Literature in the Classroom gives readers background and context for children's literature from an historical perspective and basic information on the genres through a number of brief, informative sketches on leading authors and illustrators of children's books. With the knowledge and insight gained from Part I, readers may move to Part II: Perspectives on Evaluation and Selection in Children's Literature.

In Part II, readers will find information that will enable them to make informed decisions about the books they use in their classrooms. Selection and evaluation are no longer purely personal. There are so many books published each year that it is impossible for teachers to keep up with them all. Even though book reviewers bring some order to the vast numbers, from those reviewed volumes, teachers still must decide which books to use with their classes. The chapters in this section offer general as well as specific guidelines for evaluating and selecting books for both general classroom use and more specific goals. One chapter also addresses the topic of selection and how its process may help diffuse problems caused by attempts at censorship.

Part III: Literature In and Beyond the Classroom, covers how literature can be used in a classroom reading program and how such a program compares favorably with more traditional approaches. One chapter recommends the integration of literature into the social studies curriculum, particularly when a global perspective is desired. The family-school relationship is also explored, and specific recommendations are offered for promoting this crucial partnership.

Julius Lester offers an inspiring afterword that reminds us of the immeasurable power of literature to move and influence young readers in powerful and positive ways unthought of by writers.

Foreword

Bill Martin Jr

All language is metaphor, a shorthanding of experience into skeins of sound that are stored in memory. There, in the brain's ballroom, newly acquired words, feelings, thoughts, ideas and hunches skid, slide and cavort about in search of meaningful connections. Eventually they intertwine weightlessly with other skeins of previously stored, sound-encoded memories, thereby enlarging one's hold on language, one's field of awareness.

Children begin language acquisition by absorbing the language ways of the environment in which they were cradled. Beyond that, their forays into the neighborhood, community and classroom, enlarge and flavor their language usage, but it is books, in large measure, that provide the models of finely tuned language by which they can better identify their individual worlds and focus their personal odysseys.

Becoming a booklover and an expert language user, however, is not an educational surety for a large majority of children. For some, lively access to the printed page where they perceive the linguistic models is sacrificed to the hauntings of early childhood traumas that usurp the psychological power and confidence necessary for fluent reading. Other children are thwarted in their quests for literacy by the compunctions and irrelevancies of textbook instruction that didactically orients to skills and rules, rights and wrongs, parts and pieces, subverting the necessary delight and meaning that must prelude high adventuring in books. Even able and already-into-reading children are sometimes diverted from literary pursuits by classroom procedures that hallmark

"Friday afternoon" as "our library time" and "when you have finished your lessons, you may quietly get a book and read."

Research cited in *Children's Literature: Resource for the Classroom,* a compendium of how-we-can-help-children-become-booklovers strongly suggests that the cause of books and young readers is best served by a home and classroom where reading is a joyous expectation in human ongoingness. Books are plumbed and savored as real life experiences, as are involvements with maps, globes, encyclopedia, dictionaries, newspapers, magazines, recipes, games, photo albums, pieces of art, family letters, children's writing, family conversations, and all such informative and entertaining sources of "staying alive."

Parents and teachers in these settings see themselves not as authorities, but as guides and appreciators. Children are listened to and encouraged to discuss their views of self, their dreams, aspirations and accomplishments. This leads me to believe that life itself demands a constant bolstering of language to encompass our ever emerging and gently unfolding goals and purposes. From books we lift words, phrases, and notions, as well as counsel, blueprint and model, that help the future become more immediate. From books we also borrow verbal coinage to celebrate the victory.

This biofeedback of right and left brain, together with the constancy of the social, learning environment, puts reading in a life-related context that values all children for their uniqueness and strengths and for their capacity to learn. The focus is not on grades, test scores, and other questionable evaluations. The focus is on making a go of life.

The echoing themes and language of books—books of all human dimensions and purposes, experienced in all kinds of settings and at all times of day and season—herald our lifelong and life-fulfilling pursuits. The resulting linguistic alchemy is a way of passage where otherwise none exists.

Acknowledgments

My heartfelt thanks to Kimberly Russell, who put in countless hours at the computer and in the library entering titles, locating books, typing in annotations, and, in general, supporting all of my efforts.

Thanks, too, to my entire office staff for enduring the mess and the frantic searching and rearranging of books and papers. Thanks to Lara Strassburger for handling the editing of the interviews and to the office staff for transcribing them. Kathy Boron especially deserves canonization for her patience and steady responsiveness. Thanks to the authors and illustrators for giving so generously of their time and attention.

Thanks again to the staffs of the Jones Library and the University of Massachusetts Reference Room for their always pleasant willingness to find answers to my queries and their permitting me to take away all those books for long periods of time.

Thanks to Hiram Howard and Sue Folan for their graciousness and good ideas.

Special thanks to my husband, Sy, for his unfailing understanding and love. And thanks to Sam, my grandson, for inspiring and delighting me with his love of books.

Part 1

Context and Background for Using Children's Literature in the Classroom

The first four chapters of *Children's Literature: Resource for the Classroom* provide readers with useful background information. The chapters will not only enrich their use of children's literature in the classroom by placing readers securely within an historical context but also will personalize encounters with books by sharing insights into how writers and illustrators of books for children see themselves and their work.

In Chapter 1, Jane Yolen offers an overview of the evolution of children's literature from the sixteenth century to the present day. Literature for children in each of the periods she identifies reflects general attitudes and societal concerns of the day. Understanding this, readers may judge works of children's literature in an historical context and not just with the wisdom of hindsight.

Masha Rudman introduces readers to a number of leading illustrators and authors of books for children in Chapters 2 and 3. Knowing something about the creator of a book and how he or she works makes that work more accessible to the reader. While the essence of the creative process is ever elusive, these brief biographical sketches enhance our understanding of the exceptional people writing and illustrating books for children today.

Part I concludes with a chapter by Donna Norton, author of one of the top textbooks for college courses in children's literature, *Through the Eyes of a Child: An Introduction to Children's Literature,* (3rd edition, Merrill, 1991). In this chapter, she helps readers understand how to identify, analyze, and appreciate the various genres of children's literature. She offers some basic definitions and moves to questions designed to focus on distinguishing characteristics of particular genres. For those who have had courses in children's literature, the chapter offers a brief refresher. For those who have not had formal courses and are only now beginning their joyful discovery, it is a valuable beginning.

How Children's Literature Has Evolved

Jane Yolen

The history of children's literature in the English language is as compressed as a section of rock showing the geologic eras of the past. However, instead of reading Cambrian, Jurassic, Mesozoic, we might better call the layers Pre-Lit, Golden, Gilded, and Guilty. We are also just now evolving, or resolving, into a fifth age as yet to be named.

The Pre-Lit Age

The Pre-Lit Age occurred before there was actually any thought of a special literature for child readers. Much of what passed for childhood entertainment was in the oral tradition—stories, rhymes, songs. What pieces of written material existed for children were in the form of admonitory warnings as in the New England Primer's:

> In Adam's Fall
> We sinned all.

By early in the sixteenth century the books especially for child readers were treatises on manners written in rhyme. These books, however, were meant for children of the upper classes. (Who else could read, after all?) They were harrowing little verses, pedagogical in intent, and not much fun:

> Discover not your own good deed,
> Neither for mirth, nor yet for meed.

3

This was also the time of the famous Foxe's Actes & Monuments (more popularly called *Foxe's Book of Martyrs*). Produced in 1563 and going through dozens of editions, this was the book the Puritans inflicted on their children. It contained detailed descriptions of martyrdoms by maiming, torture, burnings at the stake, implements, and quarterings, implemented by woodblock illustrations. Here is a typical passage from the 1749 edition, about the death of Dr. Cranmer, Archbishop of Canterbury:

> And when the wood was kindled, and the fire began to burn near him, he stretched forth his right hand, which had signed his recantation, into the flames, and there held it so steadfast that all the people might see it burnt to a coal before his body was touched.

The sixteenth century was also the period for wordless books. Begun by the German Comenius with his *Orbis Pictus (The Pictured World)* such picture encyclopedias proved popular since one did not need to know how to read to enjoy them.

In the next two centuries things began to lighten up a bit. The itinerant peddlers of the seventeenth and eighteenth centuries, known as *chapmen* or running stationers, sold little penny books. These books were sixteen, thirty-two, or sixty-four folded pages of old tales such as "Jack the Giant Killer" along with their regular fare of news sheets and broadsides. The chapbooks were laden with amateurish illustrations done in woodblock, the same blocks being used over and over for different stories on the theory that one giant looked pretty much like the next. Nevertheless, these little chapbooks were popular. They often had a lusty humor, quick pacing, and were written in the vernacular. The rough equivalent to today's comic books, the chapbooks were frowned upon by the upper classes because they contained lower class tales, bad grammar, and cheap pictures. But they were affordable and available, an unbeatable combination. Though they were actually published for adults (the bawdy humor attests to that), children bootlegged them.

Two miracles occurred during this time of Pre-Lit. The first was in 1697 when a French court clerk named Charles Perrault put together *Histoires ou Contes du Temps Passé* avec des Moralités, which was more familiarly known in England when it was translated as *Tales of Mother Goose*. The Perrault versions of some of the old tales so familiar to the Western world were set down, some of them for the first time in print, in such a manner as to define them forever.

For example, Perrault's version of Cinderella had a fairy godmother and the midnight warning that had never been in the popular tale before. When it was translated into English a few years later, a bad translation yielded the rest of that first miracle: the fur slipper was called a *glass* slipper, and glass it has remained to this day. Of course, Perrault was not setting down these tales for children but for the men and women of the French court who liked to pass their days dressing as shepherds and shepherdesses and playing around the formal gardens of the palace. In England, however, the children took over the tales as their own.

The second miracle occurred in 1744, and this one was *meant* for children. John Newbery, a British printer, decided to publish books "for amusement" and "by way of diversion" for young readers themselves. His first attempt was A *Little Pretty Pocket Book,* and it was a tremendous success. It was a modest little potpourri, including two moral letters from a reformed Jack the Giant Killer, some game instructions, a few fables, a number of proverbs, a couple of poems, and an ABC rhyme. It was a real miracle because by its very popularity it began the publishing of true books for children.

In Comes the Golden Age

After Newbery's first success, all sorts of books for children followed. In 1765, Oliver Goldsmith's smarmy but beloved tale of a poor little girl *Goody Two Shoes;* in 1781 Newbery's own edition of *Mother Goose's Melody,* the first collection of nursery rhymes; William Roscoe's overly long talking animal verse poem *The Butterfly's Ball* (1808); plus the Peter Parley books and the soppy Elsie Dinsmore series, both drearily pedantic and preachy and endless, as this paragraph from one of the Elsie books demonstrates:

> Yet, outwardly calm and self-satisfied as his demeanor may have been, Horace Dinsmore was even now regretting the step he had just taken; for remembering Elsie's conscientious scruples regarding the observance of the Sabbath—which he had for the moment forgotten—he foresaw that there would be a struggle, probably a severe one; and though, having always found her docile and yielding, he felt no doubt of the final result, he would willing have avoided the contest, could he have done so without a sacrifice of pride; but, as he said to himself, with a slight sigh, he had now gone too far to retreat; and then he had all along felt that this struggle must come some time, and perhaps it was as well now as at any other.

(Horace Dinsmore is Elsie's father, and she has just refused to sing for his friends because it is Sunday.)

Except for the Newbery token books and the bootlegged chapbooks, much of what was available was still wearily serious in purpose. Even what passed for fiction tended to be testimonial and instructive. The popular Parley books were barely fictionalized texts:

When I was a little boy, Boston was not half so large as it is now, and that large building which stands very high, as you see in the picture called the new State House, was not built then. And do you know that the very place where Boston stands, was once covered with woods, and that in those woods lived many Indians? Did you ever see an Indian? Here is a picture of some Indians . . . They lived in little houses called Wigwams. Here is a picture of a Wigwam.

The Indians were very ignorant; they could not read or write; their houses were very small and inconvenient. They had no such fine rooms in them as our houses have nor had they any chimnies or fireplaces. The Indians had no chairs to sit in, nor tables to eat from. They had no books to read, and had no churches or meeting houses . . .

and, as it is easy to see, packed with cultural colonialisms now unacceptable to modern readers.

For all that they were for the most part a dreary beginning, a beginning of a literature for children such books surely were. The *idea* of a branch of reading especially for young readers had arrived.

It would, however, be another century of modest and often meanspirited storybooks before a rich, full, palpable classic children's literature—the Golden Age—would be established. Meanwhile, school books, religious texts, alphabet and counting rhymes, and the books of manners sustained the young readers.

It was the nineteenth century, heralded by that most delightful of holiday stories *A Christmas Carol* by Charles Dickens, that classic children's *literature* commenced. After that, the roll call of children's books in English is a roll call of greatness. When Ebenezer Scrooge started his journeys with the ghost of Christmas past, all the children of England and America—and eventually the world—rode on his bony shoulders.

A Christmas Carol was written as a family book, to be shared *with* the children. It became so popular that Dickens tried to write several more Christmas family stories, though none was ever as successful. But after *A Christmas Carol*, look at the list:

1843: *A Christmas Carol,* Charles Dickens
1846: *Book of Nonsense,* Edward Lear
1846: *Fairy Tales,* Hans Christian Andersen (translation)
1852: *A Wonder Book for Girls & Boys,* Nathaniel Hawthorne
1865: *Alice's Adventures in Wonderland,* Lewis Carroll
1865: *Hans Brinker, or The Silver Skates,* Mary Mapes Dodge
1867: *Sing a Song of Sixpence,* Walter Crane 1868: *Little Women,* Louisa May Alcott

1876: *The Adventures of Tom Sawyer*, Mark Twain
1877: *Black Beauty*, Anna Sewall
1878: *Under the Window*, Kate Greenaway
1878: *The Diverting Ride of John Gilpin*, William Cowper
1883: *Treasure Island*, Robert Louis Stevenson
1883: *Nights With Uncle Remus*, Joel Chandler Harris
1883: *The Merry Adventures of Robin Hood*, Howard Pyle
1884: *Heidi*, Johanna Spyri (English translation)
1884: *The Adventures of Huckleberry Finn*, Mark Twain
1885: *A Child's Garden of Verses*, Robert Louis Stevenson
1889: *The Blue Fairy Book*, Andrew Lang
1894: *The Jungle Book*, Rudyard Kipling
1889: *The Story of the Treasure Seekers*, E. Nesbit
1900: *The Wonderful Wizard of Oz*, L. Frank Baum
1901: *The Tale of Peter Rabbit*, Beatrix Potter
1908: *The Wind in the Willows*, Kenneth Grahame

All of the great themes and types of children's books to come can be seen in that list: color-filled picture books, collections of rhymes and fairy tales, adventure stories, stories of children at home, animal stories, fantasy tales, historical fiction, holiday books, and the rewritten classics from the world's treasure house of story. Some of this explosion into literature has to do with what was happening in adult books. The Romantic Movement had surely fueled an interest in folklore. From the opening salvos—the printing of the Grimm collections in English in the 1820s—fairy stories in England were all the rage. Hans Christian Andersen was more popular in England and America than he was in his homeland of Denmark. Interestingly enough, England and America retained the greatest interest in a literature of childhood. (For more on this subject, read Paul Hazard's brilliant little book, *Books, Children, and Men,* 1983.)

Then, in England, an invention changed the face of publishing itself. In 1872, a London printer named Edmund Evans invented the full-color printing process and the race to produce books with color plates—especially books for children—was on.

Could a single invention and a literary movement be the only reasons why children's literature was suddenly born? Certainly they are the easy answers. The larger, more global answer, however, is this: until the nineteenth century, society's view of childhood was not one that was conducive to the development of a special literature for young readers. Medieval societies had viewed childhood as a state to be passed through quickly, merely a training ground for adulthood. One bishop in 1628 had described a boy as "a man in a small letter." Children, this view held, were only shorter than adults. Training, not entertaining, was the child's lot in life. They would soon grow out of that state so nothing was made to keep them happily ensconced there, certainly not something as expensive and important as literature. Childhood was a passage, the quicker gotten through the better.

Society's view of the child slowly changed and by the nineteenth century this newly enfranchised reader was ready for a literature directed at the under-twelves. Tentatively, one at a time, such books were produced and many of them were brilliant, destined to be classics.

As they began to succeed, a superstructure of services began to be cobbled together. Children's magazines grew up, such as the venerable *St. Nicholas.* And, in the beginnings of the twentieth century, the first children's book rooms in libraries were begun. (Before then, there simply were not enough children's books for such an idea to surface.) Then in 1910, the next logical step: the Macmillan Company in America decided to form an actual department within its publishing company specifically to produce books for children.

Between 1910 and the early 1950s, Macmillan and its eager followers (Harper, Scribner's, and the like) produced many wonderful books. The establishment in 1922 of the John Newbery Medal for the writer of the book adjudged the most distinguished of the year and in 1938 the Randolph Caldecott Medal for the illustrator of the book judged the most distinguished in its illustrations certainly helped the proliferation of books for children. Once begun, the idea of a special literature for young readers could not be stopped.

1926:   *Winnie-the-Pooh,* A.A. Milne
1928:   *Millions of* Cats, Wanda Gag
1933:   *ABC Bunny,* Wanda Gag
1935:   *Caddie Woodlawn,* Carol Ryrie Brink 1936: *And to Think That I Saw It on Mulberry Street,* Dr. Seuss
1938:   *The Sword In the Stone,* T.H. White
1939:   *Madeline,* Ludwig Bemelmans
1941:   *Make Way for Ducklings,* Robert McCloskey
1943:   *The Little House,* Virginia Lee Burton 1943: *Johnny Tremaine,* Esther Forbes
1944:   *Many Moons,* James Thurber
1947:   *Goodnight Moon,* Margaret Wise Brown
1947:   *Misty of Chincoteague,* Marguerite Henry
1948:   *Blueberries for Sal,* Robert McCloskey

and dozens of other minor classics. What is interesting about this list, as compared to the earlier one, is how they are definitely for children and not the kind of family story that Dickens had written with *A Christmas Carol.* This slight shift in emphasis to the child-readers themselves was not the only change. There was also a decided increase in the volume of books published. Children's books now meant big business and what many came to call the Golden Age of children's publishing ended awash in print.

Enter the Gilded Age

There are those who equate a loss of quality with the rise of profit and proliferation. When there is a rush to produce, the word "product" is substituted in minds for the thing produced. In fact, something of that sort happened in the 1950s to 1970s in children's books. One could hear the word "product" or "unit" instead of the word "book" in the once-ivory towers of the literary kingdom. However, in children's books, there were still a number of beautiful books brought out. It was not the numbers that changed so much as the percentage of the really fine books. Often poor books seemed to be crowding out good ones. The poor ones were being produced in glossy, glitzy, easily available numbers, and an unsophisticated public did not seem to know the difference. That is the reason the next twenty years in children's book publishing is often referred to as The Gilded Age.

With book printings at an all time high (2,500 new titles appearing yearly, not counting comic books, calendars, re-issues, etc.) the hopeful slogan of 1919's first-ever Children's Book Week— *"More Books in the Home"*—was almost mocked by the ever increasing numbers of junk books brought out by mass market publishers.

In 1965, one editor friend of mine was faced with the task of weeding out manuscripts bought by her predecessor at a major publishing company in that frenzied rush to buy-buy-buy. Her favorite rejectee was a children's book purporting to teach youngsters French by using phrases from the Bible such as "Bring me a Hebrew nurse." It was indicative of the buying spree mentality. When the Children's Book Week organizers had promulgated their "More Books in the Home" motto, it was understood to mean more *good* books in the home. But thirty years later, junk was pushing out literature on the bookstore shelves.

Still, the list of great books produced is impressive:

1952: *Charlotte's Web*, E.B. White
1952: *The Biggest Bear*, Lynd Ward
1954: *Ape in a Cape*, Fritz Eichenberg
1955: *Crow Boy*, Taro Yashima
1956: *Old Yeller*, Fred Gipson
1960: *Island of the Blue Dolphins*, Scott O'Dell

1962: *A Wrinkle in Time*, Madeleine L'Engle
1963: *Where the Wild Things Are*, Maurice Sendak

This list, just a sampling of the many good books published for children at this period, shows a continuing variety. From the psychologically adept picture-book story of a naughty young boy venturing in his imagination to a place where there are things as wild and as (seemingly) unmanageable as he to a story of a strong young woman who must make her own life alone on an island, the palpability of characters in these books, like the wonderful mothering spider Charlotte, is as fine as anything in the Golden Age. Why then Gilded?

At this time there were more than sixty publishers producing a specific body of work for children. Each publisher was equipped with a promotion department whose sole task was to publicize and promote the children's book line. An interesting relationship between the publishers (producers) and the library community (the actual buyers) had grown up. Symbiotic, it was a relationship based upon solid buying patterns. In the trade publishing (that is, the fine books, not the cheap supermarket books) 85 to 90 percent of the sales of any title was to the institutional market—public and school libraries. This had not always been the case. In the nineteenth century and well into the twentieth, children's books had sold to individuals— mothers, fathers, grandparents, even to children themselves. Many times books had been sold by subscription (Mark Twain's books sold this way) through the mails. With the rise of children's book rooms and school libraries, however, the greatest buyers of children's books became those institutions.

Such buying power conferred another kind of power. Publishers began to consult teachers and librarians regularly on the kinds of books they *should* be publishing. Curriculum-oriented storybooks arose, and even a swift perusal of the Newbery Medal Honor Books of the period 1950-60 gives evidence of this connection: *George Washington* (1949) by Genevieve Foster; *Ghandi, Fighter without a Sword* (1950) by Jeanette Eaton; *Abraham Lincoln, Friend of the People* (1950) by Clara Ingram Judson; *Americans before Columbus* (1951) by Elizabeth Baity; *Birthdays of Freedom* (1952) by Genevieve Foster; *Theodore Roosevelt, Fighting Patriot* (1953) by Clara Ingram Judson; *Men, Microscopes, and Living Things* (1955) by Katherine Shippen; *Mr. Justice Holmes* (1956) by Clara Ingram Judson; *Tom Paine, Freedom's Apostle* (1957) by Leo Gurko; *Chucaro, Wild Pony of the Pampa* (1958) by Francis Kalnay; *America is Born* (1955) by Gerald W. Johnson. This is not to say that these are bad books or badly written. They are all solid, interesting nonfiction. But it is certainly indicative of the kind of book that is produced when publishers and school curriculums go hand in hand.

From Gilt to Guilt

In the 1960s, book buying was at its height. Money flowed in from the government to small urban libraries, and special minorities previously slighted both in literature and in the library were discovered by President Johnson's Great Society.

What books were available for these newly enfranchised readers? In the basals, just Puff, Spot, Dick and Jane in whitebread America. In the trade books it was the same. Except for an *Uncle Remus* (1883) here, a *The Story of Little Black Sambo* (1899) there, and a long-running and popular series of *Nicodemus* stories (c. 1939) that were blatantly racist and caricatured, there was little in children's books with which minorities could identify unless it was with a nonracial talking rabbit or hedgehog or fox.

It is not just that racist books existed. They were highly praised. *The New York Times,* for example, said of one Nicodemus book: "Like all the Nicodemus books this latest is kindly, and childlike, and has a lively humor and much action in both text and drawings." *The New York Herald Tribune* said of another: "The most popular little black boy in recent nursery fiction is no doubt Nicodemus. . ."; and *Parents' Magazine* trumpeted: "The many children who have laughed over the adventures of that funny little colored boy, Nicodemus, will welcome this new book." Here is a passage from one of those popular stories, *Nicodemus and the Gang* (1939):

> "Heyo, Nicode-e-mus!" The whole gang was outside calling. "Come on out!"
> Nicodemus looked out of the window. He saw Petunia and Clara Belle and Rastus and Obadiah and little Sim.
> "I'se a comin," shouted Nicodemus.

Clearly there were issues that needed to be addressed in the children's books where so many youngsters were learning their cultural values. As each new advocacy articulated its hunger, a place at the literary table had to be set. Libraries asked for and got books for and about specific subjects. They asked for and got books starring strong and wonderful African Americans, native Americans, women, gays, and the elderly.

Sometimes the books were powerfully written stories, a literature scraped across the chalkboard in dayglow colors, books such as *Zeely* (1967) by Virginia Hamilton, *Dragonwings* (1975) by Lawrence Yep, *Anpao* (1977) by Jamake Highwater, *Roll of Thunder, Hear My Cry* (1976) by Mildred Taylor, *Julie of the Wolves* (1972) by Jean Craighead George, *A Figure of Speech* (1973) by Norma Fox Mazer. Often, however, they were books simply published to fill a perceived need.

Set in motion by the racial, gender, and age advocates, the trend towards specific books for specific social problems steamrolled ahead. In the 1960s and 1970s, publishers, authors, and the buying libraries took on the mantle of guilt for the entire country. The word *"bibliotherapy,"* first invented in the early 1900s, became a concept popular in library and children's literature circles: the idea that books could be invaluable in helping children deal with the major issues in their lives. Too often, though, unsophisticated dabblers did not see the books in terms of a larger therapy but as print bandages to be applied at will. Is a child suffering from abuse? Apply *Don't Hurt Laurie* (1977). Do you have a child who is having trouble recovering from a friend's death? Apply *A Taste of Blackberries* (1973). Have a child with a sibling who is dying? Apply *The Magic Moth* (1972). Have a blind, retarded, pregnant, doped out, spaced out, outraged child? Surely there was a book produced in the sixties or seventies to make everything all right. The simplistic misapplication of bibliotherapy encouraged the Guilt Age in children's literature, approximately fifteen years of publishing books with the idea of bandaids first, literature after.

Yet this was also a time when books that accurately reflected wholly forgotten segments of the reading population were produced, books that editor Richard Jackson has called "Discovery Fiction" because many children discovered themselves in books for the first time. This was a lesson that authors and illustrators and publishers would not forget.

There was something else happening in children's books. This was the time that all the young readers were also young television watchers. No one growing up in the sixties and seventies was unaware of TV. The pacing of television shows, the half-hour concept, the break for commercials, the continuing cliff-hangers, all forced children's books to take on some of those characteristics. Children wanted to read books the way they watched television. In Hollywood, a movie concept could be sold as long as it was not more than two sentences long. *Moby Dick:* Man kills killer whale, killer whale kills man. Children's books began to be sold that way to the publishers, to the librarians, and ultimately, of course, to the young readers. Yet early classics had not been produced that way. What if they had?

> *Little Women:*   A family of strong young women adjust to their sister's death.
> *Black Beauty:*   An abused horse finds a good home.
> *Heidi:* Spunky girl helps paraplegic to walk.
> *The Tale of Peter Rabbit:* Naughty bunny learns to listen to Mom.

In the early 1960s, at a library meeting, there was a parody of an easy reader performed at the American Library Association meeting:

Jane Eyre

This is Jane.
Hello Jane.
Jane is poor.
Her dress is poor.
Her shoes are poor.
Her hat is poor.
Poor Jane.

This is Mr. Rochester.
Hello Mr. Rochester.
Mr. Rochester is rich.
He has a big house.
He has a big dog.
He has a big horse.
He has a big secret.

What is Mr. Rochester's secret?
Jane cannot guess the secret.
Can you guess the secret?

This is Mrs. Rochester.
Hello Mrs. Rochester.
Mrs. Rochester is crazy.
She has a candle.
The candle is lighted.
Mrs. Rochester can laugh.
She laughs: ha ha ha.

RUN JANE RUN.

When it was performed, the audience howled. But the audience in the very guilt-ridden seventies would probably have wanted to know why Mrs. Rochester was not being helped. "Crazy" is not a seventies word. Mrs. Rochester was probably manic depressive and needed lithium, or else she was a paranoid schizophrenic. Either way, there was certainly an organization (and a book) to help her. Children must not be made afraid of people with emotional problems. Jane should probably study social work and help poor unfortunate Mrs. Rochester so that she will not burn down the mansion and can become, again, a productive member of society.

In other words, many of the books published—and by backward extension, many of the books written—in the Guilty Age were books of an educational or medical or purposive nature, as in the Pre-Lit days, only with a great deal more sophistication and a much larger distribution ability. As much as we believe in education and the art of healing, great literature is not created that way. As the ever-wise Isaac Bashevis Singer has said: "Truth in art that is boring is not true."

Where Are We Now?

We are at a crossroads once again in the literature of childhood. It will be years before we will be able to accurately chart which path is taken in the 1980s and 1990s. There are, however, some interesting trends that we can already note.

The Guilt that so assailed society has lessened. The Guilt—not the problems! Many of the writers who got their start because of the publishers' search for minority authors and illustrators are still producing, but there is a backlash of censorship alive today that keeps certain books off the shelves. The religious right and the conservative right (not necessarily the same thing) are taking their turn at trying to influence what is being published so there are rewritten fairy tales or thrown away fairy tales. ("Snow White" was recently banned by one religious group because it *encouraged mirrorgazing*.)

The composite book—a little bit for this minority, a little bit for that advocacy—the so-called "problem novel" so widely popular in the sixties and seventies is out, as is the paperback reprint for such novels. Instead, there are the highly popular "Babysitter Series" and the "Sweet Valley High" books that are distinguished more by their numbers than the writing. The publishers are looking for bright-eyed, humorous, light-weight stories because they sell well and offend no one.

Because they sell well. It is important that anyone interested in the literature of childhood understand that first and foremost publishing is a business. What comes on to the shelves gets there not because of a search for the greatest literature but because there is a perceived market for it. Along the way, of course, there are good books, even *great* books that get produced. In the eighties, we already have our classics, such as *Sarah, Plain and Tall* (1985) by Patricia MacLachlan and *The Polar Express* (1985) by Chris Van Allsburg.

As trends go, so far it is the palpable *lack* of trends in the eighties that is interesting. If there is any news, it is that Story is once again alive and well.

Storytelling, that old oral tradition, has had a renaissance. Begun in the 1970s by a hardy band of tellers who held a storytelling conference one October in the tiny town of Jonesborough, Tennessee, the National Association for the Preservation and Perpetuation of Storytelling (NAPPS) has grown into a huge and enormously influential group. Not only are there hundreds of newly converted storytellers marching on schools, libraries, hospitals, stages, coffee houses, prisons, and conventions, but they have influenced book publishers as well. Volumes of stories, books about storytellers, and, more importantly, the idea that books should be *stories* first has come around again. History, science, science fiction, fantasy, realism—all presented as *story* seems to be the watchword of the decade. Whether it will last more than a few short trendy years is difficult to say, but I suspect that if it does, we may be in for a second true flowering of books for young readers, a second Golden Age.

Works Cited in the Chapter

Alcott, Louisa May. *Little Women.* Boston: Little, Brown & Co., 1868.

Andersen, Hans Christian. *Fairy Tales.* London: F. Warner and Co., 1868.

Baity, Elizabeth. Americans Before Columbus. New York: Viking, 1951.

Bannerman, Helen. *The Story of Little Black Sambo.* New York: Harper & Row, 1899.

Baum, L. Frank. *The Wonderful Wizard of Oz.* New York: G.M. Hill, 1900.

Bemelmans, Ludwig. *Madeline.* New York: Viking, 1939.

Brink, Carol Ryrie. *Caddie Woodlawn.* New York: Macmillan, 1935.

Bronte, Charlotte. *Jane Eyre.* London: Smith, Elder and Co., 1847.

Brown, Margaret Wise. *Goodnight Moon.* New York: Harper & Row, 1947.

Burton, Virginia Lee. *The Little House.* Boston: Houghton Mifflin, 1865.

Carroll, Lewis. *Alice's Adventures in Wonderland.* London: Macmillan, 1865.

Cowper, William. *The Diverting History of John Gilpin.* Illustrated by Randolph Caldecott. London: G. Routledge, 1878.

Crane, Walter. *Sing a Song of Sixpence.* New York: John Lane, 1909.

Dickens, Charles. *A Christmas Carol.* London: Chapman & Hall, 1843.

Dodge, Mary Mapes. *Hans Brinker, or The Silver Skates.* New York: James O'Kane, 1865.

Eaton, Jeanette. *Ghandi, Fighter Without a Sword.* New York: Morrow, 1950.

Eichenberg, Fritz. *Ape in a Cape.* New York: Harcourt, Brace, 1954.

Finley, Martha. *Elsie Dinsmore.* Salem, NH: Ayer Co. Publishers, 1896.

Forbes, Esther. *Johnny Tremaine.* Boston: Houghton Mifflin, 1943.

Foster, Genevieve. *Birthdays of Freedom.* New York: Scribner, 1952.

Foster, Genevieve. *George Washington.* New York: Scribner, 1949.

Gag, Wanda. *ABC Bunny.* Coward-McCann, 1933.

Gag, Wanda. *Millions of Cats.* New York: Coward-McCann, 1928.

George, Jean Craighead. *Julie of the Wolves.* New York: Harper & Row, 1972.

Gipson, Fred. *Old Yeller.* New York: Harper & Row, 1956.

Goldsmith, Oliver. *Goody Two Shoes.* London: Griffith & Farran, 1882.

Grahame, Kenneth. *The Wind in the Willows.* Mattituck, NY: Ameron, Ltd., 1908.

Greenaway, Kate. *Under the Window.* New York: G. Routledge, 1878.

Gurko, Leo. *Tom Paine, Freedom's Apostle.* New York: Crowell, 1957.

Hamilton, Virginia. *Zeely.* New York: Macmillan, 1967.

Harris, Joel Chandler. *Nights With Uncle Remus.* Boston: J.R. Osgood, 1883.

Hawthorne, Nathaniel. *A Wonder Book for Girls and Boys.* New York: A.L. Burt, 1852.

Henry, Marguerite. *Misty of Chincoteague.* New York: Macmillan, 1947.

Highwater, Jamake. *Anpao: An American Indian.* New York: Harper & Row, 1977.

Hogan, Inez. *Nicodemus.* New York: Dutton, 1939.

Johnson, Gerald W. *America is Born.* New York: Morrow, 1959.

Judson, Clare Ingram. *Abraham Lincoln, Friend of the People.* Chicago: Wilcox and Follet, 1950.

Judson, Clare Ingram. *Mr. Justice Holmes.* Chicago: Follett Publication Co., 1956.

Judson, Clara Ingram. *Theodore Roosevelt, Fighting Patriot.* Chicago: Follett Publication Co., 1953.

Kalnay, Francis. *Chucaro, Wild Pony of the Pampa.* New York: Harcourt, Brace, 1958.

Kipling, Rudyard. *The Jungle Book.* New York: Macmillan, 1894.

Lang, Andrew. *The Blue Fairy Book.* New York: Longmans, Green & Co., 1889.

Lear, Edward. *Book of Nonsense.* London: T. McLean, 1846.

Lee, Virginia. *The Magic Moth.* New York: Seabury Press, 1972.

L'Engle, Madeleine. *A Wrinkle in Time.* New York: Farrar, Straus & Giroux, 1962.

MacLachlan, Patricia. *Sarah, Plain and Tall.* New York: Harper & Row, 1985.

Mazer, Norma Fox. *A Figure of Speech.* New York: Delacorte Press, 1973.

McCloskey, Robert. *Blueberries for Sal.* New York: Viking, 1948.

McCloskey, Robert. *Make Way for Ducklings.* New York: Viking, 1941.

Melville, Herman. *Moby Dick.* New York: Harper & Row, 1851.

Milne, A.A. *Winnie-The-Pooh.* London: Methuen & Co., 1926.

Nesbit, E. *Story of the Treasure Seekers.* New York: Frederick A. Stokes Company, 1889.

Newbery, John A *Little Pretty Pocket Book.* London: John Newbery, 1744.

Newbery, John. *Mother Goose's Melody.* London: John Newbery, 1781.

O'Dell, Scott. *Island of the Blue Dolphins.* Boston: Houghton Mifflin, 1960.

Perrault, Charles. *Tales of Mother Goose.* Translated by Charles Welsch. Boston: D.C. Heath & Co., 1901.

Potter, Beatrix. *The Tale of Peter Rabbit.* New York: Frederick Warne & Co., 1901.

Pyle, Howard. *The Merry Adventures of Robin Hood.* New York: Scribner, 1883.

Roberts, Willow Davis. *Don't Hurt Laurie.* New York: E.P. Dutton, 1977.

Roscoe, William. *The Butterfly's Ball.* London: J. Harris, 1808.

Sendak, Maurice. Where the Wild Things Are. New York: Harper & Row, 1963.

Seuss, Doctor. *And to Think that I Saw it On Mulberry Street.* New York: Vanguard, 1936.

Shippen, Katherine. *Men, Microscopes, and Living Things.* New York: Viking, 1955.

Smith, Doris Buchanan. *A Task of Blackberries.* New York: Crowell, 1973.

Sewall, Anna. *Black Beauty.* London: Jarrold and Sons, 1877.

Spyri, Johanna. *Heidi.* Boston: De Wolfe, Fiske & Co., 1884.

Stevenson, Robert Louis. *A Child's Garden of Verses.* London: Longmans, Green, and Co., 1885.

Stevenson, Robert Louis. *Treasure Island.* London: Cassell & Company, 1883.

Taylor, Mildred. *Roll of Thunder, Hear My Cry.* New York: Dial, 1976.

Thurber, James. *Many Moons.* Columbus, OH: Scarlet Mask Club of Ohio State University, 1922.

Twain, Mark. *The Adventures of Huckleberry Finn.* New York: Harper & Row, 1884.

Twain, Mark. *The Adventures of Tom Sawyer.* San Francisco: A. Roman & Co., 1876.

Van Allsburg, Chris. *The Polar Express.* Boston: Houghton Mifflin, 1985.

Ward, Lynd. *The Biggest Bear.* Boston: Houghton Mifflin, 1952.

White, E.B. *Charlotte's Web.* New York: Harper & Row, 1952.

White, T.H. *The Sword in the Stone.* London: Collins, 1938.

Yashima, Taro. *Crow Boy.* New York: Viking, 1955.

Yep, Lawrence. *Dragonwings.* New York: Harper & Row, 1975.

2

People Behind the Books: Illustrators

Masha Kabakow Rudman

A number of artists have made enormous contributions to contemporary children's literature. They are a varied group and approach their work from diverse perspectives. Their illustrations demonstrate the use of many media, including tissue-paper collage, oil paint, watercolor, pencil, pen-and-ink, and woodcuts. All of them are extraordinarily talented; all understand people's feelings; all are distinctly in tune with their audience of children and adolescents.

Ashley Bryan

Ashley Bryan has a commanding presence and demonstrates his many abilities in a variety of ways. His paintings and blockprints stand alone as works of art, his musical ability includes a rich singing voice, and his writing is widely acclaimed, as evidenced by his many popular books. He lives on an island in Maine, where his studio and home are frequently visited by neighbors and guests from all over the world. His congenial and sincere responses to other people's feelings are hallmarks of his personality.

Bryan's family came from Antigua to New York City, where he was born and brought up. He found, at an early age, that his artistic talents were assets that helped him survive in that tough Bronx community. He recalls that his mother sang throughout the day and that his father, a printer, was very musical and loved birds. Bryan says, "With the birds trilling, my mother singing, and the general music-making that went on at home, it is only natural that I would one day do books of the songs that had special meaning for me, the black American spirituals." His books of spirituals include *Walk Together Children: Black American Spirituals; I'm Going to Sing; What a Morning; All Night, All Day;* and *Climbing Jacob's Ladder.*

Byran remembers creating his very first book in kindergarten. It was an alphabet book that won rave reviews and appreciation from his family at home. Because of this favorable response, he continued to write, illustrate, bind and publish one-of-a-kind editions to give as gifts to family and friends. Bryan was very close to all of his siblings. "My older sister and I always did work together. We made marionettes as children together, we did drawing, and we did patchwork things. I would cut and design, and she would stitch and put together patchwork skirts and vests and other things.

"The younger of my two sisters, to whom I dedicated one of my books, died in her forties. I was very close to her and always gave her materials for drawing. She had a child-like way of seeing, in drawing, and I always loved that kind of art. When she was ill in the hospital, when I was teaching at Dartmouth, I took a year off from teaching so I could visit her regularly. I would create little watercolors based on the drawings that she had been doing. She was so pleased with them that I continued to do some for each visit. Since her death I have used her drawings as a way of just calming myself. These watercolors keep me in touch with what I do when I do not have the time to pursue things in an ongoing, concentrated way. I could begin one of those little watercolors that I was doing to her drawings; I could pick it up and put it down at intervals, and so work a month, two or three, and create little paintings from the inspiration of her drawings. I've continued doing that over the past ten years. That was my major source of inspiration for illustrating my first book of poems."

Bryan attended the renowned Cooper Union Art School and then went on to Columbia University, where he majored in philosophy. His paintings and illustrations of books he had read attracted the attention of Jean Karl, an editor at Atheneum, who encouraged him to illustrate African tales and tell the stories in his own words. *The Ox of the Wonderful Horns and Other African Folktales; The Adventures of Aku; Beat the Story-Drum, Pum-Pum;* and *Lion and the Ostrich Chicks* are several of those he has both retold and illustrated.

Although Bryan has visited several countries in Africa, researched the tales of specific African sources, and has studied African sculpture, masks and rock painting, he likes to recreate the tales and translate the art in his own style and interpretation. He is more interested in preserving a sense of African heritage than depicting specific groups.

When Bryan is at home on his island he paints during the day and works on the book projects in the evenings. "Sometimes when deadlines are close, I will spend more time with the book, working things out. But since painting is the center, if painting doesn't go, very little else will go. I must give myself to painting sometime during the day and the other things will flow out of that. I find that one has different kinds of energies in a day. There is a point when I can turn from painting, feel very fresh, and work on a story or an illustration, or perhaps a puppet or a glass piece. You just tap into different areas of energy as one approach or another becomes exhausted."

With all of his talents, Bryan considers himself primarily a painter. "Everything has grown and developed out of that center. My love of doing pictures for books and everything else I do stems from my love of drawing and painting, so the books have been a natural outgrowth of that. Artists have always seen images in what they read and have always painted pictures or drawings of those images. That's why you enter a museum and you see so much of literature there. It's from the Bible, and mythology, from novels, historical pieces, whatever. It's from literature, from books, that so much of art has developed."

Bryan's techniques are as varied as his talents. "My work is always reviewed as woodcuts. Actually, my illustrations for the African folktales stem from African masks and sculpture and the rock paintings of Africa. They were meant to give the feeling of being as carefully shaped and formed as those works of African art, but they were actually paintings. They are painted neatly, from the roughs, on illustration boards. The book illustrations in *Beat the Story-Drum, Pum-Pum, Lion and the Ostrich Chicks, The Adventures of Aku, Ox of the Wonderful Horns and Other African Folktales* are one-of-a-kind, unique paintings. In painting them in that way I could get almost a 100 percent approximation from my original to the thousands that were printed. And that's always exciting to the artist, to get as close as you can from your original to the book. Now, I've been doing work in color, in watercolor, in the poster colors which are tempera, because today more work is being done in full color. The new printing techniques reproduce color closely, more closely to the originals than ever before. But those first books that I mentioned of African tales are paintings, very strictly painted, thus always reviewed as block prints or silkscreens."

"The block prints are *Walk Together, Children*, and *I'm Going to Sing*, my first two books of the black American spirituals. Those two are also always reviewed as wood blocks. They are cut to look like the early medieval wood blocks. I had to carry the thirty or forty blocks for each book with me wherever I went, from teaching at Dartmouth to coming here in Maine in the summer, or visiting my family, who had retired to

Antigua in the West Indies, so I devised a way of working with linoleum. I use unmounted linoleum, which is thin and light, and I can carry those thirty, forty blocks with me over the two years it takes me to cut the blocks for one of those books. They are cut in the tradition of wood blocks, and so I don't mind if those are always reviewed as wood blocks. Even when I've sent them to exhibitions and specified them as lino-block prints, they have always come into the exhibition labeled as wood blocks."

"That was the look they were meant to have. The early religious books were cut in blocks and printed by hand. I did that because I wanted the books to relate visually to that period. You need not know that my initial inspiration for illustrating the spirituals wood block illustrations of the early books, but when I talk to people I tell them that was my inspiration. That is the source that gives me the spring from which I am working for that whole series."

"In early medieval times all art was created for the greater glory of God. The great Gothic cathedrals, the stained-glass windows, the music, the illuminated manuscripts, the block prints, the theater—everything was created with that spirit. It is said that the only time in Western civilization that this occurred again was when black slaves created this tremendous body of song—the spirituals. For me, making that identification with the spiritually inspired art of the black slaves was important. That approach is one that really has meant a lot to me, and those first two books, I hope, will come back into print."

"*What a Morning,* the five Christmas spirituals, and *Climbing Jacob's Ladder,* its companion, the Old Testament spirituals, are both done with tempera paints, the little poster color jars, the paints that children use in their art classes. With those paints, I can put down a color and paint into it as one paints with oils. You can get a clean statement of color each time. You can build to a density of color, or you can even have a lighter quality. With the tempera paints, you can paint over areas of color and build up in that way to create the ultimate painting."

"*All Night, All Day* is in watercolor, used in a lighter way so the feeling of the paper is more evident. Because I often place color close to color, I must control the painting of the color on the page. Now, most watercolor is free-flowing, with the colors intermingling. Some of my illustrations have it more than others. In many of them I've worked the colors close to one another, sometimes using little areas of color, one next to the other, separated by a white line, such as in 'This Little Light of Mine, I'm Gonna Let It Shine.' "

When Bryan is on his island in Maine he keeps busy with many projects. "I had started many years ago, over thirty-some, forty years, now, that I've been coming to the islands, picking up things on the beach. They were always suggestive to me—the driftwood, bones, glass, shells—

and I began making forms from them, which became the puppets which I developed over the years. I have a whole collection of puppets made over a period of more than thirty years which are based on materials picked up on walks along the beach.

"With the glass I collected, I began making stained-glass panels. I developed a method of using papier-mache to hold the pieces in place. I tried it as an experiment with some very small forms at first, in the shape of simple gingerbread patterns of birds, flowers, stars, fish, whatever. When that worked, I then decided I'd do scenes from the life of Jesus. I did a whole series, maybe twenty feet long and four feet tall. They're made from sanded pieces of beer bottles, wine bottles, and soda bottles that I gathered on walks along the island shores. Rare colors from broken glasses, bowls, and vases are given to me by friends, so I have quite a range of colors. Because of the variations of thickness and thinness, you get a tremendous play of the light through the glass. They're now in a stretch of windows in the bedroom."

"The puppets are on shelves and different areas of the house as well. I love making them. I did a number of puppet shows with friends on the island, to show the islanders how beach finds come alive when they're recreated as puppets acting on stage. It takes about six to eight people working along with me when I do a story. These puppets are gesture puppets; they're not in the Punch-and-Judy style of theater; they're more in the ritual style of a medieval mystery play. They move slowly and deliberately and use carefully chosen, well-spoken language, so there is a stately quality that comes out in the performance. The audience is very much involved in making it real because the characters in the story are cast from whatever the forms are. They can be made from shells, driftwood, bones, or glass, but whatever you say they are becomes believable because the audiences involve themselves in the play. People often say afterwards, when I've done the plays, 'That felt more real than real!' What they meant was they had given so much of themselves to make it real that they could feel it in themselves. I enjoy all kinds of puppet theater, but that style of theater especially interests me. If I had time, that's what I would pursue, but, with the painting and working on the books, I just don't have time to do puppet theater in an ongoing way as well."

Bryan's life is rich and filled with opportunities to practice his many talents. His remarkable skill as a storyteller is not the least of these. For Bryan, storytelling is the art of bringing the music and flavor of African heritage to young audiences, and it is not confined to the making of books. When he visits schools or conferences for teachers and librarians his performances of the stories and poetry of African Americans are powerful and unforgettable. His prowess as an actor is formidable. Many of his readings include the works of such African American poets as Paul Laurence Dunbar, Gwendolyn Brooks, Nikki Giovanni, Eloise Greenfield, and Langston Hughes.

As Bryan "reads" (in truth, he has committed the words to memory and does not need the text to remind him) he holds the book aloft, symbolically indicating the high esteem in which he holds the printed word. He believes "There is life in the printed word just waiting to be given breath." Many adults in his audiences say that he has changed their lives and influenced how they will bring poetry and story to their students. Children, too, are moved to laughter, tears, and cheers by his presentations and are affected forever in how they approach literature.

Bryan's life and his art blend well into a mosaic of energy, interaction with people, and the creation of many art forms. Music, language, painting, and drama all support his continuing quest to bring the beauty of black culture and an appreciation of all cultures to his audiences.

Books Written and Illustrated by Ashley Bryan

(all published by Macmillan)

All Night, All Day: A Child's First Book of African-American Spirituals, 1991.

Beat the Story-Drum, Pum-Pum, 1980, 1987.

The Cat's Purr, 1985.

The Dancing Granny, 1987.

Lion and the Ostrich Chicks & Other African Folk Tales, 1986.

Ox of the Wonderful Horns and Other African Folktales, Athenum, 1971.

Sh-Ko and His Eight Wicked Brothers, 1988.

Sing to the Sun. Poems, HarperCollins, 1992.

Turtle Knows Your Name, 1989.

Books Illustrated by Ashley Bryan

(all published by Macmillan)

Climbing Jacob's Ladder: Heroes of the Bible in African American Spirituals, by John Langstaff 1991.

What a Morning! The Christmas Story in Black Spirituals, by John Langstaff 1987.

Trina Schart Hyman

From her drawing board in the nineteenth century New Hampshire farmhouse where she lives, Hyman moves out through her art into worlds both magical and real. The house and its setting form the foundations for much of her art work. The apple tree in the backyard shelters the wounded knight who will become St. George; the woman who lives up the road finds the voice of Norma Farber's narrator and tells us *How Does It Feel to Be Old?*

Hyman's work day is a long one. She not only works at her art, she also researches so as to be accurate in her depictions, and she is always thinking about her current projects. Even when she goes for a walk with her dogs, she is working. "I no longer work the very long hours and the very many projects all at once that I used to. I literally can't. I used to work twelve hours a day, seven days a week, and I can't do it anymore. My eyes stop focusing at ten o'clock at night. And I just decided, quite recently, that life is short and I should take a little time out to live it. I work about eight hours a day now, five days a week. Quite a cutback."

Hyman and her friend and colleague, Barbara Rogasky, live in a "beautiful, old, rambling, falling-down farmhouse with dogs and a cat and other animals. I love nature very much. I guess that's from my German background. I like to walk, I love weather, I love to travel—I don't get enough chance to do that because my work takes a lot of time. I'm a workaholic out of habit; if I don't sit down and work, I don't feel right. I'm an addictive personality: I smoke cigarettes and drink coffee like crazy. Ahh, I don't know what else, I know everybody loves to talk about themselves. I'm basically a kid at heart. I get along with children very well, they get along with me because I'm like them, we share kind of wacky things."

Her daughter, Katrin, is married to a prince of Cameroon, West Africa. They have a two-year-old son, Michou, and live in Burlington, Vermont, where Katrin's husband is finishing up his degree. Trina enjoys romping with her grandson. "He's very beautiful and very smart. I think he's wonderful, and he thinks I'm wonderful, too. We like to do the same kinds of things. What we like to do is get in the red wagon together and go really, really fast downhill and bang into a tree and fall out and lie on the ground screaming for a while. Barbara and my daughter, Katrin, will come out of the house and be all upset. That's the kind of thing I mean when I said I'm a kid at heart."

Hyman's relationship with her daughter is also an excellent one. "My daughter is a wonderful woman. We're good friends. I feel like we are kind of holding hands going through life, finding things out and helping each other, searching through things, like sisters."

Hyman decided during childhood that she wanted to become an

illustrator and grew up to study at art schools in Philadelphia, Boston, and Stockholm, Sweden. Editor Astrid Lindgren (the writer of the *Pippi Longstocking* books) gave Hyman her first children's book to illustrate, a book in Swedish, titled *Toffe Och den Lilla Bilen* (Toffe and the little car) in the early '60s. By the mid-'60's she was beginning to illustrate children's books regularly. About this time, editor Helen Jones gave her a book by Ruth Sawyer to illustrate: *Joy to the World: Christmas Legends.* The book won recognition as an ALA Notable Book and a Horn Book honor list book but what Hyman prized most was having found a mentor in Jones, "a tough, clear-eyed, no-nonsense Yankee lady," as Trina later described her. "She cared deeply about children's books and knew everything there was to know about publishing them."

Through the seventies and eighties she illustrated all kinds of books, from Kathryn Lasky's story of Jews escaping the Russian pogroms, *The Night Journey,* and Norma Farber's reflection on life and aging, *How Does It Feel to Be Old?,* to the stunningly illustrated fairy tales for which she is best known. One of these, *St. George and the Dragon,* won the Caldecott medal in 1985.

Hyman saturates her illustrations with details. "I'm a compulsive filler-in of space," she says, and certainly her fairy tale illustrations are rich with items to look at, often even illuminated. Even when her style is somewhat sparer her art still brims with the results of her acute observation skills. Hyman thinks deeply into her characters, imagining the personalities and motivations behind their actions in the story and also their lives beyond the story. Although she often uses friends and family as the starting point for characters' physical appearances, she knows a book's characters thoroughly as people on their own terms. This knowledge is the spark of life that her characters carry. Whether the Hyman illustration shows the enchanted princes and evil older brothers in Barbara Rogosky's retelling of *The Water of Life* or the patrons of a colonial Boston tavern in Jean Fritz's *Why Don't You Get a Horse, Sam Adams?,* there's a story in every face.

The natural surroundings, architecture, and clothing are all as closely observed and rendered as the people who inhabit them. Hyman's research gives her the insight into the details of time and place that make solid the worlds of the stories she illustrates. She makes these story worlds sumptuous not only with what she puts into her pictures but also through how she surrounds them—framing pictures and text with illumination-like borders (in her retelling of *Little Red Riding Hood* or Margaret Hodges' retelling of *St. George and the Dragon*) or framing pictures within pictures (as in Margaret Hodges' *The Kitchen Knight*).

In an interview with David White (*Language Arts,* September, 1983) Hyman said that she didn't feel that she had "achieved a slot or niche" for herself. When questioned about that now she reflected, "I think that I feel that I have certainly achieved a niche. I've been around long enough; I've been illustrating for over thirty years. I feel that my name is well-known, my work is well-known, and there are lots of people out there who like my books very much. I am at the point in my career where I certainly can think of myself as a well-known children's book illustrator. I get the chance to more or less make my own way, not be nervous about asking people's permission. If I don't want to do sketches, I don't do them, and that's it. I'm one of the old pros. But as far as being someone who the general public, the children's literature general public, thinks of in a particular way, I don't get that, I don't see that. I don't think I have a definite personality as an illustrator. I think that my work has evolved and changed very much over the years, and I think the evolution and changing maybe doesn't leave a very clear image or picture in my audience's mind, except maybe for the fairy tales."

Hyman's doubts notwithstanding, the strength of her people and the force of the detail make her always recognizable, from *How Does Feel to Be Old?*, which she has said a number of times she views as her best work, to *Saint George, Little Red Riding Hood, The Kitchen Knight*, and, indeed, all of her work. "It's true that I think my main strength, which is also my major interest, is human beings. I like to watch people. I like to look at them and then guess what their reactions are going to be. I think that the human face and form is endlessly interesting and I like to portray it. I like to set real people in fantasy situations, and I kind of like playing goddess at the same time. I think I'm a natural sharer; I'm a sort of creative dibbledabbler, the kind of person who likes to say, 'Oh, look at that, isn't that fascinating, isn't that interesting, isn't that fun.' And, I kind of like to say what I see and share my own reactions with people.

"It gratifies me when people like my work. It feels wonderful when somebody sees something in one of my books and gets it, you know, really gets what I was trying to say. A lot of children have written and said, 'You know, I love the books, I want you to know there's something about it that's really true, that reminds me of myself, that's exactly what I wanted to say, it's a very frightening story, really spooky,' and so on. "Every single one of my books has something special for me. I wouldn't deliver the art if it didn't feel personal and special and precious. Of course, there are a lot of books that I don't like anymore; there are a lot of old books that I'm not proud of. I did them for money. I like *How Does It Feel to Be Old?* pretty much. I'm very touched by family feelings, by the relationship between the very old generation and the young one."

Although the character of the old woman was inspired by a neighbor, Hyman doesn't use models to pose for her work. "I don't take pictures. I don't set people up in the pose and take a Polaroid of them and work from photographs or have people come and pose. But I usually, not always, but I usually have a real person in mind for the character."

Hyman works "first in pencil, on one piece of paper, and then I add the color with acrylics or oil. I don't do 'fill-in-the-sketches.' I do most of the preliminary work in my head. When I've tackled the picture in my head and it's the way I want it to look, then I just sit down and go right into it, drawing in pencil on paper or board, or whatever. If it doesn't work in the pencil drawing, then I might do some sketches or some rearranging on paper. When I get a pencil drawing then I finish it off with India ink and a brush. Then I put in the colors. In the past, I've done the color mostly with acrylic paint. Now I'm kind of into mixed media: I use acrylic, but I also use colored pencils, some Crayola crayons, and whatever looks best, whatever feels best.

"In *The Fortune-Teller*, a book just coming out this fall, I worked with crayons, and it was so much fun. It's published by E.P. Dutton. That's Lloyd Alexander's publisher. Lloyd Alexander and I have not worked together before, but we've been friends for a long time. We've always said we should do a book together. This is that book. I've worked for Dutton in the past two years, and they know my work. We did something very bold and brave. Lloyd had written a very witty little cautionary tale, and it was set in just your basic generic fairy-tale setting. When I read the manuscript, I thought we could set it in Cameroon. I know and love the country, and I was dying to get the pictures from there. Lloyd said, 'Sure!' All he had to do was change five nouns and it became a West African tale. I did the pictures, and they are inspired by the part of Cameroon where my daughter lived. And I just had a good time with it. And so, here we have an original folktale set in Africa, done by two very white people."

"Of course we're not pretending that it's an authentic Cameroon tale. It's such a pretty book that we haven't had any complaints. I'm excited about the book, and I'm curious to see what the reaction's going to be. They have already had to go into a second printing. I guess that advance sales must be wonderful."

"So, at this point I'm still experimenting. At one point I felt soundly dissatisfied by my own work. I was in a real rut, and two years after that, I started drawing to please myself. Then I felt alive, I felt able to change very slightly in my approach and I had a little more courage. I'm one of these artists that just makes it up from my head; I'm not going to draw it until it looks right, which is not the organized way that most professional artists go about things, so it takes some courage for me to decide to try something new. And that's where I am now. Whatever is happening inside my head at the moment, I can't help it, it's automatically translated into what I'm working on. So, if I am in a place in my life where I find I'm angry, or frightened, or something is going on that I don't understand, maybe I take it out on my work in a way that is an expression of me."

When Hyman was asked if she has an audience in mind when setting out, she replied, "Of course. I am my audience. I'm the one who makes it up and gets to look at it first. I have to please myself. On the other hand, I always have an audience looking over my shoulder. Right in the forefront of that audience is children. Now, I can't say what children are or what they want or what I think they would like, but I do think of kids and what would make them want to read the stories, what would help stretch their imaginations. There's also the influence of reviewers, and parents, and their reaction to little jokes that I used to play that I don't do anymore, like sexy carvings on a table. I just thought that was funny, kind of an 'in' joke to people who could understand it. But I have found that this kind of a joke gets people so bent out of shape that I can't deal with it anymore, so I've stopped doing it. It's not so important anymore, being a joker or a trickster, just to prove something. I think you can do a perfectly great book without it."

Hyman's decision on whether or not to do a book is based on many factors. "Truly, it's just my own purely emotional response. If I read this story and it gets me excited and it makes me want to do a lot of pictures in my head, then I want to do it. I have to respect my own background and what I know, and that helps to inform me about what I'll take on, although I do a lot of research as well. I can't say that I was alive in medieval England, although I've done lots of books connected with that period. But I think that I have a feel for it. I've visited England many times. It's the kind of country that, if you've been there, you feel part of it. I feel connected with western European philosophy, my own background. This recent foray into Cameroon was connected to me because I visited there. I had several wonderful, meaningful, personal experiences there. My daughter married a Cameroonian; I got to know people who lived there, so I felt like, okay, at least I'll try and tell something of my experience through my pictures."

Hyman's daughter, Katrin, paid tribute to her in a *Horn Book* article in June/July, 1985. She described her mother as uncompromising in her sense of self and in her artistic vision. She affirmed that her mother had taught her to "value human beings for their humanness, their ability to feel strongly, to work hard and to care for each other." Hyman's dedication to her work and her sense of ethics shine through the entire article, as does her warmth as a human being and her success as a mother.

Her sense of humor and playfulness is exhibited in her Caldecott Medal acceptance speech, reprinted in that same 1985 edition of the *Horn Book*. In this speech Hyman also reveals how difficult her early schooling was because of her vivid imagination, her "need to draw pictures all day long," and her demonstrated ability to read beyond the expected flat fare of the schools. Fortunately for us all, her passion for reading stories and drawing continue to this day and her illustrations are evidence of her wit, her intelligence, and her enormous talent.

Books Illustrated and Written by Trina Schart Hyman

How Six Found Christmas. Holiday, 1991.

A Little Alphabet. Little, 1973. WM. Morrow, 1993.

Little Red Riding Hood. Holiday, 1982.

Self-Portrait: Trina Schart Hyman. HarperCollins, 1989.

The Sleeping Beauty. Little, 1983.

Books Illustrated by Trina Schart Hyman

Among the Dolls, by William Sleatar, Dutton, 1975. Knopf, 1991.

The Bad Times of Irma Baumlein, by Carol R. Brink. Macmillan 1972, 1991.

Caddie Woodlawn, by Carol R. Brink. Macmillan, 1973.

Canterbury Tales, by Barbara Cohen. Lothrop, 1988.

Cat Poems, compiled by Myra C. Livingston. Holiday, 1987.

A Child's Christmas in Wales, by Dylan Thomas. Holiday, 1985.

A Christmas Carol, by Charles Dickens. Holiday, 1983.

Christmas Poems, selected by Myra C. Livingston. Holiday, 1984.

A Connecticut Yankee in King Arthur's Court, by Mark Twain. Morrow, 1988.

Fairy Poems, edited by Daisy Wallace. Holiday, 1980.

The Fairy Tale Life of Hans Christian Andersen, by Eva Moore. Scholastic Inc., 1967.

The Fortune Tellers, by Lloyd Alexander Dutton, 1992.

Hershel and Hanukkah Goblins, by Eric A. Kimmel. Holiday, 1989.

A Hidden Magic, by Vivian Van de Velde. Crown, 1988.

How Does It Feel to Be Old? by Norma Farber. Dutton, 1988.

King Stork, by Howard Pyle. Little, 1973.

The Kitchen Knight, by Margaret Hodges. Holiday, 1990.

Let's Steal the Moon, by Blanche Serwer-Bernstein. Shapolsky, 1987.

Magic in the Mist, by Margaret M. Kimmel. Macmillan, 1975.

The Man Who Loved Books, by Jean Fritz. Putnam, 1981.

The Night Journey, by Kathryn Lasky. Puffin, 1986.
Rapunzel. retold by Barbara Rogasky. Holiday, 1982.
A *Room Made of Windows*, by Eleanor Cameron. Puffin, 1990.
St. George and the Dragons, adapted by Margaret Hodges. Little, 1984.
Snow White, adapted by Paul Heins. Little, 1979.
Star Mother's Youngest Child, by Louise Moeri. HM, 1980.
Swan Lake, by Margot Fanteyn. HBJ, 1989.
Tight Times, by Barbara S. Hazen. Viking, 1979. Puffin, 1983.
The Water of Life, retold by Barbara Rogasky. Holiday, 1986, 1991.
Why Don't You Get a Horse, Sam Adams? by Jean Fritz. Putnam, 1982.
Will You Sign Here, John Hancock? by Jean Fritz. Putnam, 1982.
Witch Poems, edited by Daisy Wallace. Holiday, 1990.

Brian Pinkney

Brian Pinkney was born in 1961. His first illustrations for picture books were published in 1989. Before that he was an illustrator for such publications as *The New York Times Magazine, Woman's Day*, and other popular journals. His art work has been exhibited by the School of Visual Arts, the Society of Publication Designers, the National Coalition of 100 Black Women Art Show, and the Afro-American Historical and Cultural Museum in Philadelphia. The inclusion of his work in the National Arts Club Exhibition in 1990 earned him the National Arts Club Award of Distinction. He won the Parents' Choice award four times and the Society of Children's Book Writer's Golden Kite Award for illustrating for *Where Does the Trail Lead?*, published in 1992 by Simon and Schuster. His illustrations for *The Dark Thirty* (by Patricia McKissack) earned him a Caldecott Honor for 1993.

To date, Pinkney has illustrated thirteen children's books and as of February of 1993 he is hard at work on at least six more. The books that he has illustrated so far and several he has in mind for the future deal with themes of African American heritage or context. "I tend to like the African-American story because I know I can connect with that right now. I learned a lot about myself and my heritage researching *The Boy and the Ghost*. It's kind of like finding my roots. I really feel like I'm researching myself. To research other stories, like *The Ballad of Belle Dorcas*, I bought books on slavery and the South. Ironically, *The Ballad of Belle Dorcas* takes place in North Carolina, which is where my mother grew up. When my mother and I went down for a family reunion I used the opportunity to take photographs for research. I didn't know too much about the South, and I kept thinking I didn't know where this story took place. Then I found out that the story took place miles from where my mother grew up."

In response to the question of how he decides to illustrate a particular book Pinkney responded: "I think of myself first probably as an artist. When I pick a story I want to illustrate I try to find something that I feel I can get involved with personally. With the first two books that I was offered I was just lucky because I loved both of those stories. Since then I've received a lot of manuscripts to read through, so I've started to become very selective. Publishers say to me, 'Give us an idea of what type of manuscripts you like.' I don't know unless I read them because sometimes there may be something personal that I could never have suspected. For example, I was offered *Where Does the Trail Lead?* because it was about the ocean. I previously illustrated with watercolors so they thought my style would be perfect for the book. In the meantime I had started working on scratchboard. I knew that that's how I wanted to work from now on, at least until something new comes along."

"The connection I found to this story was that I used to stay in a house on Cape Cod. I recognized that the story was my autobiography. When I read the poem at first (for *Where Does the Trail Lead*) I just kind of sat back and thought about different images that I remember from when I was a kid. I ended up with about ten of them: running away from the waves, jumping off dunes, and things like that. Then I went back and said, 'Okay, now where can I fit these into the story?' Of course there were some that had to be changed slightly, but that's how I approached that book. The whole book is a map of the boy's journey. If you were in a helicopter and watched the action, it actually makes sense that the boy leaves the house and goes to the left and circles back around the house and then comes back in from the right and meets his family in the same spot where he started from."

Family is very important to Brian Pinkney. His sense of family figures largely in all of his illustrations. His father, Jerry Pinkney is a well established, talented, and renowned illustrator of children's books. They often talk shop when they are together at family gatherings. Pinkney's wife, Andrea Davis Pinkney, has served as a model for many of his characters. One notable example of this is in the book, *The Ballad of Belle Dorcas,* in which Andrea is Belle. Pinkney served as his own model for Belle's husband, Joshua.

The two-page spread in *The Ballad of Belle Dorcas* where Joshua is turning into a tree is an astounding work of art, capturing the horror Joshua feels at losing his human form. "Originally that book was supposed to be done in pencil and watercolor. I had done a sample in watercolor and sent it to try and get the illustration assignment. They liked what I gave them and we went ahead with the project. Halfway through the project I started working on scratchboard and I told them that I wanted to do the book in this medium. They were a little taken aback, but they said, 'Well, okay, fine; show us a sample.' So I did the spread that now appears in the book, and when they saw it they loved it."

"Another book I am working on is a biography of Alvin Ailey, which my wife wrote. It will be published by Hyperion in 1993. I was having problems with it because I kept trying to do the book as though you're watching Alvin perform. I just couldn't make it work until I started changing the reference. I decided what I needed to do was to find a model who looked like Alvin Ailey, and then I realized I was the best model. As soon as I became Alvin the book came alive to me. Then I was kind of acting out his life; I was doing a kind of autobiography, a self-portrait. Just as I was that little boy in the dunes in *Where Does the Trail Lead?* and I knew I had to be Joshua in *The Ballad of Belle Dorcas,* I was Alvin Ailey. That's when I started getting all the action and dynamics I wanted. I was thinking, 'What does it feel like to be Alvin?' as opposed to, 'What does Alvin look like?' "

The scratchboard technique that Pinkney uses becomes versatile in his hands. "It started when I was a master's degree student at the School of Visual Arts in New York City. I had been working in pencil and watercolor for about five years, doing a lot of editorial work for magazines. I had just been assigned *The Boy and the Ghost* so I was doing that in the early technique. I went back for my master's basically because I knew that I wanted to take my art work to the next step, the next level. I figured I'd have two years away from the world to do my art work. The same week I was accepted into the School of Visual Arts master's program, I received *The Boy and the Ghost* manuscript. I actually did *The Boy and the Ghost, The Ballad of Bell Dorcas,* the *Harriet Tubman* book, and the beginning of *Where Does the Trail Lead?* while I was at school getting my degree."

"During the second half of the first semester I had an instructor who kept saying, 'Now is the time to experiment with different techniques.' He kept telling me to try scratchboard. People don't use it much for art work and I decided to just try it. At the time I used to ride my bicycle to school every day and after a while I was riding in the middle of traffic. I'd get to school and I'd want to ride down to the Village and back again, so I just kind of did an essay on this transformation of me into this bicycle messenger in pencil drawing."

"Someone said they liked the pencil drawing the way it was and they didn't want me to add watercolor to it. I thought that was interesting so I thought, 'Let me try something different.' I decided to do it in scratchboard. When I was drawing with pencil the drawings would get heavy. The more lines I put down the darker they would get. With scratch board it worked in reverse. The more lines I scratched out the lighter the image got and I was able to build volume, movement, and form at the same time, kind of like sculpting, and I just fell in love with it. From then on I did all my projects that way. I was working on *The Ballad of Belle Dorcas* at the time and knew I couldn't continue in watercolor. I think I tried to do one piece in the pencil and watercolor afterwards and my heart just wasn't in it."

Pinkney describes the process as follows: "It starts out with a white board that I buy already prepared with a coat of black ink on it. (I buy it already prepared because it is a lot easier. You can make it yourself by taking a white board and painting black ink on it.) At that point I use one of three sharp tools: a #11 Xacto blade (which is a regular art-cutting tool) or either of two scratchboard bits, one that looks like an arrow head and one that looks like a spoon. The spoon is for scraping away large areas and the arrow head is for fine detail."

"What happens is you scratch into the black and the white shows through. You end up with a white line on a black background. Then I just keep scratching and I get a rhythm going. I think of it as sculpting so I start out trying to make whatever I am drawing look round and look like it has volume to it. After I get black and white rendering done I go back in to add color by using oil pastels that come in little sticks. I rub the oil pastel onto the scratchboard and the color goes into the cracks. Sometimes there is color on the black also. I use a liquid which dissolves the pigment of the oil pastel so it goes into the cracks. Then I can wipe the excess from the black with a paper towel. That's basically how I do color. Lately I've scratched away all of the background or I've gessoed it out. I am struggling with new techniques of this sort right now. I like to sit back and experiment."

"Most of the books I had done in scratchboard took place outside or they were inside a log cabin. The technique made sense for that because I could scratch the logs in it and it could look like wood grain. It made sense. I'm working now on a Kwanzaa book that my wife wrote, and it's set in contemporary homes where the walls are flat and there is no grain to the wood. I had to figure out a way to render that in scratchboard and I can't even tell you how I resolved that. I can tell you I'm oil painting them and that's starting to work."

"Sometimes I enjoy taking on a challenge, like *The Elephant's Wrestling Match*. I like drawing animals but I had never done an animal book before. The reason why they suggested I do that book was because of the drum in it. I play the drums and have always played different types of drums. As a matter of fact, I have lots of African drums around me now.

I liked this story not because of the fact there was a drummer in it but because of the monkey, who is kind of the antagonist in the story." The book, published in 1992, demonstrates not only Pinkney's proficiency with scratchboards but also his deftness in drawing the animals so that their particular features are conveyed to the viewer: the strength of the elephant, the energy of the monkey, and the menacing nastiness of the crocodile, for example.

Pinkney is involved with many projects at this time, including the illustration of two books written by his wife, Andrea Davis Pinkney: *Seven Candles for Kwanzaa* and *Alvin Ailey*. He is deluged with manuscripts from publishers and is working on a book writing his own stories. He would very much like to do books with a multicultural theme. "I'm African-American but I grew up in a multicultural environment. I want to do books that show my story. As I think about it, when I was a kid growing up, there were Asians, blacks, whites, and Hispanics on the streets in my neighborhood. That's the world I grew up in. I haven't received manuscripts like that."

We can be assured that whatever Pinkney endeavors, he will display the sense of movement, strength, and universality of experience that stamp his work.

Books Illustrated by Brian Pinkney

Alvin Ailey, by Andrea Davis Pinkney to be published by Hyperion in Fall, 1993.

The Ballad of Belle Dorcas, by Willaim H. Hooks, Knopf, 1990.

The Boy and the Ghost, by Robert D. San Souci, Simon and Schuster, 1989.

Cut From the Same Cloth, by Robert D. San Souci, Philomel, 1993.

The Dark Thirty, by Patricia McKissack, Knopf, 1992.

The Elephant's Wrestling Match, by Judy Sierra, Silver Press, 1992.

Happy Birthday, Martin Luther King, by Jean Marzollo, Scholastic, 1993.

Harriet Tubman. by Polly Carter, Silver Burdett, 1990.

Max Found Two Sticks, by Brian Pinkney, to be published by Simon and Schuster in Spring, 1994.

Seven Candles for Kwanzaa, by Andrea Davis Pinkney, to be published by Dial in Fall, 1993.

Sukey and the Mermaid, by Robert D. San Souci, Four Winds Press, 1992.

A Wave In Her Pocket, by Lynn Joseph, Clarion, 1991.

Where Does the Trail Lead? by Burton Albert, Simon and Schuster, 1991.

Maurice Sendak

Maurice Sendak is a very private man whose work has drawn on his personal psychology and emotions. Nevertheless, his stories and images connect with the inner lives of so many of his readers that they have become widely cherished. He is considered a giant in children's literature, partly because his work has provided a breakthrough in redefining what children's literature and the illustrations in children's books can accomplish. He manages to achieve this new and fresh approach while at the same time drawing on sources from the eighteenth and nineteenth centuries. Each of his books touches in some way on children's (and adults') anxieties and dreams, capturing in an unsentimentalized way the emotional quality and passion of childhood.

Sendak has earned many honors, among them the three most prestigious awards in the world of children's literature: the Caldecott Medal for perhaps his most famous book, *Where the Wild Things Are*, the Laura Ingalls Wilder Medal and the Hans Christian Andersen International Award for the excellence of his entire body of work. He was the first American to receive this impressive award. Most of his books have been designated ALA notables.

Maurice Bernard Sendak was born in Brooklyn, New York, the youngest of three children. His childhood was not a carefree one. He was sickly and frail and, therefore, had to stay at home most of the time. He remembers hearing his mother worry aloud that he might die. He drew pictures and observed the world rather than participating in it. He recalls looking out the window a great deal when he was a child and it is no accident that windows figure strongly in all of his books. He loved the imaginative stories that his father invented for him and his siblings. He and his brother Jack collaborated on his first book, *They Were Insepa-rable*, when he was six years old. His sister Natalie gave him his first book, *The Prince and the Pauper*, when he was nine years old, starting him on his love for beautifully made books. His other reading consisted mostly of comic books. The young Sendak also loved music, movies, Mickey Mouse, and the radio show, "Let's Pretend."

While Sendak was still in high school he began earning money as an illustrator for All-American Comics. He hated school and vowed never to go to college. Perhaps part of his discomfort was due to the fact that he is left-handed and was made to feel inadequate because of this and totally retreated into himself. He found for himself those models he wished to emulate. The work of such artists as William Blake, George Cruikshank, Wilhelm Busch, Bouter de Monvel, Philip Otto Runger, and other German romantic painters inspired many of his works.

The important breakthrough in Sendak's career came in 1950 when he was working as a window-display artist for F.A.O. Schwartz, a famous toy store in New York City. (He was also attending evening art classes at the Art Students' League.) Ursula Nordstrom, a renowned children's book editor at Harper, saw some of his paintings in the window of the store and was very impressed with his talent. She offered him the opportunity to illustrate *The Wonderful Farm* by Marcel Ayme. Nordstrom became a mentor and friend to the young artist. She recognized his remarkable talent and encouraged and believed in him. He credits her with training him to be a children's book illustrator. She decided to engage Sendak to illustrate Ruth Krauss's now classic book, *A Hole Is to Dig*, a book that immediately upon publication changed the face of children's book illustrations. The book also established Sendak as a leading artist.

In 1963, after having published a number of books that he wrote and illustrated, Sendak produced his most successful book, *Where the Wild Things Are*. In this book the pictures and text equally share in the telling of the story. Some adults were fearful that the book would frighten children and sought to keep it out of libraries when it was first published. Its earning the Caldecott Medal ensured its purchase by libraries across the country. The enormous readership it immediately garnered assured the public that most children, frightened or not, were fascinated by and attracted to the book. The story, about the fantasy trip of a child who is naughty and a little rebellious and who eventually returns to the loving and familiar comfort of his own home, is ultimately reassuring to readers.

Sendak tells us that the wild things are modeled on his Brooklyn relatives who used to visit his family. He and his sister and brother used to have to entertain these "cheek-pinching relatives" while his mother was in the kitchen preparing meals for them.

The round-edged look of Maurice Sendak's characters and the crosshatched shades and tones in much of his work evoke for many readers a sense of the wildness of a dream, a wildness that never becomes chaos and always comes under control by story's end. This dream-sense can be found throughout Sendak's work, but it is most fully realized in the picture book trilogy, *Where the Wild Things Are, In the Night Kitchen,* and *Outside Over There*. He considers these three books to be "all variations on the same theme: how children master various feelings such as anger, boredom, fear, frustration, jealousy, and manage to come to grips with the realities of their lives." The third book of the trilogy afforded the artist a great sense of inner peace. He is not known for being a happy person but this book satisfied him enormously. He felt that he had resolved some very strong emotions in this work.

In the cross-hatching and other elements of his technique he draws on nineteenth century illustrators such as William Blake, Randolph Caldecott and George Cruikshan. He is also influenced by twentieth century popular art and design. From Walt Disney and comics to the advertising, architecture and product packaging that formed a backdrop to his Brooklyn boyhood, these modern influences touched him early. Some of them can be seen in the cityscape/kitchenscape of *In the Night Kitchen.*

Dear Mili, published in 1988, based on the Grimm brothers' story as represented in an 1816 piece of correspondence to a young child, reflects Sendak's involvement with nineteenth century art, music, and literature. It also represents his anguish over the Holocaust. His father lost every one of his family members in the Holocaust and the events of World War II hung over Maurice's childhood like a dark cloud.

Sendak comments, "My Jewishness is something that I don't seek out intellectually but that I respond to emotionally. It's a kind of drenched feeling which just surfaces in anything I do. I don't set out to do it, but I do admit, it happens each time do a book. I don't know when a book is going to happen; it's like a quiet explosion. I'm doing a book right now, and there it is again. I start at one end and you think, 'It can't possibly touch there,' but it always somehow touches there. And it touches the Holocaust, and yet the Holocaust not in the literal sense of what happened (I've already been through that in the creative sense) but now meaning something else, meaning the world, the present day decay of the world, and the atrocious disinterest in children who are dying all over the world. It drives me crazy; it must drive, I assume, any thinking person crazy."

"The core is my incredible, traumatic experience as a boy of living through the war, of hearing my father scream, and knowing that there were no more Sendaks in the world but us. That of course is the core and always will be. And somehow, me having to make up for that."

Sendak's talents extend well beyond picture book production. Maurice has long had a fascination and love for the theater. Many of his books look as if they take place on a proscenium stage. When asked if this was a purposeful image, Sendak replied, "It was there almost unwittingly; I wasn't aware of the double meaning. I had to actually get to a theater to realize that I had been doing it all the time."

He has designed the sets and costumes for operas and ballets, including adaptations of his own works. Throughout the eighties, Sendak became increasingly involved in opera and theater, not only writing librettos and scripts and designing costumes and sets but also serving as artistic director for a children's theater company. "It's called The Children's Theater because we have no other words for it—just the way my books are called children's books, but I think of them as books that are for everybody, mostly children and parents. I'd like The Children's Theater to have the same breadth and vision. It isn't precisely children's theater as we know it in the general sense but a more complicated theater experience, acknowledging that children can use their emotions and their brains in a vigorous manner and also be something that would intrigue grownups."

The theater, located in the State University of New York at Purchase, New York, "is based exactly on the kind of books I've done for forty years so I know what the pattern is and I know how to achieve it. Having had roughly twelve years of stage experience designing operas and ballets, and having experimented with some of my particular ideas on stage, I know that they work."

At this point in his life Sendak acknowledges that working very hard is part of his plan. He values creative labor. "I've decided to be to others what Ursula Nordstrom was for me." And he takes his mission very seriously. In this world where there is so much that is mediocre and pedestrian, Maurice Sendak shines as an innovator, a man of principle and intelligence, and a creative genius whose work continues to delight and tantalize audiences of all ages.

Books authored and illustrated by Maurice Sendak

(All published by HarperCollins)

Alligators All Around, 1962, 1991.

Chicken Soup with Rice, 1962, 1991. Scholastic Inc, 1986.

Hector Protector, 1965.

Hector Protector and As I Went Over the Water: Two Nursery Rhymes, 1990.

Higglety Pigglety Pop: Or, There Must Be More to Life, 1967, 1979.

In the Night Kitchen, 1970, 1985.

Kenny's Windows, 1956, 1989.

Nutshell Library, 1962.

One Was Johnny: A Counting Book, 1962, 1991.

Outside Over There, 1981, 1989.

Pierre: A Cautionary Tale, 1962, 1991.

Seven Little Monsters, 1977.

Sign on Rosie's Door, 1960.

Some Swell Pup Or Are You Sure You Want a Dog? Farrar, Straus & Giroux 1985, 1989.

Very Far Away, 1962.

Where the Wild Things Are, 1985, 1988.

Books Illustrated By Maurice Sendak

Along Came a Dog, by Meindert DeJong, HarperCollins 1958, 1980.

Animal Family, by Randall Jarrell, Pantheon, 1985, 1987.

The Bat-Poet, by Randall Jarrell, Macmillan 1967.

The Bee-Man of Orn, by Frank Stockton, HarperCollins, 1987.

The Big Green Book, by Robert Graves, Macmillan, 1985.

The Birthday Party, by Ruth Krauss, HarperCollins, 1957.

Dear Mili, by the Brothers Grimm, Farrar, Straus, & Giroux, 1988

Father Bear Comes Home, by Else Minarik, Harper Collins, 1959, 1978.

Fly By Night, by Randall Jarrell, FS&G, 1985.

The Golden Key, by George MacDonald, FS&G, 1984.

The Griffin and the Minor Canon, by Frank R. Stockton, HarperCollins 1986, 1987.

A Hole is to Dig, by Ruth Krauss, Live Oak Media 1990. HarperCollins 1952, 1989.

House of Sixty Fathers, by Meindert DeJong, HarperCollins, 1956, 1987.

Hurry Home Candy, by Meindert DeJong, HarperCollins, 1953.

I Saw Esau, by Iona and Peter Opie, Candlewick, 1992.

I'll Be You and You Be Me, by Ruth Krauss, HarperCollins, 1954. Bookstore, 1973.

In Grandpa's House, by Philip Sendak, HarperCollins, 1985.

The Juniper Tree, by the Brothers Grimm, Farrar, Straus, & Giroux, 1973.

King Grisly-Beard, by the Brothers Grimm, Farrar, Straus & Giroux, 1973.

A Kiss for Little Bear, by Else Minarik, HarperCollins, 1968, 1984.

Let's Be Enemies, by Janice Udry, HarperCollins, 1961, 1988.

The Light Princess, by George MacDonald, Farrar, Straus & Giroux, 1969.

Little Bear, by Else Minarik, HarperCollins, 1957.

Little Bear's Friend, by Else Minarik, HarperCollins, 1960.

Little Bear's Visit, by Else Minarik, HarperCollins, 1961, 1985.

Lullabies and Night Songs, edited by William Engvick, HarperCollins, 1965.

Mister Rabbit and the Lovely Present, by Charlotte Zolotow, HarperCollins, 1962, 1977.

Moon Jumpers, by Janice Udry, HarperCollins, 1959.

Mrs. Piggle-Wiggle's Farm, by Betty MacDonald, HarperCollins, 1954.

No Fighting, No Biting! by Else Minarik, HarperCollins, 1958, 1978.

The Nutcracker, by E.T. Hoffman, Crown, 1984, 1991.

Open House for Butterflies, by Ruth Krauss, HarperCollins, 1990.

Pleasant Fieldmouse, by Jan Wahl, HarperCollins, 1964.

Sarah's Room, by Doris Orgel, HarperCollins, 1991.

Seven Tales by Hans Christian Andersen, HarperCollins 1959, 1991.

Shadrach, by Meindert DeJong, HarperCollins 1953, 1980.

Somebody Else's Nut Tree and Other Tales from Children, by Ruth Krauss, Shoe String, 1990.

A Very Special House, by Ruth Krauss, HarperCollins 1953, 1990.

What Can You Do With a Shoe? by Beatrice DeRegniers, HarperCollins, 1955.

What Do You Do, Dear? by Sesyle Joslin, HarperCollins, 1958, 1986.

What Do You Say, Dear? by Sesyle Joslin, HarperCollins, 1958, 1986.

The Wheel on the School, by Meindert DeJong, HarperCollins, 1954.

Zlateh the Goat and Other Stories, by Isaac Bashevis Singer, HarperCollins,

3

People Behind the Books: Writers

Masha Kabakow Rudman

The field of children's literature is blessed with an abundance of dedicated, talented, thoughtful, and perceptive writers. Some are teachers or librarians as well as writers; some have served or work now as editors of other authors' work. Their writing takes the form of fiction, nonfiction, and poetry. There are many more authors and artists who write and illustrate movingly and effectively than are described here. We have chosen to highlight a few notable people who are actively and outstandingly involved in creating books for children today, to provide readers with some insight into the creation of books that are important to today's children and how the creators view themselves. We also want our readers to get to know these authors and artists as the interesting, dedicated, humorous, and thoughtful people they are.

They all have in common a remarkable clarity of vision, the ability to portray diverse people with sensitivity and accuracy. Not one of them writes books empty of meaning or demeaning to any group or individual. Each is a prolific and popular writer.

Children often decide what book they will read next based on work they have already read by a particular author. They may build on this practice when they know some personal facts about the authors. A number of resources are listed at the end of this chapter for teachers' and librarians' use in searching out information about the authors described here as well as others.

Arnold Adoff

Arnold Adoff holds fast to his appreciation of youth, justice, music, painting, photography, and poetry. All of these serve him well as a poet and anthologist. He started writing poetry when he was eleven years old, growing up in the South Bronx, in New York City. In college (City College of New York) he was active in civil liberties causes, wrote for the campus newspaper, and studied history. His passionate commitment to social justice, his experiences as a teacher in New York City's Harlem and Manhattan West Side and as manager for jazz great Charlie Mingus, and his life with his wife, Virginia Hamilton, and their children have flavored his work and informed his vision.

All of Adoff's anthologies include work by African American poets. He first became interested in collecting these poems as a very young man, "I was a non-black anthologist of black poetry for many years" Adoff put his research capabilities to good use in tracking down the material. His first anthology, *I Am the Darker Brother: An Anthology of Modern Poems by Negro American*, was published in 1968. At least seven more anthologies followed (see list at end of this chapter).

"Once you decide that America's your country and that you'll try to make the dream of equality a reality, then you have to be inclusive. When I was growing up there was no question as to what was western civilization and what was culture. So many factors bred separation and a feeling of superiority—the so-called majority group over the minority group—that my sense of outrage was peaked at an early, early, age. That's why I became an anthologist of black literature, because the books I found were totally exclusive, or a single or two token poems, no knowledge of parallel cultures. W.E.B. Dubois did a study of social studies textbooks fifty, sixty years ago coming to the same conclusions that people came to again in the '60s and still again in the last or 4 or 5 or 6 years. Literature, poetry, the art forms that make the least amount of profit are the ones that are controlled the most closely by the smallest number of people."

"It was much, much worse in the 1950's. Expand from black and white to Hispanic and AmerIndian, and further to male/female and you still have a situation only slightly improved, not quite as bad as it was in the 1950's. When we were in college we did not study very many women writers, no live women writers at all, and had few women professors. As a matter of fact, we still have women struggling for tenure today. The list goes on and on and on, whether it's the stuff like the making and disseminating of a poem or getting a job and a decent house—those are all the reasons I write as I do. It was a natural development for me to combine history and literature (reading Dubois and then Langston Hughes and going back to Claude McKay and going forward.)"

In the 1970's Adoff began publishing his own poetry, much of it reflecting his family configuration. The warmth and vibrancy of the family members accompany what he calls "shaped colloquial speech" to form very carefully designed structures. Each word and the very placement of each syllable makes sense in the integration and balance of the piece. The effect is one of freshness and spontaneity, while the underlying base is a firm one. There is nothing haphazard about the design. The techniques of flowing from one poem to another so as to create a continuous narrative, the repetition of key words and images, the capturing of what Adoff calls "crystal moments," and the sometimes startling physical layout all combine to provide a complex synthesis of meaning and shape.

Arnold calls his writing a "process of vision and revision." He feels that "less is more." His favorite way of working is vertical rather than horizontal: His poems hang in scrolls of drafts all over his room so that he is forced to look at them daily and, eventually, to act upon them. He finds the most difficult element of writing to be the selection process: what to leave in and what to take out.

"I think probably the operative word in my work and my world view is 'change.' I look to change and to create change. I think I see my work from several different perspectives, but certainly stylistically I attempt to bring many of the innovative techniques of so called 'adult poetry' from the early parts of this century into poetry for children rather than verse for children, which is traditionally the case. Most post World War II poets are creating open form, free form, or free verse, and every time my books of poetry are published reviewers use one of those three terms. But I don't create any of those poems; I create 'shaped speech' and those are my poems—they have form and they have semantic lines of force and they have rhythmic lines of force."

"Most free form poetry breaks the line at the natural breath pause. That is a prose overlay and does not create a form that's unique to poetry and to the individual poem. I believe that a poem has, very simply, to 'sing' as well as say, and most poets are not interested in having their poetry sing and say at the same time. I was influenced by the kinds of approaches I studied, particularly with a poet called Jose Garcia Villa. He was a professor at the New School who was a Filipino-American. These are some of the techniques that I impart, and when teachers are receptive they do many of these process techniques of mine, and kids love them, and it's a lot of fun. My theories and my aesthetics don't garner great hordes of followers, but I've enjoyed developing them over the years and when I have a chance to teach, I do." Adoff continues to practice the craft of teaching. He regularly visits classrooms and helps young writers with their work. He believes that teachers should make poetry an integrated part of each day so it will become part of each child.

"Whether it's a book called *Greens*, where the mother is driving the truck and playing the traditional, supposedly male gender role, to *Black Is Brown Is Tan*, I think I try to change the reader's perceptions of stereotypical views of human beings. In writing for children in general I try to change society for the better. That's my motivation. So *Black Is Brown Is Tan* is about an interracial family, but the mother chops wood and the father cooks hamburgers. It isn't a single theme, subject, or 'problem book'; it's an attempt to view human beings very much as whole people. That's kind of what I've been doing all these years. Even the recent ones, for example, *Hard To Be Six*, about going to the cemetery and a dead grandfather, has nothing to do with any particular culture or race and yet it's illustrated (by Jerry Pinkney) as African-American. This is an attempt again to present universals, rather than to separate out, let's say, the black experience into black experience books."

"That's basically what I've been doing—there's usually a political subtext to everything I do. *Flamboyan* is a perfect example of a beautiful and decorative picture book that is very much on one level to be enjoyed in a relaxed, loving, wish-fulfillment manner by young children and on another level is a very powerful story of force of will and self-empowerment. Everything is done consciously, whether I decide how to flush my lines, punctuate, do upper and lower case, or whatever, right down to the statement. I always have been that way. There is no mimicking of the various traditional, classical Eurocentric nineteenth century forms, and there's no mimicking, obviously, of white, male, Christian dominance, so-called dominant cultural attitudes, in any of my work."

"Flamboyan flies because she wishes to fly and look deeply and strongly into the center of this tree's beauty. Combining the force of the flamboyan flowers with the force of her own will *she* creates *her own* magic. She's not a sorceress; it's not abracadabra; it's not even the good witch with the red shoes. Look at your European fables, parables, or fairy tales, and she does not come out of any of those, or even out of African or Asian folk material. She's a consciously constructed person who uses will to create her fantasy."

In response to a question about what he thinks makes a book worth doing, he responded, "Work develops... the bottom line is I can't tell you why a wonderful idea or wonderful title or wonderful single poem never goes beyond that stage. That part of it I cannot tell you. What I can tell you about is what I've just done, which is the process of living and revision that takes those beginnings and makes a whole collection out of them. The book I just finished for a Willa Pearlman book at HarperCollins is... *Music*—it probably won't be out 'till '94. We've just signed on Karen Barbour to do the art."

"Those notes were begun—so this is an example—in '86. I had notebooks of scribbles and notes and tape recordings... Virginia and I were living in New York City and then going back and forth—New York to Ohio—for two years. Every two weeks we'd fly back to Ohio. It was exhausting. It began in '86 and was finally finished by the end of '91. So that's four or five years of scribbling, neglect, other things getting in the way, other books written and published, and then going back to process to completion. That's how it is."

Adoff is committed to continuing the publication of poetry for child audiences. He has been fortunate, for the most part, in his illustrators. His books, like *Flamboyan, Hard to Be Six,* and *In for Winter, Out for Spring,* have also been beautifully produced. Even though it is not commercially lucrative, he says, "Poetry is always at the back of the bus in today's publishing world. Real poetry for young people is not a healthy and flourishing form in youth literature... It's too expensive to print poetry (even verse, which makes a lot more money) with expensive four-color art. But with the advent of the '80s and a larger share of disposable income, the wordless picture book, hundreds of new children's book-stores in America, and the big bookstore chains coming along with children's departments, the publishers can now sell full-color books of my poems."

His own popularity has been enhanced by winning the National Council of Teachers of English Award for Poetry for Young Children (the only medal for poetry) in 1988. "It was not a big help in allowing me to publish more of my innovative work, but it was a big help in getting a more beautifully produced book, being 'assigned' an artist with a bigger reputation and, therefore, generating bigger sales. My finest work is still not published, my most innovative work, my most controversial. I still circulate it to publishers. On the one hand I get the best production and color and artist that I've ever had; on the other hand, there still are censorship pressures on publishers, whether they admit them or not. There are real struggles and battles going on in a very chaotic time in American society. So many times when there's less profit margin publishers play it safe. That's just where things are. There are so many young people really attempting to say and create such beautiful work. I've always done just what I wanted to do, and I continue to do just what I want to do. I have the luxury to pursue my work the way I want to."

In response to the comment that his work shows a refreshing honesty and understanding of how children feel, Adoff says, "You really have to relax and play like a kid plays, and that's the beauty and the fun of it. It's very much more of a free way to live. I've reached the top and I continue to try to be innovative and to stay at that top level." But, he adds, "I still have books of mine censored around the country, books about black and female issues that are not welcomed by school systems."

"Gender issues are crucial. When you deal with young kids, particularly in picture books, it isn't only the out and out blatant didactic story that's censored. Sometimes it's the (perhaps) more subtle and oblique kind of thing, like a girl flying, interracial families, or a poem in a collection dealing with youths and their feelings that runs into trouble."

Adoff says, "It's the circle of the family that is a very important factor in my work as well, and love—all that good stuff." He continues to work toward the increasing publication of authors and illustrators of parallel cultures and to bring the passion and substance of his views to the reading public.

Works by Arnold Adoff

All the Colors of the Race. Lothrop, 1982.

Anthology of Modern Poems by Negro Americans. Macmillan, 1970.

Birds. HarperCollins, 1982.

Black Is Brown Is Tan. HarperCollins, 1973.

Black on Black: Commentaries by Negro Americans

Black Out Loud: An Anthology of Modern Poems by Black Americans. Macmillan, 1970.

Brothers and Sisters: Modern Stories by Black Americans

The Cabbages Are Chasing the Rabbits. HBJ, 1985.

Chocolate Dreams. Lothrop, 1989.

City In all Directions. Macmillan, 1969.

Eats: Poems. Lothrop, 1979.

Flamboyan. HBJ, 1988.

Friend Dog. HarperCollins, 1980.

Greens. Lothrop, 1988.

Hard to Be Six. Lothrop, 1990.

I Am the Darker Brother. Macmillan, 1968.

I am the running girl. HarperCollins, 1979.

In for Winter, Out for Spring. HBJ, 1991.

it is the poem singing into your eyes: An Anthology of New Young Poets. HarperCollins, 1971.

MA nDA LA. HarperCollins, 1971.

Make a Circle, Keep Us In. Delacorte, 1975.

Malcolm X. HarperCollins, 1985.

My Black Me: A Beginning Book of Black Poetry. Dutton, 1974.

OUTside INside Poems. Lothrop, 1981.

The Poetry of Black America: Anthology of the Twentieth Century. HarperCollins, 1973.

Sports Pages. HarperCollins, 1986, 1990.

Today We Are Brother and Sister. Lothrop, 1981

under the early morning trees. Dutton, 1978.

Where Wild Willie. Harper, 1979.

Eve Bunting

Eve Bunting's work is as diverse as she is prolific. She has written more than a hundred picture books, middle grade books, and young adult novels. Her stories take place in every time from the distant past of magic and legend to the present of contemporary concerns and problems. They are set everywhere from the Ireland of her birth to Southern California where she and her husband, Ed, have lived for the past three decades.

Bunting was born and raised in the small town of Maghera in the north of Ireland. Her father was the postmaster: "a tough Irishman, a horse trader and a cattle dealer, who wore his cap on the back of his head and stood out on market days making deals with the other farmers around the place." She connects her father's love of poetry and the impassioned way he read it to her with the beginnings of her own love of words.

She didn't begin writing until her own children were in junior high school but she has been writing steadily since, an average of six books annually. She and her family had settled in California, and it was a "Writing for Publication" class at Pasadena City College that eventually led to the publication of her first book, *The Two Giants,* based on the legends of Finn McCool, in 1972.

Bunting involves herself intensely in each book she writes. She thinks through each book thoroughly before she begins to write it down. Once she starts a book she commits herself to finishing it. She alternates among picture books, middle grade books, and young adult books, enjoying each kind of writing. She finds that the shift among age levels lets her relax and collect herself as she moves from one project to the next. She has said that a picture book is sometimes "like taking a little vacation." She elaborates on this: "Unfortunately, it seems the older the child you write for the grimmer the subject. This doesn't always hold true, of course, but when I was writing *Face at the Edge of the World*, I just couldn't write that book all the way through. I had to stop and give myself a little break; it was just a little too grim. There were parts of it that were breaking my heart. The same thing occurred with *Such Nice Kids*. What was going to happen at the end? I couldn't bring myself to write it."

"When that sort of thing happens, I will stop, and if I have an idea for one of my lighter picture books, then I will leave the young adult book and go to the picture book. The writing of the picture book does not take that long when I get time to write it, but the thinking of the picture book takes a long time for me because I have to have it absolutely right in my head before I start it. I'm working on a really difficult one now with a difficult subject—the sort of subject that's handled in *The Wall* and *Fly Away Home*. I've been agonizing over it, and it will probably be very short. The time level in the thinking is not consistent but is ever there with me while I am doing other things. It is there with me and it will probably be quite awhile before I ever get it written."

Her inspiration comes from many sources: "First of all something has to excite me. I don't ever lose track of something that is important to me that I know I want to write about. It's there waiting to pop out. Many of my ideas come from some sort of print or magazine. Or maybe I'll think, 'That would be a nice peripheral character in a book.' I find that I am lucky because when things excite me I don't have to worry about the age level. There are people who are wonderful writers who are purely young adult writers or who are purely picture book writers. For me, if an idea comes along, something that is exciting and wonderful, which is the only way I write, I can immediately say, 'Oh that will work really well for a picture book,' or "That would work really well for a young adult book.' The subject matter makes it fairly obvious which age level I would write for."

Many of Bunting's young adult novels highlight contemporary concerns, such as surrogate motherhood in *Surrogate Sister*, the tragic effects of negative peer pressure in *Such Nice Kids*, and teen suicide in *Face at the Edge of the World*. Sometimes a newspaper article will spark an idea for a book; Bunting says that 90 percent of her ideas come this way. This was the source for *Sharing Susan*, about babies who were switched at birth in the hospital, and *Going Against Cool Calvin*, about illegal aliens.

Many of her picture books also address present day issues and often do so movingly. *Terrible Things: An Allegory of the Holocaust* conveys its powerful anti-war message through the allegorical story of woodland animals and their inexorable, systematic destruction by shadowy form-less monsters, alluded to only as "the terrible things." At the end of this tale only the little rabbit remains alive. He wonders if he and his fellow creatures of all species could have done something to prevent the terrible things from overwhelming all of the other animals in the glen. Although the author had not seen or heard of the Reverend Niemuller speech about people's responsibility for each other, the story bears out the message of the speech, which is, essentially, "When they came for the others I distanced myself from them; when they came for me there was no one left to help."

Bunting was moved to write *Terrible Things* because, she says, "I came from Ireland where I only knew one Jewish person. I didn't know a lot of Catholics either because we are Protestant and I went to a Protestant school. You know how it is in Northern Ireland—they are both segregated in a different way, by religion. I'm sure there must have been other Jewish people, but in my school there was one Jewish girl, and when I think back on it, it must have been very sad for her because she walked alone. There probably were not any Jewish schools. Because she was excused from prayers we knew she was Jewish. Then when I came to the United States, of course I began to meet many Jewish people.

"In my writing group there were several Jewish writers, and I got pretty friendly with them. It was just about that time or a little bit after that the mini-series of the Holocaust was on TV. It made a deep impression on me because I'd always known about it, but it was far away and it didn't seem to affect me as I didn't know anybody directly affected by it. When I came here I knew all these people. I remember sitting next to these two elderly women who had numbers on their arms, and realizing the horror of all of this and wanting to talk to them and yet not knowing what to say. It was about then that I decided that I wanted to write a book for the very young because I think that's where everything starts. I certainly came from a country that knew all about prejudices, and it starts very young there."

"I think you write what's important to you and you write your concerns. It's a catharsis and what you are comes out. If there is something that upsets me terribly in our system, and a lot of things do, I can vote; but it seems that everybody I vote for loses. So I have this other forum which I use. I don't necessarily want to preach from any podium; it's just my own concerns coming out—that's what it is. I call it the jolt—something jolts me out of my complacency. Here I am sitting in my nice old home looking out at my nice garden and it is so pleasant, so peaceful, but I'm really aware that it's not that way for everybody. When I read something, or hear something, whatever, that jolts me away from this setting, then that's what I write about."

All of Bunting's books, including *Fly Away Home*, about a homeless father and son living in an airport, and *The Wall*, about a visit to the

Vietnam Veterans Memorial, convey strong values that are as much a part of the plot as the events that take place. One might imagine that *The Wall* would be for much older children than the usual picture book audience. Most people agree that there is no upper age limit for that book. "From the letters I receive and from the response from teachers and others, they read it not only with young children, where it can be used along with some adult explaining, talking or discussing, but it can also be used right up through high school. When I first conceived the idea of writing this book it was because I heard some teachers talking about class trips that their students had made to Washington, D.C. and the most impressive thing the children felt, the thing that really excited them and also the best learning experience, was going to the Vietnam Veterans' Memorial. It has really affected the children enormously."

"These children were fifth and sixth-graders, and originally I thought I wanted to write a book for them about that topic. One teacher said to me, 'My son will never be the same again. For the first time he realizes that these names on the wall represent the live people who are now dead who have died in war.' She said, 'This is a kid who plays war a lot; he likes war movies; he likes to look through magazines about war, and I really think that experience changed him.' Originally I had thought of it for that age level, but I wanted it to be simple; I wanted it to state simply the effect the wall had. I wanted to convey this, but I thought, 'The younger the age group I can reach in this the better; it's just a simple monument and it does so much. I need to write it really simply.' "

The protagonists in *The Wall* are a Latino family, and those in *Fly Away Home* are Caucasians, contributing to the erosion of stereotypes in both cases. "I do try to have a certain consciousness about that. I've had letters saying, 'Thank you for making the father and son be Latino because they don't get the recognition that they should get in respect to serving their country.' I've had, I think, two adult letters on that, not from teachers or librarians but from the ordinary population here who have seen the book in a bookstore and have commented that they were so pleased to see that I did it that way. In *Fly Away Home*, I thought it was important that that family be Caucasian. I pondered that quite awhile and I thought that it was good to have a Mexican-American family be their friends. Of course all of the illustrations are out of my hands, so I have to trust to the sensibilities of the illustrator. I sometimes get an opportunity to see the page proofs before the book is actually finalized and to say, 'Look, I don't think we have a proper personal representation here in these illustrations.' But usually illustrators are quite wise and notice this."

Given the fact that authors are not usually permitted to select their illustrators, Bunting has been fortunate in the publishers' choices for her picture books. "What I try to do when I am talking with my editor is suggest that a certain illustrator be invited to do the pictures. Demanding doesn't do any good because the illustrators that one knows from their other books are usually well-established, and they're booked up for ten years ahead! It's difficult, but I do sometimes suggest a name, especially if it's someone who has worked for me before, whose work I know. What happens is you trust the editor and the art director to have a knowledge of young, upcoming, wonderful artists who have not really hit the mainstream yet."

Of her entry into writing after her children were in school, Bunting says, "I was facing that time in my life that I guess women of my generation faced a lot: My husband was a successful professional businessman; my children were in school and didn't really need me that much anymore, so I found that I had a lot of time on my hands. I had dropped out of college to marry my Ed, which was smart, but it wasn't smart to drop out, I should have finished first. So I found myself in my middle thirties coming up to forty with, as I thought, the interesting and exciting part of my life over. I didn't know what to do with the rest of it."

"I had always been a good writer. I had never written for a newspaper, we didn't have one. I had never written for a magazine; I'd never had any real desire to do that. Yet I loved English in school and I loved writing essays as homework... loved it so much that I would do other people's essays for fun. I thought it was great so I used to make a lot of bargains with people and do their essays for them and of course always got found out. This was something that I enjoyed a lot so when I saw a class being offered in my local junior college (Pasadena City College) which was close, just a few blocks away—this catalog had come probably every year in my mailbox but somehow I had never looked at it before—somehow I was ripe to have it come and I looked and saw several things that were being offered that were interesting. Among them was writing for publication. In those days extension classes were free and it was like a little club. All these people had been in this class for years and years and I was just a new girl coming in."

"It was a little awkward at first fitting into that group, but pretty soon I began writing. I thought I was going to write adult books, but I soon found out that what I really liked to do and what I had most success at almost immediately was in writing for children. I began sending out and I began selling. There's a nucleus of that class that all held together; we have been together for all these years. At the beginning we were all unpublished, then maybe one or two might have published a story in a children's magazine or something like that, but as it turned out we all began to publish. I think I am the most published of anyone in the group, but the group has stayed together. We call ourselves the lunch bunch because we don't have a class anymore, but we meet on Tuesday mornings. We meet and criticize one another's work. We've known each other so long we're good friends and good professional friends. I'm also on the Board of the SCBW (Society of Children's Book Writers) and am involved in their activities."

One of Bunting's current projects is a book about her childhood. "I am not as involved in it as I should be. I just finished a middle-grade book—actually it's even younger than middle-grade. It came about in an interesting way: I get so many letters from kids and I answer them all, God help me, I really do. It's a job I equate with my ironing; it is never empty to the bottom. But I love to read them and I enjoy hearing the children's reactions. Maybe a month ago I got this big bunch of letters from students in a school in Illinois. These were kids who had corresponded with me before on various things. A long time ago I did a book called *Black Birds Singing* and I had worked with the teacher in the school, so we'd kept up a correspondence over the years. These students, about a month ago, had a frog jumping competition at school and they sent me maybe twenty letters about their frogs and their experiences catching them, their jumping, etc. I really loved them because some of the things in them were so kid-like that I decided to stop what I was doing. (I am quite easily stopped from the more serious book I'm working on at the moment.) So I've just finished a book called *Some Frog*, not yet sold, I may add, and mailed it off yesterday. I don't know if it will sell, but it's finished."

"In the fall I have a book coming out with HarperCollins. It's a story for the middle grades about a boy whose father is a detective and who fancies himself a detective when his father is not around. According to my editor, it reminds him a little bit of "Home Alone." It may be the first of a series, but I'm not sure. I also have two picture books coming out in the fall with Clarion: One is *The Day Before Christmas* with Beth Peck illustrating it, and the other one is *Our Teacher Is Having a Baby*, inspired by a real case, of course, and the illustrator is Diane De Groat. In the spring next year I will have a picture book called *Flower Garden*, illustrated by Kathy Hewett, from HBJ and a picture book called *Someday a Tree* illustrated by Ron Himler, with Clarion."

Even with her busy writing and speaking schedule Bunting has time to enjoy her four granddaughters, two of whom are twins. She loves the work she does and, although she works hard at her craft, enjoys every moment of it. She says, "I would like people to know that I enjoy writing for children; that it's hard and I put a lot of effort into it, but there isn't anything I'd enjoy doing more than what I am doing." In an interview in *Something about the Author* (1991) she said, "Each of us has a choice of what we do with our lives. I hope the children make the right choice, whatever it is, and in my books I try to help them make it."

Books by Eve Bunting

The Big Red Barn. HBJ, 1979.

The Cloverdale Switch. HarperCollins, 1979.

Coffin on a Case. HarperCollins, 1992.

The Day Before Christmas. Clarion, 1992.

Demetrius and the Golden Goblet. HBJ, 1980.

Face at the Edge of the World. Ticknor and Fields, 1988.

Fly Away Home. HM, 1991.

Ghost Behind Me. PB, 1986.

The Ghost Children. Ticknor and Fields, 1989. Bantam, 1991.

Ghost's Hour, Spooks Hour. HM, 1987, 1989, 1990.

The Ghosts of Departure Point. HarperCollins, 1982, 1984.

Happy Birthday Dear Duck. HM, 1988, 1990.

The Happy Funeral. HarperCollins, 1982.

The Haunting of SafeKeep. HarperCollins, 1985.

The Hideout. HBJ, 1991.

How Many Days to America? A Thanksgiving Story. Ticknor and Fields, 1988, 1990.

If I Asked You, Would You Stay? HarperCollins, 1984.

In the Haunted House. HM, 1990.

Is Anybody There? HarperCollins, 1990.

Jane Martin, Dog Detective. HBJ, 1988.

Janet Hamm Needs a Date for the Dance. Bantam, 1987.

Jumping the Nail. HBJ, 1991.

Karen Kepplewhite is the World's Best Kisser. HM, 1983, 1986.

The Man Who Could Call Down Owls. Macmillan, 1984.

The Mother's Day Mice. Ticknor and Fields, 1986.

No Nap. HM, 1989.

Night Tree. HBJ, 1991.

Our Sixth-Grade Sugar Babies. HarperCollins, 1990.

Our Teacher Is Having a Baby. Clarion, 1992.

The Perfect Father's Day. HM, 1991.

The Robot Birthday. Dutton Children's Books, 1980.

St. Patrick's Day in the Morning. HM, 1983.

Scary, Scary Halloween. Ticknor and Fields, 1988.

The Sea World Book of Sharks. HBJ, 1984.

The Sea World Book of Whales. HBJ, 1987.

Sharing Susan. HarperCollins, 1991.

Sixth-Grade Sleepover. HBJ, 1986. Scholastic Inc., 1987, 1988.

The Skate Patrol. Whitman, 1980.

The Skate Patrol Rides Again. Whitman, 1981.

Someone is Hiding on Alcatraz Island. HM, 1984

Such Nice Kids. HM, 1990.

A Sudden Silence. HBJ, 1988.

Summer Wheels. HBJ, 1992.

Surrogate Sister. HarperCollins, 1984.

Terrible Things: An Allegory of the Holocaust. Jewish Publication Society, 1989.

A Turkey for Thanksgiving. Ticknor and Fields, 1991.

The Valentine Bears. HM, 1985.

The Waiting Game. HarperCollins, 1981.

The Wall. HM, 1990.

The Wednesday Surprise. Ticknor and Fields, 1989. HM, 1990.

Will You Be My POSSLQ? HBJ, 1987.

Winter's Coming. HBJ, 1990.

Virginia Hamilton

Virginia Hamilton sees herself as a storyteller and a link in a chain of tellers and tales that stretches back to her grandfather, Levi Perry. As a boy he escaped from slavery in the late 1850s and settled in the small Ohio town where Virginia was born and still lives. Her connection goes even further back through the time of enduring under slavery, back even as far as her ancestors' forced journey from Africa. Through her writing, Virginia brings the history and lore of African American experience to the printed page. From there, the stories live for readers of all backgrounds.

Hamilton weaves memories from her childhood into her books, tales she has heard and read added to the details she has gathered from extensive research and personal experiences and thoughts. Her stories deal with the great problems of the time, the small, personal, significant features of daily life, and the real people of parallel cultures who form America into "a multicultural world village."

Hamilton has said that her people, the characters that she creates, live in more than one time. "I think I wanted in some of my books to give the impression of time continuing. That is, I've often said that I see where I live here in Yellow Springs not only through my eyes but through my mother's eyes and my grandmother's and so forth because I know how they saw it. So what I try to express is this generational continuity, this generational consciousness or unconsciousness, that doesn't end when there's a long family line in one place. So many of my characters are families, you know. You see the same things through generational eyes."

Indeed, the sense of family comes through strongly in all of her work. "Family has always had a strong influence on me." She presents her characters with loving respect, no matter what their weaknesses. "I think I learned that from my family because when you have a large extended family—lots of cousins, lots of aunts and uncles who have all kinds of foibles and weaknesses and strengths—you become very tolerant of them. And I think a lot of times stories, storytelling, came out of that because people were concerned about one another and had respect for one another even though everybody had certain weaknesses. (Uncle Joe drank too much, or Uncle Larry liked too many women, or whatever, you know what I mean.) Everybody had some understanding for that and told stories, and the stories expressed this feeling of family and tolerance. That's what I learned—how to get along."

Hamilton has commented on how she writes first for the pleasure of it. In response to being asked how much this pleasure is driven or informed by her own societal or global vision, she answered, "I think the pleasure is a combination of things: It's partly in making a morass of words into good writing or literature." As an author she immerses her readers in the "joys of literate language. I come from a literary background. I majored in writing at Antioch College, so I was very, very focused on language. The pleasure for me is getting to what I consider a clear literary level while also making the work available to as large a population as might want to read it. It takes considerable skill to combine those two sometimes opposing forces. What I want to create in every book is a style that expresses the book as clearly as possible. The pleasure is in being able to do that as close to the vision as I can. I'm aware that each book I do has its own line of force or its own power, and I try to find a tone and a style that fits that force."

"For example, I see *Cousins* as a much more gentle book than, say, *Sweet Whispers, Brother Rush* and it demands a simpler style. Every book has its own definition. The pleasure for me is bringing it to its fulfillment. I think when it's all done correctly it's a particular that goes to the general. Whatever I am or whatever I believe, you will find in the characters and in the stories. I really think that I am very much a part of every character. The final solution or the final statement is really what I feel, you know, no matter what it is because it all comes from me."

"It's all so simple and complicated at the same time. It never ceases to fascinate me—how it comes out and why it comes out and why I tell stories. I really think it has to do with the fact that I'm solving problems of my own. It works for me to write whatever I'm thinking or whatever problem-solving I'm doing. It must be very basic to people because people relate to it so closely and so intimately. They enjoy it so I feel that I'm very much a part of the world in that sense."

Hamilton's fiction comes from deep inside her and it moves along the two paths of fact and tale as it works its way into being told. In her Newbery acceptance speech she described some of the creative process behind *M.C. Higgins the Great.* On the one hand, she felt the story drifting towards the mythic: "How do I keep mountains, rivers, and, yes, black people from turning into myths or emblems of themselves?" she wondered. At the same time, however, she knew the pull of concrete details: the pole M.C. sits on, the way "...before one can see the mountain, one must know its heat, its flies, its wind, its place against a total breadth of sky."

Hamilton has said, "If you're going to be an outlandish writer you have to be a good one." She explains, "I decided to go to Antioch even though I had an older sister who went there who was very brilliant. Every time I tried to get into a class the professor would say, 'Oh, you're Nina's sister? Okay.' It would infuriate me. In addition, I was surrounded by all those intellectuals posing as writers and drama students and I felt very inadequate. I felt that if I was going to get any attention at all I had to be really different. So what I did was write this story, my first story at Antioch, and the professor read it in class. I had to be outlandish. It was called, 'The John.' I became famous overnight on campus with that story. My professor always told me, 'Virginia, your stories are outlandish or weird, or strange enough—you don't have to create a new style, too!'"

But Hamilton *is* always creating a new style. "Yes. I think I really have to for the way I write. I have to do things in order to contain all the people and ideas that are, I suppose, not usual, or weren't when I started in children's literature. I mean how do you contain a six and a half foot black woman, a pig herder, in a story with a night traveler and all these different kinds of things that I don't think appeared in the literature before *Zeely?* Plus, all of this evokes a kind of history of a people, you know. This wasn't done for children so I had to find a way to do it, and I had to find a style that would convey all this stuff. That's what I keep doing in various ways and in different kinds of books. *Anthony Burns,* for example, demanded a certain kind of style, because his early life was not documented, so I had to find a style that would allow me to write this part of the story anyway. A lot of his life was documented and I *really* wanted to do it. It took me a long, long time to figure that out. When I did write it, I could render his early life through supposition, historical knowledge, and what little source material I had. Then I created those sections on the past, and that required a different style."

Each one of Hamilton's books requires a different style. *Sweet Whispers Brother Rush*, with its movement back and forth in time and its very palpable ghost, certainly demanded something new. "In order to obtain a ghost who acts as a method of getting into a past for the young person to learn from it, I needed a special device and also very strong characters. No one questioned the reality of the ghost. It's fascinating to me because that book was autobiographical, or very close to it, in many ways, and all of it came together. It's utterly amazing to me that it works."

Sometimes Virginia writes biographies, using historical detail to build up portraits, such as *Anthony Burns: The Defeat and Triumph of a Fugitive Slave* or *Paul Robeson: The Life and Times of a Free Black Man*. Sometimes she collects folktales, as in *The People Could Fly*, and gives witness to the spirit that African Americans summoned to carry themselves through the time of slavery. Both genres convey truths that were vital parts of their time and are just as important for understanding today's world.

Hamilton's versatility ensures that she won't be classified solely as a writer of African-American stories. She comments, "I've done twenty-seven books about African Americans and at some point I felt frustrated, I think, that I was being limited. But I don't feel that way now because I've been able to find a publisher that is enthusiastic about my doing things that aren't African American particularly, like *In the Beginning*, or *The Dark Way*, that don't have a specific racial content but include something from everybody. Not all publishers are interested in that. They wanted me to do black books, period. I thought I was capable of doing all kinds of books. I love the research for my collections of folk tales. For example, I ran across the book of *Beginning Stories in Hebrew* translated into English, in which in the beginning God laughs and the world is created. This is a translation of one of *The Dead Sea Scrolls*. I find that just wonderful.

"Nevertheless, books on African-American themes are important. My companion book to *The People Could Fly* is coming out in January specifically to hit Black History Month. Several of my books can be very lucrative for publishers who want to market that way. One reason cultural diversity books are becoming so popular is that publishers have figured out that they can do many different kinds of things with them; that's something rather new. Some publishers have been doing a lot of promoting of black books, but only in that sense. I think that I have transcended that internationally."

Hamilton has said that often when she approaches a book the pictures come first. "Most of the time, even with the nonfiction books, I get an image of what the book should be. It happened with *M.C. Higgins the Great*. It happened to *Whispers*, although that started out to be a tape recording of a girl telling the story. Of course, it goes through many transitions, from those early ideas on; it's almost like you're stumbling, you're learning to walk when you get the first ideas. Something compels you to write it down. I think that's instinct, knowing that you trust yourself to find the story. It's not given to you, you sort of have to find it. I get these pictures and start writing what I see. I think that painting and writing are a great deal more similar than most people realize. "I really have this strong urge just to paint. I used to paint, and that desire is coming back ever more strongly. I have a friend down in Culebra [an island off the coast of Puerto Rico where Virginia and Arnold have a home] who is a professional painter, and every time I see her work I want to do it again. Then we talk painting. She expresses herself in words very differently than I do because she sees in a different way, but I know how to see that way, too. I'd love to start painting again, if I ever have time."

In response to the question about what makes her decide that a book is worth writing, Hamilton said, "I think it's not my decision. I think that you're overwhelmed by the vision or the impression, and you start. It's endlessly mysterious—the whole process—and I suppose that's why Freud wrote so much about it and never could find an answer. He studied creativity in Michelangelo and all sorts of people and he could never conclude how it was done or why it was done or where it started. I think that's one of the things that keeps one doing it—the fact that it's out of your control. When you discover that it's there in your consciousness then you exert control, but before that it's almost primordial—it comes from some kind of well, or some kind of connection you have. I think Jung called it our 'archaic heritage' and Freud called it the 'collective unconscious.' There are things that I know and that I do in books and then I find out they are African, or they go back to another world or a country where I never was. Whether that comes through the mine of knowledge of my family or what, it's almost as if I inherited it unconsciously. So that interests me—I don't think anything is impossible.

"I think I really learned a lot from my teachers. My early publishers taught me a great deal. I didn't know what a children's book was when I started. I learned by writing and from my editors. I hope it's still happening in publishing that an editor will work with the writer for a long, long time. That's what was done with me. Susan Hirschmann started with my twenty-page story called 'The West Field' and we turned it into Zeely. Nobody ever told me what to write, but they would say, 'Between this sentence and the next is a chapter; figure it out,' and that's what I had to do. Those kinds of mentors and those kinds of teachers are people who really knew what writing was all about, and still do. I'm fortunate to be working with just such an editor now. Between us we're very creative and it's very nice to see somebody come along who cares about literature as well. It's very nice when that happens and I hope it's going on with other young writers. I came in knowing how to write, but I didn't know how to form, and that's something you learn."

Hamilton receives hundreds of letters from young readers. In commenting on the changes in their content over the years, she says, "The change over twenty-five years has been astonishing! Where white kids used to say, 'Why do you always write about black kids?' they now say, 'I felt just like him, or I felt so and so...' They don't talk about color at all—they don't care. The difference is that they're so familiar with people, whether it's through television or sitcoms or films, that another color or writing about somebody black is no longer surprising or different or threatening. Maybe it's still threatening to come into your neighborhood but not to read about.'"

"I've learned a lot through my writing and it's been quite fulfilling. I just kind of hope that people know that I really care about what I do. I want young people to be entertained by my books and to find out things that they didn't know. It's not that I'm trying to teach them anything specific, but I want them to discover new things about the human condition (although they wouldn't put it in those terms), about themselves, and about the possibilities available for them. I think that I've come to want that. When I started out I certainly wasn't thinking like that. I was simply telling stories."

Hamilton's many awards and accolades speak to her popularity and acceptance in the world of children's literature. Her vision and her work are consistent evidence of her humanity, her humor, and her joy.

Books by Virginia Hamilton

All Jahdu Storybook. HBJ, 1991.

Anthony Burns: The Defeat and Triumph of Fugitive Slave. Knopf, 1988.

The Bells of Christmas. HBJ, 1989.

Cousins. Putnam, 1990.

The Dark Way: Stories from the Spirit World. HBJ, 1990.

Drylongso. HBJ, 1992.

Dustland. Greenwillow, 1980. HBJ, 1989.

The Gathering. Greenwillow, 1980. HBJ 1989.

The House of Dies Drear. Macmillan, 1984.

In the Beginning: Creation Stories from Around the World. HBJ, 1988,1991.

Junius Over Far. HarperCollins, 1985.

Justice and Her Brother. HBJ, 1989.

A Little Love. Putnam, 1984.

M.C. Higgins, the Great. ABC-CLIO, 1988.

The Magical Adventures of Pretty Pearl. HarperCollins, 1983, 1986.

Many Thousand Gone: African Americans From Slavery to Freedom. Knopf, 1993.

The Mystery of Drear House. Greenwillow, 1987. Macmillan 1988.

Paul Robeson. HarperCollins, 1974.

The People Could Fly: American Black Folk Tales. Knopf, 1985, 1988.

The Planet of Junior Brown. Macmillan 1971, 1986, 1988.

Sweet Whispers, Brother Rush. Putnam, 1982.

W.E.B. DuBois: a Biography. HarperCollins, 1987.

A White Romance. Putnam, 1987. HBJ, 1989.

Willie Bea and the Time the Martians Landed. Greenwillow, 1983. Macmillan, 1989.

Zeely, Macmillan 1968, 1987.

Milton Meltzer

Born in Worcester, Massachusetts, and educated at Columbia University, Milton Meltzer, a distinguished biographer and historian, is the author of more than eighty books for adults and young people. He has written and edited for newspapers, magazines, books, radio, television, and films. Meltzer and his wife, Hildy, live in New York City. They have two daughters, Jane and Amy, and two grandsons.

Among the many honors for his books are five nominations for the National Book Award as well as the Christopher, Jane Addams, Carter G. Woodson, Jefferson Cup, Washington Book Guild, Olive Branch, and Golden Kite awards. Many of his books have been chosen for the honor lists of the American Library Association, the National Council of Teachers of English, and the National Council for the Social Studies.

Meltzer decides to write a book when he finds a subject that piques his curiosity. "I think every child is born with innate curiosity. Unfortunately, too often, schooling squelches this quality in the students. I feel that anything that interests me is fit material for a book. Many people mistakenly believe that writers of books must be longtime experts before they begin or they would never have presumed to try and write the book. I write in order to find out all I can about a subject that's interesting to me but which I want to know a lot more about."

"Of course that changes as you write a number of books that cluster in a certain field. For example, by now I have done maybe four or five books—biographies and documentaries or narrative histories—revolving around the American revolutionary era. With each successive one I've learned more about the period. Each book is of course a research problem in itself, but I start it with a big bank of knowledge."

Meltzer is the author of some twenty biographies, which feature such people as Columbus, Washington, Jefferson, Franklin, Lincoln, Andrew Jackson, Mark Twain, Langston Hughes, Mary McLeod Bethune, and Dorothea Lange. Meltzer's biographies do not necessarily depict only those people the author admires. His Columbus book leaves the reader with a sense of how cruel and greedy the explorer was. His recent work on the life of Andrew Jackson introduces readers to the contradictory views of the President held by his contemporaries. "Some saw him as a great, benevolent hero of democracy, while others considered him to be despotic, tyrannical and even murderous. What is the truth? Who was the real Andrew Jackson? I came to my own conclusions during my research, and the book traces the process."

Asked about the difficult challenge of writing the book recently completed, *Lincoln: In His Own Words*, Meltzer said, "Anyone would have a right to groan, 'What! Another book on Lincoln?' But what I've done is different from all the others. Lincoln was one of the greatest masters of the English language. He had a gift for writing that placed him far above most of his contemporaries. Yet for young readers there is little or nothing of Lincoln in his own words, except perhaps for the Gettysburg Address. I wanted to present what he said or write about what he thought, felt, and did, so I read through the million or so words of his speeches, state papers, letters, and so on. People who had conversations with him often ran home and scribbled down the conversation. Using his own words I've woven together the narrative of his life and bridged the gaps and supplied background in my words. In cases where his views changed over the years on a given subject, I've sometimes pulled them together in one chapter so that readers can see how and why his attitudes changed as circumstances changed."

"The other new thing about the Lincoln book is my concept of the illustrations which the publisher, Harcourt Brace Jovanovich, welcomed. Instead of using all those well-known photos of Lincoln which are great but who have been published so often, I thought, 'Why not commission an artist to read Lincoln's story in his own words and come up with his or her own visual interpretation of that life?' The publisher asked a young artist, Stephen Alcorn, to tackle the assignment. He's done very powerful work that carries the story as he sees it. It isn't only action scenes and Lincoln portraits, but portraits of many of the important figures of that time who influenced Lincoln's thought or played a role in the great events of his era. Stephen shared in the design of the book, too, and I believe it will be an extraordinary work. It will be published in the fall of 1994."

Meltzer is a meticulous researcher. He does all of his own research because, he says, "I love the research almost as much as I enjoy writing, so I would be giving up half the fun if I commissioned others to do it. I don't see how anyone who is not as closely attuned to what the author is trying to do could possibly respond to unforeseen, unpredictable things that pop up while you're doing research. It's happened to me many times: I am looking for a particular thing, say, in archives or in documents, and my eye catches something totally unexpected, but suddenly I could see fresh possibilities in it and find ways to weave it into the story I'm telling."

His research has carried him all over the country, although he often finds all he needs in the magnificent library resources of New York. In recent years, however, he has cut down on projects that might take him far afield. Now in his seventies, "I still have plenty of energy to do my writing but I don't like to be on the road a long time. Although I don't mind going to speak at schools and universities or professional meetings for a day or two at a time."

Meltzer's books are directed at various age groups—some for readers as young as eight and others ranging up into the adult category. "I've often found that a book reaches beyond the intended audience. In talking to kids in the schools (and I've done that quite a lot) I'm constantly surprised by the age of kids reading a particular book. Sometimes a book meant for young adult category is being read by kids not only in middle school, but even in elementary school. I've found that books I wrote for kids aged eight to eleven, such as my four titles in the *Women of Our Time* series, are being read by older boys and girls. Those brief biographies are also used in adult literacy classes because the tutors find that the content and interest level are high, but they are happily short books. I don't mean that the books talk down—I never limit myself in vocabulary or in sentence structure. On the other hand, books like *The Black Americans: A History In Their Own Words,* are used in college classes. That's true of other histories I've done."

Meltzer's recent book, *The Amazing Potato* (1992), is somewhat of a departure in form from many of his other books. "It's a new venture for me—a cross-cultural study of how a lowly object like the ordinary potato has enormous implications for world history. People may say, 'What? A book about the potato? What's interesting about that?' But the book demonstrates that there's an enormous amount that is fascinating. Just listen to my subtitle: *A Story in Which the Incas. Conquistadors. Marie Antoinette. Thomas Jefferson. Wars. Famines. Immigrants. and French Fries all play a part.* It's a little different from the forms I've used before, but it works as social history. I so enjoyed doing it and Harper liked it so much that I've promptly followed up with another one in the same form, this time on the subject of gold. From vegetable to mineral—and maybe animal next time."

Meltzer usually works on two projects at a time. "Since it's non-fiction based on research, when I've completed the research I spend mornings writing the book. In the afternoon I often will be doing research on an upcoming book. Sometimes I have contracts for two or three books beyond the current project.

"Right now I'm completing work on a book for Viking-Penguin on the theme of child labor. The heart of it is child labor in America today, which is far more extensive and terrible than most people realize. People usually think of the nineteenth century as the bottom of the pit for that, but it's almost as bad now in many ways, and worse in some respects. The book goes way back to antiquity. It really is a book about children who work, from enslaved kids in Greek and Roman times, and moves on through the early industrial revolution in England and then traces child labor from our own colonist times to today. About half of the book is about working children today, but young readers will, I hope, benefit from the broad frameworks I've provided."

In discussing the body of his work, Meltzer says, "I think every one of my books reflects my opinions or my feelings. When I speak before professional groups people sometimes say challengingly, 'Shouldn't you be more objective in what you write?' My answer to that is, 'I don't think there is any such thing as objectivity.' What you write about comes out of who you are, what your genetic makeup is, what your upbringing was like, what your political or economic development was like as you grew to maturity. You choose your own subjects and your background shapes both that choice and the way you handle the material. You must be careful not to rule out things that don't suit a premise or a conviction you started with when you find evidence to the contrary. You have to be fair about that and let the reader know there is a controversy over this or more than one way to look at it."

What about the response to his books? Meltzer says, "That falls into two categories: response by mail and response in person. My mail is quite small. I have found in matching notes with other writers of non-fiction and with popular fiction writers that the fiction writers get far more mail. Non-fiction writers—no matter how well-established or widely used their books may be—hear less from readers. Sometimes what we do get is the result of a teacher telling the kids what to write. That's usually unproductive for both the students and the author. I try to answer everything that comes in, especially letters from individual kids moved to write on their own. Those are the ones that are far more meaningful to me."

"Once I got a dozen letters in one week, all in response to my biography about Mary McLeod Bethune. They came from young girls who were in middle or elementary school and who loved that book. They were very deeply moved by the story of a black child like themselves, who had come out of poverty and reached great heights. These letters were from several parts of the country, not from one school or district."

"The other kind of response, of course, is when you go out and speak to kids in the school or to adults in colleges or professional meetings. I get much more of a feedback then. It's almost always an enthusiastic response. When I come home, my wife says as I come in the door, 'Well, how did it go?' And then she answers for me—Terrific!' Those visits recharge my batteries. Working at home is a lonely business. I don't teach and am not in touch with other people a lot of the time, so going out in the field where your work is being read is exciting and refreshing. I often get questions that show that what I've written has shaken people up, illuminated some corner of life they weren't aware of, raised questions they hadn't thought about. Those are the responses I value more than anything. At this age, I come across people who are now adults who tell me they read my stuff twenty or thirty years ago and how much it meant to them."

In response to a question about whether he ever goes back to his home town of Worcester, Meltzer describes a rare experience: "I was invited by two teachers in one of the high schools to come up and speak to a class, which I was glad to do since it was my home town. I checked into a motel the night before, and one of them picked me up in the morning and drove me to school. There was a crowd outside, and I said, 'What's going on? Is there something special?' She just smiled. I went through the crowd and she said, 'We're not going to class; we're going to the auditorium.' And there was the mayor and the city council people and people from the board of education, and an auditorium full of kids, and some people my age who had been classmates long ago. The mayor, who was also a professor of history at Holy Cross College, introduced me by talking about work of mine he had read and used in his classes. Then he gave me the symbolic key to the city mounted on a piece of mahogany. It's on the wall of my study now. After that I gave my prepared talk and answered questions."

"I just wish my immigrant parents, working class people, had been there to see it. My mother never forgave me for dropping out of college. Even after I had published often, she would still regret that I was never able to hang a diploma on my wall."

Meltzer says, "I prefer that young readers come to my books on their own and not necessarily as part of class work. But an author's books don't lie around everywhere, easy to pick up, so it's important to have teachers and librarians introduce your books to young readers. If that's done well, in the right setting, it can open doors to young minds, help them to new experiences, to rewarding insights."

In his article, "The Social Responsibility of the Writer" in *The New Advocate*, (Summer, 1989) Meltzer wrote, "The books I've written for children are intended to do more than simply convey facts. I hope they are works of revelation as well as information that help young readers to understand the world as it is and to realize that we need not accept the world as it is given to us." He has certainly fulfilled his intention and his hope.

Books by Milton Meltzer

African American History: Four Centuries of Black Life. Scholastic, 1990.

Ain't Gonna Study War No More: The Study of America's Peace Seekers. HarperCollins, 1985.

All Times. all Peoples: A World History of Slavery. HarperCollins, 1980.

The Amazing Potato: a Story In Which the Incas. Conquistadors, Marie Antoinette, Thomas Jefferson, Wars, Famines, Immigrants, and French Fries All Play a Part. HarperCollins, 1992.

American Politics: How It Really Works. Morrow, 1989.

The American Promise: Voices of a Changing Nation. Bantam, 1990.

The American Revolutionaries: a History in Their Own Words. HarperCollins, 1987.

Benjamin Franklin: The New American. Watts, 1988.

Betty Friedan: A Voice for Women's Rights. Viking, 1985.

The Bill of Rights: How We Got it. and What It Means. HarperCollins, 1990.

The Black Americans: A History in Their Own Words. HarperCollins, 1984, 1987.

Black Magic: a Pictorial History of the Negro in American Entertainment. Prentice-Hall, 1967.

A Book About Names. HarperCollins, 1984.

Bound for Rio Grande: The Mexican Struggle. 1845-1850. Knopf, 1974.

Bread and Roses: The Struggle of American Labor. Facts on File, 1990.

Brother, Can You Spare a Dime. Dutton, 1977.

To Change the World: A Picture History of Reconstruction. Scholastic, 1971.

The Chinese Americans. HarperCollins, 1980.

The Collected Correspondence of Lydia Maria Child. Kraus Microform, 1980.

Columbus and the World Around Him. Watts, 1990.

Crime in America. Morrow, 1990.

Dorothea Lange: a Photographer's Life. FS&G, 1978, 1985.

Dorothea Lange: Life Through the Camera. Viking, 1985. Puffin, 1986.

The Eye of Conscience: Photographers and Social Change. Follet, 1974.

Freedom Comes to Mississippi. Follet, 1970.

George Washington and the Birth of Our Nation. Watts, 1986.

The Hispanic Americans. HarperCollins, 1982.

The Human Rights Book. FS&G, 1979.

Hunted Like a Wolf: The Story of the Seminole War. FS&G, 1972.

In Their Own Words: A History of the American Negro. Crowell, 1964, 1965, 1967.

The Jewish Americans: a History in Their Own Words. HarperCollins, 1982.

The Jews in America: A Picture Album. JPS, 1985.

The Landscape of Memory. Viking, 1987.

Langston Hughes: a Biography. HarperCollins, 1988.

A Light In the Dark: The Life of Samuel Gridley Howe. Crowell, 1964.

Lydia Maria Child: Selected Letters, 1817-1880. UMASS Press, 1982.

Margaret Sanger: Pioneer of Birth Control. Crowell, 1969.

Mark Twain. Watts, 1985.

Mark Twain Himself. Crowell, 1961.

Mary McLeod Bethune: Voice of Black Hope. Viking, 1987.

Milestones To American Liberty. Crowell, 1961.

Never to Forget: The Jews of the Holocaust. Harper Collins, 1976, 1991.

A Pictorial History of Black Americans. Crown, 1956, 1963, 1968, 1973, 1983.

Poverty in America. Morrow, 1986.

Remember the Days: A Short History of the Jewish American. Doubleday, 1974.

Rescue: The Story of How Gentiles Saved Jews in the Holocaust. HarperCollins, 1988, 1991.

The Right to Remain Silent. HBJ, 1972.

Slavery: From the Rise of Western Civilization To Today. Regnery, 1971, 1972.

Starting from Home: a Writer's Beginnings. Viking, 1988. Puffin, 1991.

Taking Root: Jewish Immigrants in America. FS&G, 1974.

Thadeus Stevens and the Fight for Negro Rights. Crowell, 1967.

The Terrorists. HarperCollins, 1983.

Thomas Jefferson: The Revolutionary Aristocrat. Watts, 1991.

Thoreau: People, Principles and Politics. Hill & Wang, 1963.

A Thoreau Profile. Crowell, 1962.

Time of Trial, Time of Hope: The Negro in America. 1919-1941. Doubleday, 1966.

Tongue of Flame: The Story of Lydia Maria Child. HarperCollins, 1990.

The Truth About the Ku Klux Klan. Watts, 1982.

Underground Man. HBJ, 1990.

Violins and Shovels: The WPA Arts Projects. Delacorte, 1976.

Voices from the Civil War: A Documentary History of the Great American Conflict. HarperCollins, 1989,1990.

Winnie Mandela: The Soul of South Africa. Viking, 1986. Puffin, 1987.

World of Our Fathers: The Jews of Eastern Europe. FS&G, 1974.

Cynthia Rylant

Cynthia Rylant grew up in West Virginia, in the heart of Appalachia, and much of her writing springs from this background. Her first book, *When I Was Young in the Mountains,* reflects her memories of the time she lived with her grandparents and conveys their language, thought, and general attitude toward the world. (She lived with her grandparents for four years, until she was eight years old, while her mother was studying to be a nurse.) The setting is presented in such a palpable way as to make each reader feel a part of it, no matter what the reader's heritage.

That same setting and her rendition of the sounds and tone of the people and other inhabitants of her childhood home won her the *Boston Globe-Horn Book* Award for non-fiction in 1991 for her *Appalachia: The Voices of Sleeping Birds.* In her acceptance speech Rylant says of the people who raised her, "I wanted to thank them for teaching me their profound love of work and of family, for teaching me their faith and grace in waiting patiently for the wheel to turn. I wanted to thank them for their gentleness and for their quiet ways, for their mystery."

Another of her books that is a reminiscence of her family is *The Relatives Came,* a merry romp of a story that describes an extended family gathering in which everyone makes room for everyone else. Clearly, not only each individual but also a sense of family togetherness is treasured. Although this is a true story about Rylant's family, the illustrator, Stephen Gammell, drew pictures of his own family, including his father, mother, wife, and himself, underscoring the personal involvement each reader feels.

When Rylant was eight, she moved with her mother from her grandparents' house to a less rural area, where she encountered sidewalks and indoor plumbing for the first time. Her *Waiting to Waltz* depicts in poetic form her teen years in Beaver, West Virginia. The poems are portraits of people she knew as well as reflections of her feelings as a teenager. The very moving poem "Forgotten" addresses the painful fact of her father's absence from her life and his early death.

Rylant began writing in her early twenties after having graduated from college and earned a master's degree in English. Her work in a children's library put her into contact with children's books, a new experience for her. As a result of reading books like Donald Hall's *Oxcart Man*, which delighted and enthralled her, she decided to become a writer. After a few months of sporadic writing, when her son Nathaniel was six months old, Cynthia reports, "I crawled into my bed with a pen and some yellow notebook paper, and I wrote these words: when I was young in the mountains. I don't know where they came from. I guess from the twenty-four years I had lived, from all the fine books I had read, from angels." Rylant completed the manuscript in one hour. She sent it to E.P. Dutton without revision, and it was a great success as soon as it was published.

Indeed, that is the way Rylant writes all of her books; she doesn't write and rewrite. She has said that the "writing springs like magic." She is not at all conscious of "cooking" the writing in her head during the time that she is between books. "When I'm going through the weeks or months of not writing, I don't even think about the books or what I'm going to write next. When I'm ready, I'll think about it and sit down and do it. The picture books have all been written in just a sitting. I probably get up only to refill my teacup. I do it without an outline and just go from one sentence to the next. I don't revise much, maybe a word or two, then I send it in.

"I know that a lot of writers have file cabinets crammed with manuscripts and ideas for books. If you came to my house you wouldn't find a thing. I don't write for fun, though the picture books, poetry, and short stories come easily to me. The novels are harder. I needed to write the novels in order to get the respect that I wanted as a writer. I don't want people to pick up a book of mine and say, 'Oh, I could have written that,' and they do that with the picture books a lot. You have to have a gift for picture books. You have to have a natural feel for them. I don't think it's a thing that anyone can learn if they don't already have that natural gift."

"With the novels I make a decision to write a novel. I say to myself, 'I am going to write a novel this fall and I am going to start in September.'

Then in September I will start thinking about it and something will come into my head and I will work on that. With the novels I obviously can't do them start to finish in a sitting, but I will write them much like the picture books in that I generally do a chapter at a time in one sitting. Then I will wait a little bit and sit down and write another full chapter and see what happens.

"Like most authors, my own personal life affects what I write. I wasn't raised on children's books, on the happily ever after kind of literature. I did read Nancy Drew books and comic books, but the literature that influenced me was the literature I read after I was grown. The books that teach me as a writer are books by writers like James Agee and William Maxwell, and much of their writing is influenced by their childhood experiences of loss. That's the only training I've had as a writer, reading people like that. It could be that I was influenced by the themes that my favorite writers were dealing with."

"I really have had a very happy life. The picture books, *The Relatives Came, When I was Young in the Mountains,* and the Henry and Mudge books reflect the celebration of life that I also feel. It's in the longer novels that I deal with more serious subjects, and that's where the writers who are my favorites may have influenced me."

"*A Blue Eyed Daisy* and a *Fine White Dust* (a Newbery Honor book) were in some ways autobiographical, but *A Kindness* was just pure fiction. However, I was influenced to write *A Kindness* by my feelings as the only child of a single parent. Any kid who's struggling with the feeling of being the person left in a parent's life... even though the parent is independent of you otherwise... even though that parent has a very full and happy life... the child feels a whole lot of responsibility. I certainly felt that weight." Then I grew up and had a baby and was divorced soon after. Now that I have been raising my son on my own, I understand the sacrifice and the loss of freedom when you have a child to raise by yourself so I used all the elements in *A Kindness.*"

"*Missing May* is another book that I invented. But I empathize with Summer when she describes being taken home by Ob and May and feels that she has found Heaven. I guess there's still a part of me that identifies with the child who is nurtured by an older couple. When I was writing this books Summer's voice came through very clearly in my head. All I had to do was sit and listen. Toward the end when May finally speaks, the mother that I am now responded to May's voice and her absolute devotion to Summer. I read this section to a friend and we both cried and cried, so I knew I had written something powerful." *Missing May* deservedly won the 1993 Newbery medal.

When asked about the recurrence of animals in her books, Rylant responded, "I grew up with a lot of them. When I was growing up with my mother, just the two of us, we had puppies and kittens just flowing out the front door. These animals were very important to me. They kept me company when my mother wasn't there. I still have a houseful of animal—dogs and cats... We had a tortoise, but he walked away one day. The animals fill the house with life and they make us laugh." Rylant makes the animals characters readers can identify with, but they are presented without a sliver of sentimentality.

In discussing what makes a book worth writing, Rylant said, "It is not so much the subject; it is how it sounds after it is written. If I can read it aloud over and over again and am thrilled with the sound of it and never get tired of it, then I know it is good. It is the same thing with fabrics. I make quilts sometimes just for fun and there are certain pieces of fabric I can look at over and over and they are so beautiful that I will never get tired of them. It's the same way with my writing. If I can hear it again and again and it is so beautiful every time, then I know that I have written something really good. If it isn't beautiful then I toss it out and I don't send it in to an editor."

"I never told stories to my son when he was younger; I always read books to him. I can't tell stories out loud and I am not a good joke teller. If I try to tell somebody about a movie I just saw I get it all messed up. For me it is all on the paper. I never took a writing class, and I don't go to writers' retreats. I have never taught writing. Whatever I do, I don't really have anything to compare it with. I think that has probably worked out really well for me. In fact, I think maybe if I had been influenced by the market and trends and whose book was popular during what season I might not have found my natural voice for a long time. I might have tried just to mimic."

"I think every writer's greatest nightmare is rejection—not just a rejection slip in the mail, but the editor having to call you and say, 'I am sorry, this book isn't good enough.' You are very vulnerable. People react in different ways: I cry; other writers get angry; still other writers say, 'I don't care because I know I am good and I don't need validation from anybody.' One way or another we all have to find ways to protect ourselves because writing is so personal."

"It is really terrifying for me to write novels. The picture books are almost like writing songs... joyful and easy, but the more serious and longer stuff is daunting. Several years ago, Richard Jackson, my editor at the time, helped me to begin writing novels. He took away much of my fear. I trusted that he wouldn't hurt me in his response and he was a very sensitive teacher. When I wrote *A Fine White Dust,* my first real novel (*A Blue-eyed Daisy* came out before that, but I wrote *A Blue-eyed Daisy* as a series of stories), I was really lost because I was used to finishing what I had to say in five pages. It didn't work the first time I wrote it. I did have to make a lot of major revisions. It was the first time I had ever tackled anything of that length, and if I hadn't been working with Dick, who could teach me without devastating me, I might not have continued. I owe a lot to him for the risks that I took."

Because Rylant has recently moved to a different publishing house, Richard Jackson is no longer her editor. "It was very hard, and it still is hard. It has been a great loss and a great adjustment for me. I still haven't really gotten over it. It is like religion. Some people believe in the preacher instead of believing in God; your faith has to be your own regardless of who is at the pulpit. I feel the same way about writing. I have to write, and I will write regardless of who my editor is, but there is no question that I owe a great debt to Dick."

Rylant confesses that, "I really enjoy sitting at home with my dogs and my son just making books. I don't go to conferences much, and I don't much enjoy speaking publicly. I just enjoy the writing. I'm always surprised when people say that I am famous, because I didn't know that I was." As the numbers of her books increase and as her versatility becomes more and more established, there is no doubt that Cynthia Rylant will continue to be a well-known, sought-after, and deeply admired writer.

Books by Cynthia Rylant

All I See. Orchard, 1988.

An Angel for Solomon Singer. Orchard, 1992.

Appalachia: The Voices of Sleeping Birds. HBJ, 1991.

Birthday Presents. Orchard, 1987, 1991.

A Blue-Eyed Daisy. Macmillan, 1985. Dell, 1987.

But I'll Be Back Again: An Album. Orchard, 1989.

Children of Christmas: Stories for the Season. Orchard, 1987.

A Couple of Kooks, and Other Stories About Love. Orchard, 1990.

Every Living Thing. Macmillan, 1985,1988.

A Fine White Dust. Macmillan, 1986. Dell, 1987.

Henry and Mudge and the Bedtime Thumps. Macmillan, 1991.

Henry and Mudge and the Forever Sea: The Sixth Book of Their Adventures. Macmillan, 1989.

Henry and Mudge and the Happy Cat. Macmillan, 1990.

Henry and Mudge Get the Cold Shivers: The Seventh Book of Their Adventures. Macmillan, 1989.

Henry and Mudge and the Long Weekend. MacMillan, 1992.

Henry and Mudge in Puddle Trouble. Macmillan, 1987, 1990.

Henry and Mudge in the Green Time. Macmillan, 1987.

Henry and Mudge in the Sparkle Days: The Fifth Book of Their Adventures. Macmillan, 1988.

Henry and Mudge Take the Big Test. Macmillan, 1991.

Henry and Mudge: The First Book. Macmillan 1987, 1990.

Henry and Mudge Under the Yellow Moon: The Fourth Book of Their Adventures. Macmillan, 1987.

Henry and Mudge and the Wild Wind. Macmillan, 1992.

A Kindness. Orchard, 1988.

Miss Maggie. Dutton, 1983.

Missing May. Orchard, 1992.

Mr. Griggs' Work. Orchard, 1989.

Night in the Country. Macmillan, 1986.

The Relatives Came. Macmillan, 1985.

Soda Jerk. Orchard, 1990.

This Year's Garden. Macmillan, 1984, 1987.

Waiting to Waltz: A Childhood. Macmillan, 1984.

When I Was Young in the Mountains. Dutton, 1985.

4

Genres in Children's Literature: Identifying, Analyzing, and Appreciating

Donna E. Norton

Literary genre means different things to different groups. To the early Greeks, genre was identified according to the interaction with the audience. In this categorization, an epic was a form of poetry that required an oral recitation by the poet. A drama was a form of literature that concealed the author from the audience, and the lyric was a form of literature that concealed the audience from the poet. Contemporary literary critics Northrop Frye, Sheridan Baker, and George Perkins (1985) compare genres in literature to "species" in biology: both biology and literature have primary and secondary classifications.

Although such classifications of genre are frequently discussed in college classes, authors of children's literature texts usually follow a genre approach that is easier for children to understand. The broad types or genres of literature in texts by Zena Sutherland and May Hill Arbuthnot (1986), Charlotte Huck (1987), and Donna Norton (1987) include picture books, traditional literature, modern fantasy, poetry, contemporary realistic fiction, historical fiction, biography, and informational books. Within these are subgroups such as folktales, myths, and legends identified within traditional literature.

Writers of all high-quality literature use basic literary elements to create stories that are interesting, engrossing, and believable to the reader. There are specific requirements, however, related to each genre of literature. Helping students identify, analyze, and appreciate these distinctions will improve their critical evaluative skills as well as enhance their ability to enjoy all genres of literature.

The approach recommended and developed in this chapter encourages children to read and enjoy books within the specific genre, to discuss characteristics of that genre, to describe any techniques that authors use to enhance that genre, to identify lists of questions that help them make decisions about genres, and to compare books across genres. Picture books, traditional literature, modern fantasy, and contemporary realistic fiction were chosen to exemplify this approach. The techniques discussed, however, may be used to develop an understanding of other literary genres.

Picture Books

A picture sequence that complements text or takes the place of words, a visual exploration that encourages interpretation and reflection, and a dramatic experience that resembles theater or film are all descriptions that are used to distinguish the picture book genre from other types of literature. All of these descriptions infer specific characteristics of the genre and suggest responses from the reader.

Although many children's books are illustrated, not all illustrated books are classified as picture books. If the illustrations are merely extensions of a self-sufficient text, the book is an illustrated book, not a picture book. The illustrations in a picture book play a livelier role and are an integral part of the action of the book. Zena Sutherland and Betsy Hearne (1984) state that in a picture book the illustrations are either as important as the text or more important than the text. Lyn Lacy (1986) extends this definition to include reader response by describing a picture book as a vehicle for providing "visual exploration, interpretation, and reflection" (p. 2). Barbara Bader (1976) points out the drama connection between text and illustration in her definition of picture books. According to Bader a picture book is an art form that "hinges on the interdependence of pictures and words, on the simultaneous display of two facing pages, and on the drama of the turning page" (p. 1).

Uri Shulevitz (1985) explains this drama connection when he states that a picture book is closer to theater and film, silent films in particular, because the picture book is a dramatic experience that is immediate, vivid, and moving. In this context, Shulevitz describes picture books as having "actors" and "stages" in which the characters, settings, and actions are shown through pictures rather than through textual descriptions.

In an excellent picture book there is a complete interaction between illustration and text. Shulevitz compares words in a picture book with the sound track of a movie. In this context, the rhythmic sounds of words in Maurice Sendak's *Where the Wild Things Are* (1963) augment the action. The descriptions of gnashing teeth and rolling eyes also provide information that cannot be fully shown in the illustrations. The integration between illustration and text is complete, according to Shulevitz, if the words emphasize a detail, clarify an action, or link pictures together. This is a good description of Sendak's book.

Some Examples of Picture Books

Let us consider several books that meet these definitions for the picture book genre. The impact and the importance of the illustrations are heightened by sharing and discussing books in a sequence that proceeds from totally wordless books to books with minimal text and to books in which the illustrations and the text are equally important. Finally, we will consider illustrated texts that are not classified as picture books.

Emily Arnold McCully's wordless book, *Picnic* (1984), shows the importance of illustrations in developing both plot and characterization. *Picnic* follows a family of mice as they jubilantly go on a picnic, unhappily discover a small mouse is missing, and joyfully reunite the whole family. The detailed illustrations depict home, woodland, and picnic settings. Characterization of the lost mouse is especially revealing as the illustrations show a tearful mouse child clutching his mouse toy. Other sides of his character are revealed as he considers his surroundings and searches for food. The importance of the mouse toy is revealed in the end as the mouse returns for his misplaced toy after he is found by his family. This is an example of a picture book in which the illustrations totally depict plot, conflict, characterization, setting, and mood. The text encourages interaction by the reader and develops drama through such techniques as contrasting a happy picnic scene on one page with the tearful lost mouse on the facing page.

The impact of illustrations in books with minimal texts is shown in Kate Greenaway's A Apple Pie (1979), Julian Scheer's *Rain Makes Applesauce* (1964), and Maurice Sendak's *Where the Wild Things Are* (1963). Greenaway's alphabet book is a good choice to share with students because the written text provides minimal content, but the illustrations provide detailed information. Without the illustrations, the reader would not be able to follow the actions of children as they interact with a pie. For example. the G page states "G got it." Without the illustrations we would not know that G is a boy who got the pie by chasing seven children with a stick, that the children range in age from very young to fairly mature, and that they are dressed in clothing from the 1800s. The type of action and the supporting characters are revealed only through the illustrations.

Rain Makes Applesauce shows how the written text in a picture book can become part of the illustrations. The nonsensical mood of the book is enhanced by words that change in size, flow with the pictures, and become part of each illustration.

The illustrations in *Where the Wild Things Are* show how illustrations in picture books enhance developing conflict. Notice how the illustrations increase in size as the plot changes from reality to fantasy and proceeds to the land of the wild things. At the height of the wild rumpus no words are shown. Now the illustrations become the total text. This is also an example in which the text provides minimal information and the illustrations clarify and expand the written words. For example, the author tells us that Max "made mischief of one kind and another." The illustrations show the magnitude of the mischief as we see Max pounding a large nail in the wall to hang a tent and on the next page chasing a dog with a fork. In this example, drama is added by the pause at the end of the first page and by the need to turn the page to identify a second type of mischief. This pause not only increases the drama but also suggests a lapse in time. Consequently, the mischief seems to be even more serious because it occurred over a longer duration.

Arthur Yorinks' *Hey, Al* (1986) and Wanda Gag's *Millions of Cats* (1928, 1956) exemplify books in which the text and the illustrations play more equal roles. Although the text for *Hey, Al* is longer than the text for *Where the Wild Things Are,* the illustrator, Richard Egielski, uses some of the same techniques to show developing conflict. For example, the illustrations increase in size as the setting becomes fanciful and the plot nears the climax. Double-page spreads illustrate the island experience and one of these illustrations has no words. The illustrations also clarify and expand the text. The text states that the house is a dump; the illustrations show just how small, crowded, and dingy the house actually is. One of the most interesting impacts of illustration is shown on the wordless double-page spread. An observant viewer sees foreshadowing as one of the birds shows human hands and carries a cane. Of course, Al and Eddie are not so observant. They remain in paradise unaware of the inevitable consequences of their choice. Children's responses are heightened by this illustration. They can vicariously join the illustrator and predict what they believe is likely to happen. Illustrations such as these enhance observation and increase interaction with books. They meet Lacy's requirement that picture books encourage visual exploration, interpretation, and reflection.

Gag's illustrations and text create a feeling of movement and enhance the repetitive quality of the "hundreds of cats, thousands of cats, millions and billions and trillions of cats." Our eyes do not allow us to consider the written text without the illustrations.

One of the best ways to teach students to identify the picture book genre is to have them compare the previously discussed books with highly illustrated books that are not considered picture books. For this comparison, it is easiest to proceed from books with fewer illustrations to books with extensive ones. For example, Lillian Gish's *An Actor's Life for Me!* (1987) contains at least one illustration per chapter. From this minimally illustrated text, you can proceed to Rhoda Blumberg's *Commodore Perry in the Land of the Shogun* (1985), which averages an illustration on every second page, to Patricia Lauber's *Dinosaurs Walked Here: And Other Stories Fossils Tell* (1987), which contains an illustration on almost every page. Although all of the illustrations in these books add information to the literature, none of the illustrations can stand alone or are equal in information to the written text.

Questions for Identifying Picture Books

It is helpful if students compile a list of questions that should be considered when they decide if a book is a picture book or merely an illustrated book. The following questions and discussion topics may be used to help students compare picture books and illustrated books and to decide if a book belongs in the picture book genre:

1. Describe the picture sequence in the book. Does the book contain a picture sequence that complements the words or even takes the place of the words?
2. Use the illustrations to describe the setting and the characterizations. Are the illustrations an integral part of the settings, the actions, and the characterizations?
3. Describe the importance of the illustrations and the text. Are the illustrations of at least equal importance when compared to the written text?
4. Describe how you respond to the illustrations. Do the illustrations encourage interpretation, reflection, and viewers' response?
5. Compare, if possible, the illustrations to theater or film. Do the illustrations provide a dramatic experience that resembles theater or film?

Traditional Literature: Folktale, Myth, and Legend

Defining this genre of children's literature and distinguishing the genre from other genres of literature is enhanced by developing an

understanding of the oral tradition; by identifying the general characteristics related to traditional literature; by analyzing the similarities and
differences among folktales, myths, and legends; and by interacting with
the literature through a literary analysis of setting, characterization, plot
development, and style.

Students need to understand the importance of the oral tradition
and to realize that long before recorded history, ancient peoples on every
continent developed mythologies that speculated about human beginnings, attempted to explain the origins of the universe and other natural
phenomena, emphasized ethical truths, and transmitted group beliefs
and history from one generation to the next.

In addition to tales about human beginnings, heroic deeds and
perilous adventures became part of the group heritage and were transmitted to future generations as legends. Tales reporting human foibles
and virtues or desires of peasants to overcome injustice were told around
the same camp fires and in the same halls as the myths and legends.
Many of these folktales required magic or magical objects to balance
injustice. This oral tradition, which has existed since the first oral
communication among human beings, goes back to the very roots of
civilization.

Some Characteristics of Traditional Literature

We can make several broad generalizations about traditional literature. (This section will use the terms traditional tales or folklore to
designate the broad genre; the terms folktale, myth, and legend will
designate specific categories of traditional literature found in this genre.)
First, traditional literature provided spiritual, moral, social, and educational guidance as the tales helped conduct individuals through the
important stages of life. The tales provided guidance as the members of
the group went from childhood to the responsibilities of maturity, and on
to old age, and to the ultimate passage into death.

Second, traditional tales have been handed down from generation to
generation by word of mouth. In contrast to modern stories, traditional
tales have no identifiable authors. Names such as Charles Perrault,
Wilhelm and Jakob Grimm, and Peter Asbjornsen and Jorgen Moe are
collectors of tales from oral sources. They are not authors of original
stories such as E.B. White and A.A. Milne.

Third, the traditional tales in this genre are universal and ancient.
Similarities in the types of tales, in the narrative motifs, and in the
content of traditional tales from varied peoples throughout the world
constitute tangible evidence, according to folklorist Stith Thompson
(1946), that traditional tales are both universal and ancient. For
example, variants on the Cinderella story have been found throughout

the world. The names may vary, magical objects may differ, and settings may change, but basic elements of the story remain the same.

Fourth, the art of the traditional storyteller has been cultivated in every rank of society and reflects the culture, the nature of the land, and the social contacts of the storyteller and the audience. Consequently, the themes and characters in this genre range from the noble deeds of the ruling classes as found in the King Arthur legends and "The Song of Roland" to the harsh, unjust, and often cruel circumstances surrounding the peasants whose tales center on overcoming social inequality and attaining a better way of life. Tales such as "The Flying Ship" reveal how a poor peasant lad outwits the nobleman, wins his daughter in marriage, and gains lifelong wealth.

Types of Traditional Literature

In addition to broad generalizations, there are specific qualities for the types of literature found in this genre. Analyzing the specific characteristics of folktales, myths, and legends and comparing literature within these categories helps students understand this genre and encourages them to distinguish the genre from other genres. William Bascom's (1965) characteristics of folktale, myth, and legend help in this analysis. Bascom differentiates among the folklore types according to belief, time, place, attitude, and principal characters.

Folktales

Folktales, according to Bascom, are prose narratives that are regarded as fiction by the original narrator and the original audience. These tales are not considered as dogma or history; they are set in anytime and anyplace; they are secular in nature; and they are stories about both human and nonhuman characters. Let us use this definition to analyze the folktales in Grimm's *Household Tales* (1973). First, the tales are all considered fictitious. Second, the majority of the tales infer that time is unimportant by beginning in some version of "Once upon a time," "Long, long ago," or "One summer morning." Third, any place where magic is possible is inferred by descriptions such as "Hard by a great forest dwelt a woodcutter," "In a country village, over the hills and far away:' and "In an old castle in the midst of a large and thick forest." Fourth, all the tales are secular in attitude. Finally, the principal characters may be either human or nonhuman. The human characters may be poor peasants who search for riches, princes who quest for thrones or objects of power, or heroines who complete impossible tasks. The nonhuman characters may be supernatural adversaries such as ogres and witches who entice human characters into dangerous circumstances, or they may be supernatural helpers who support the human characters during their quests. Animals play similar roles in folktales. They may be adversaries such as the cunning wolf in "The Wolf and the Seven Little Kids," or they may be loyal companions such as the horse in "The Goose-Girl." Magical objects, spells, and transformations frequently assist or hinder the characters as they complete their tasks. Students may analyze other folklore collections to decide if the stories meet these definitions.

Myths

Myths, according to Bascom, are "prose narratives which, in the society in which they are told, are considered to be truthful accounts of what happened in the remote past. They are accepted on faith; they are taught to be believed; and they can be cited as authority in answer to ignorance, doubt, or disbelief. Myths are the embodiment of dogma; they are usually sacred; and they are often associated with theology and ritual" (p. 4). Let us use this definition of myth to analyze the selections in Ingri and Edgar Parin D'Aulaire's book of *Greek Myths* (1962). First, the myths were considered factual accounts by the early Greeks who accepted them on faith and worshipped at temples dedicated to these gods and goddesses. Second, the myths are set in the remote past when the world was created and are in locations such as on Olympus, the dwelling place of the gods, on earth, the place where gods interact with humans, or in the underworld, where Hades reigns in his dismal underground palace. Third, the stories are considered sacred because the principal characters are deities such as Zeus, the Greek lord of the universe, and Demeter, the goddess of the harvest.

Legends, according to Bascom, are "prose narratives which, like myths, are regarded as true by the narrator and his audience, but they are set in a period considered less remote, when the world was much as it is today. Legends are more often secular than sacred, and their principal characters are human" (p. 4).

Legends

Legends about King Arthur and Robin Hood are among the best known legends, and they meet Bascom's characteristics. For example, King Arthur (Pyle, 1903) is considered by many people to be an early British tribal leader. The legend takes place in the recent past, in a Britain that is basically the world of today. The story is secular, and the principal character is human.

Folktales, myths, and legends are found in all cultures throughout the world. Comparisons may be made using folklore from such diverse cultures as those found in Africa, Europe, Asia, South America, and North America (native American). More extensive comparisons of similarities and differences among these folklore types are found in Norton's *Through the Eyes of a Child: An Introduction to Children's Literature* (1987).

Analyzing the various folklore types according to the literary characteristics of setting, characterization, plot development, and style provides additional characteristics of the traditional literature genre. This analysis also encourages students to interact with and respond to the characters and their conflicts. Because folktales are readily available and are enjoyed by younger children, we will use folktales for our examples.

In contrast to other genres in literature, folktale settings are not carefully developed. Instead, the settings are briefly identified in the introduction. These settings place the reader in the realm of the unknown forest or castle where anything is possible. The universal nature of these unknown settings is reflected in folktales from various cultures. For example, the introduction to a Brazilian folktale places the setting "In the endless wild jungle forest, where ants, animals, and butterflies make their world" (Jagendorf and Boggs, 1960, p. 55). A Russian tale introduces the setting as "Outside in the forest there was a deep snow" (Ransome, 1916, 1985, p. 1). Likewise, a Chinese folktale places the setting "On the plain at the foot of a huge mountain" (He, 1985, p. 23). Students can read or listen to these tales and consider why the original storytellers would want to place their audiences immediately into this realm where anything is possible and where the storyteller does not need to develop long descriptions of the settings. These settings are known as symbolic settings because the reader or listener is placed there without requiring detailed descriptions to make the locations believable.

In addition to being either human or nonhuman, folktale characters are less fully developed than are the characters in other genres of literature. Folktale characters are essentially symbolic and flat, that is, they have a limited range of personal characteristics and rarely change in the course of a story. The witch is usually wicked; the youngest son is usually honorable, kind, and unselfish, even if he is considered foolish; and the heroine is usually fair, kind, and loving. Even when the characters do change, as happens to the king's daughter in "King Thrushbeard, the plot centers on the lessons that must be taught to the proud and haughty girl rather than on an indepth look at her personal struggles.

The nature of the oral tradition made it imperative that listeners be brought quickly into the action. Consequently, folktales immerse readers or listeners into the major conflict within their first few sentences. For example, the German tale, "The Peasant and the Devil," introduces both principal character and conflict within the first sentence: "Once upon a time there was a far-sighted, crafty peasant whose tricks were much talked about, and especially the story of how he once made a fool of the devil" (Grimm, p. 149). The next paragraph introduces the devil, who is sitting on a treasure. Within the next few sentences a wager is reached in which the devil bargains for half the produce grown in the field in exchange for the treasure. Conflict increases rapidly as the peasant clarifies the wager to include half the produce grown above the ground. He then lives up to his crafty nature by planting turnips. The conflict supposedly continues during the following year. Now the devil reverses the wager to include half the produce grown below the ground. This time the peasant plants wheat, not turnips. The conflict concludes as the devil angrily walks away because he has only wheat stubble as the result of his wager. The peasant, however, gleefully collects his treasure because "That's the way to cheat the Devil" (p. 150).

This conflict between good and evil characters is characteristic of many folktales. In addition, the actions that recur in folktales form recurring patterns. The conflict and plot development in folktales may be analyzed according to recurring patterns identified by F. André Favat (1977). This activity provides additional characteristics of folktales and encourages older students to compare and contrast folktales from many different cultures.

The rapid plot development in folktales leads to a style that is characterized by simplicity of language, by direct dialogue, and by few distracting details or unnecessary descriptions. The oral language style is frequently enriched by rhymes and verses. These rhymes may be repeated as in Grimm's German version of "Cinderella:"

> Shiver and quiver, little tree,
> Silver and gold throw over me. (p. 236)

or in Ashley Bryan's adaptation of the African tale The Cat's Purr (1985):

> Pit-tap-a-la-pat
> Pit-tap-a-la-pum
> Who's that knocking
> On my drum? (p. 25)

Questions for Identifying Traditional Literature

The following list of discussion topics and questions helps students decide if a literature selection belongs to the traditional literature genre. These topics and questions can also help students decide if a traditional tale is a folktale, myth, or legend.

1. What is the original cultural source for the tale? Is the tale part of a body of literature that was originally passed down through the oral tradition? Does the adapter identify the original cultural source for the tale?
2. What is the narrative motif? Are similar types and narrative motifs found in other folklore?
3. If the tale is identified as a folktale, how does it meet the characteristics of folktale? Is it fictitious, set in anytime and anyplace, secular in nature, and human or nonhuman in characterization?
4. If the tale is identified as a myth, how does it meet the characteristics of myth? Is it considered factual, set in the remote past or in an earlier world near the time of creation, considered sacred, and nonhuman in characterization?
5. If the tale is identified as a legend, how does it meet the characteristics of legend? Is it considered factual, set in a more recent time that resembles the world of today, considered secular or sacred, and human in characterization?
6. If the tale is identified as a folktale, how does it meet the following literary characteristics of a folktale: The setting is symbolic, not carefully developed; the characters are flat and rarely change during the course of the story; the plot development is rapid and the conflict and the characters are easily identifiable; and the style is simple and direct.

Modern Fantasy

Literary fairy tales, heroic quests, and articulate animal stories are all terms used to describe certain types of modern fantasy stories. These terms, which sound like the realm of traditional literature, show the strong connections and numerous similarities between traditional literature and modern fantasy. This connection is so strong that Joyce Thomas (1987) refers to folklore as the great-grandparent of children's literature. She explains her belief by stating that folktales lay the foundation for many of the classics of children's literature. Writers such as C.S. Lewis, J.R.R. Tolkien, and Ursula LeGuin create their works on the cornerstone of traditional literature.

If folklore is the cornerstone of modern fantasy, we would expect both similarities between the genres and difficulties distinguishing modern fantasy from traditional literature. The problem of distinguishing modern fantasy from traditional literature is compounded because authors of modern fantasy frequently develop their original stories on very strong folklore foundations. For example, Lloyd Alexander (1986) clarifies the connection between mythology and his Prydain Chronicles, "In the Prydain Chronicles, the world stems, to a degree, from Welsh mythology.... Following the timehonored tradition of storytellers, I felt free to use what bits and pieces suited my purposes, without violating the essential spirit of the myth" (p. 165).

For the purpose of this chapter, we will identify modern fantasy as fiction in which the author takes the reader into a time and a setting where the impossible becomes convincingly possible. This definition allows us to identify books that belong to the modern fantasy genre and also to make comparisons with the next genre of literature discussed in this chapter, contemporary realistic fiction.

To create a fantasy experience authors alter or manipulate one or more of the literary elements from what is expected in the real world. The elements that are most apt to be changed are setting, characters, and time. Note that all of these elements do not need to be altered; many fantasy writers manipulate only one of these elements.

Setting in Modern Fantasy

When settings are altered or manipulated the action occurs in a world or place other than our own. In this secondary world, the author creates through realistic details a world where things that are impossible in our world seem possible. In contrast to the "once upon a time, in a land far, far away" symbolic settings in folktales, the settings in many modern fantasies are integral to the story. They are carefully developed with extensive detail. Consequently, we can describe the worlds of Narnia, Middle Earth, Earthsea, and Prydain. In many cases we know about the major rivers and other geographical formations, the inhabitants, and the history and cultural heritage that formed the world.

After reading well developed modern fantasies, we may be able to use the details to draw a map of the fantasy world. In J.R.R. Tolkien's *The Hobbit* (1938) we may even trace Bilbo Baggins' journey as he and his fellow companions leave the comfortable hobbit hole in the Shire, traverse the Misty Mountains, wander through the dangerous Mirkwood, and finally reach Long Lake and the Lonely Mountain where the terrible dragon Smaug lies on the treasure.

Students identify and appreciate the importance of an integral setting in fantasy by writing descriptions and drawing maps of the worlds as they might appear in nonfictional reference sources. Teachers may use Alberto Manguel's and Gianni Guadalupi's *The Dictionary of Imaginary Places* (1980) as a model for such an activity. Fantasy kingdoms that contain enough setting descriptions for such activities include Damar in Robin McKinley's *Hero and the Crown* (1984) and *The Blue Sword* (1982), Prydain in Lloyd Alexander's *The Book of Three* (1964), Middle Earth in J.R.R. Tolkien's *The Hobbit* (1938), Earthsea in Ursula K. LeGuin's *A Wizard of Earthsea* (1968), Narnia in C.S. Lewis' *The Lion, the Witch, and the Wardrobe* (1950), and Wonderland in Lewis Carroll's *Alice's Adventures in Wonderland* (1865, 1984).

After completing this activity, students may try a similar approach with several folktales. This activity helps students understand major differences between the well developed settings in the fantasy genre and the more symbolic, less carefully developed settings in folklore.

Characters in Modern Fantasy

Authors writing in the fantasy genre frequently choose to have their characters depart from what we know is possible in the real world. If the characters are normal, human characters, they may have a fantasy experience and believe in their fantasy world. In this category are Lucy and Edmund who go through a wardrobe into Narnia, Alice who goes down a rabbit hole into Wonderland, and Meg Murry and Charles Wallace who travel the cosmos in Madeleine L'Engle's *A Wrinkle in Time* (1962).

Instead of normal, human characters who live fantasy experiences, the characters themselves may be contrary to reality. These characters include Natalie Babbitt's Tuck family who gain immortality after drinking from a spring in *Tuck Everlasting* (1975). Mary Norton's Clock family are contrary to reality because they are only six inches tall and live a precarious life by borrowing food and furnishings from the human occupants of the house in *The Borrowers* (1952). There are many animal stories that are contrary to reality because the animals talk and sometimes act like people. On a humanization continuum, these animal characters range from articulate animals who retain their animal characteristics (E.B. White's *Charlotte's Web*, 1952), to more humanized animals who demonstrate human frailties (Kenneth Grahame's *The Wind in the Willows*, 1908), to the very human mice who manage the ancient Redwall Abbey and fight the intrusion of the evil rats (Brian Jacques' *Redwall*, 1986).

Like the characters in folklore, modern fantasy characters may be in conflict with supernatural powers and may even solve their problems with magical objects. Unlike the flat characters in folklore, however, the characters in the fantasy genre are usually well developed. They demonstrate several sides to their personalities and frequently change in the course of the fantasy. Students can gain understanding and appreciation for this characteristic by comparing folktale characters such as "Cinderella" with fantasy characters such as Lady Aerin in McKinley's *The Hero and the Crown.* We must emphasize, however, that it is not well developed characterization that differentiates modern fantasy from other genres of literature; it is the departure of the characters from what we know to be possible in the real world.

Time in Modern Fantasy

In addition to altering settings or characters, authors of modern fantasy may manipulate time. Authors may use time warps to send their characters into the distant past or to propel them into a future as yet to materialize. When characters go into the past, as in Janet Lunn's *The Root Cellar* (1983), they frequently live in authentic historical backgrounds and face authentic historical problems. It is the time warp experience, however, not the authentic historical background that places this literature in the modern fantasy genre rather than in historical fiction. All time warp stories that take their characters into the future are obviously fantasy. In Margaret Anderson's *The Mists of Time* (1984) characters are brought into the twenty-second century after they encounter mists encircling ancient stones.

Believable stories in the modern fantasy genre are created through the author's ability to suspend disbelief. The author must make the reader believe that, even though the reader knows that the story is fantasy, the story could be possible in the world created by the author. Consequently, descriptions such as writing with a point of view that is consistent in every detail; developing integral settings that encourage readers to see, to hear, and to feel the surroundings; and developing characters who encourage readers to believe in the fanciful world are used when evaluating an author's ability to write modern fantasy. Helping students evaluate the author's ability to suspend disbelief will help them understand and appreciate the unique characteristics of the modern fantasy genre.

Some Questions for Identifying Modern Fantasy

Discussion questions that help students identify the modern fantasy genre include the following questions that are centered about the altered literary elements:

1. How has the author manipulated or altered the literary elements so that the story takes place in a world other than the real world of today?
2. What is the evidence that the setting has been altered? How was the setting altered? How does this setting differ from the real world? (The author does not need to alter all of these elements.)
3. What is the evidence that the characters are different from characters living in the real world? How are the characters altered? How do these characters differ from characters that you know in the real world?
4. What is the evidence that time has been altered? How was time altered? How is this experience with time different from experiences with time in the real world?
5. How did the author suspend disbelief and encourage readers to believe in the fanciful experience?

Contemporary Realistic Fiction

Moving from modern fantasy to realistic fiction takes us from the realm of the impossible in the world as we know it to the realm of the plausible and possible in the world of today. According to Zena Sutherland and May Hill Arbuthnot (1986) this genre of fiction includes stories in which

> everything that happens could happen. Sometimes the adventures of the hero or heroine may seem rather improbable but still merit the classification of realistic because they are possible. A realistic story is a tale that is convincingly true to life. (p. 332)

Contemporary realistic fiction infers that everything in the story, include setting, characters, and plot, could happen to real people living in our contemporary world. Realistic fiction does not mean that the story is true; it means that it could have happened.

Comparing Modern Fantasy and Contemporary Realistic Fiction

Comparative studies between the modern fantasy genre previously discussed and contemporary realistic fiction help students define the genre and understand and appreciate characteristics of setting, characters, and plot development. Comparing differences in how authors create believable stories also helps students differentiate realistic fiction from other genres of literature.

In contrast to modern fantasy in which writers alter and manipulate settings that may be in the past, the present, or the future, settings in contemporary realistic fiction must be in the contemporary world as we know it. For our analysis let us consider the settings in four recently published contemporary realistic novels: Beverly Cleary 's *Dear Mr. Henshaw* (1983), Marion Bauer's *On My Honor* (1986), Gary Paulsen's *Hatchet* (1987), and Norma Mazer's *After the Rain* (1987). The setting in Cleary's *Dear Mr. Henshaw* is the contemporary world of a ten-year-old boy. This world includes his school, his mother's small house in Pacific Grove, California, and the world he describes in his letters to his favorite author. Bauer's *On My Honor* is set in a town in Illinois and along a river between the town and a state park. Paulsen's *Hatchet* is set in the Canadian wilderness of lakes, forests, and wild animals. Mazer's *After the Rain* follows a girl and her grandfather as they walk the streets of a city and as she lives with her parents. Although these settings are quite different, they have one thing in common: they all describe the contemporary world as we know it.

In contrast to the modern fantasy characters who have fantasy experiences, characters in contemporary realistic fiction must act like real people. If the characters are animals, they must behave like animals, not personified versions of people. Cleary's character, Leigh Botts, acts like a child who is unhappy after his parents' divorce. His changing character, as reflected in the letters and diary entries, progresses from an unhappy boy who cannot accept his parents' divorce to a boy who can at least understand and accept the changes in his life. Bauer's character, Joel, shares a challenging day with his best friend and then faces the consequences of his disobedience and his friend's death. Joel progresses through various stages of nonacceptance and self-accusation before he reveals the truth. Paulsen's character, Brian Robeson, faces both unhappiness after his parents' divorce and terror resulting from a plane crash that leaves him alone in an alien wilderness. Brian's physical survival during his ordeal helps him face the emotional reaction to his parents' divorce. Mazer's character, Rachel, changes from a girl who is alienated from her terminally ill grandfather to a character who understands her grandfather and feels deep loss after his death. These characters all act like people we know, experience contemporary problems, and change in the process of facing their problems.

The conflicts faced by these characters, their adversaries, and the ways they overcome their conflicts are quite different from those found in modern fantasy. In modern fantasy, the conflicts may be against supernatural powers and supernatural adversaries and may be solved through magic or magical objects. In contrast, the conflict and plot development in contemporary realistic fiction must revolve around problems that are possible in today's world. The problems must also be resolved in ways that are possible in this world. Our examples include personal conflict related to divorce, accidental death, survival, and family relationships. Most of the conflicts encompass person-versus-self as the main characters face their problems and gain strength from this interaction.

Finally, there are differences in the ways authors create believable stories. In modern fantasy, authors must encourage readers to suspend disbelief, to believe in the settings and the characters who are impossible by our knowledge of the real world. In contemporary realistic fiction, authors rely on relevant subjects, everyday occurrences, and realism. Authors frequently refer to common contemporary knowledge to help readers understand the contemporary characters and to reveal information about characterization. For example, Mazer's character watches "The Cosby Show" every Thursday evening and then compares her family with the television family.

Paulsen uses a similar technique to encourage readers to understand Brian's new situation in the wilderness. Memories of books he read or programs he saw help him solve some of his problems. Without these memories it would not seem plausible for a young boy to survive in this harsh environment. Contrasts between how he would handle a problem at home and how he must solve the problem in this dangerous environment allow readers to understand the magnitude of his task and the consequences of any mistakes. Paulsen also reveals Brian's reasoning processes as he solves his problems. Again, without these thought processes the reader might decide that the boy's responses go beyond the realm of reality.

Some Questions for Identifying Contemporary Realistic Fiction

A comparative study between modern fantasy and contemporary realistic fiction shows students unique differences between these two genres of literature. Questions and discussion topics that will help students decide if a book is contemporary realistic fiction include the following:

1. Describe the setting. Is everything in the setting possible in the contemporary world as we know it?
2. Describe the characters. Do all the characters act like real people or real animals?
3. Describe the conflict and the plot development. Are they problems faced by the characters problems that seem real in the contemporary world? Do the characters solve their problems in ways that could actually happen in the real world?

4. Describe how the author creates believable stories. Are the subjects relevant to today's readers? Does the author use everyday occurrences to make comparisons? Is there a sense of realism?

Sharing children's literature in a classroom and allowing students to respond to the various genres of children's literature is exciting. Appreciation of literature and enjoyment of reading are two goals that will be gained by sharing interesting picture books, traditional literature, modern fantasy and contemporary realistic fiction as well as the other genres of literature.

References

Alexander, Lloyd. "Future Conditional," *Children's Literature Association Quarterly-*Vol. 10 (Winter 1986): 164-166.

Bader, Barbara. *American Picturebooks from Noah's Ark to the Beast Within.* New York: Macmillan, 1976.

Bascom, William. "The Forms of Folklore: Prose Narratives." *Journal of American Folklore.* Vol. 78 (Jan.-Mar. 1965): 3-20.

Favat, F. André. *Child and Tale: The Origins of Interest.* Urbana, Ill.: National Council of Teachers of English, 1977.

Frye. Northrop: Baker, Sheridan; and Perkins, George. T*he Harper Handbook to Literature.* New York: Harper & Row, 1985.

Huck, Charlotte; Hepler, Susan; and Hickman, Janet. *Children's Literature in the Elementary School.* 4th edition. New York: Holt, Rinehart and Winston, 1987.

Lacy, Lyn Ellen. A*rt and Design in Children's Picture Books.* Chicago: American Library Association, 1986.

Manguel, Alberto and Guadalupi, Gianni. T*he Dictionary of Imaginary Places.* New York: Macmillan, 1980.

Norton, Donna E. *Through the Eyes of a Child: An Introduction to Children's Literature.* 2nd edition. Columbus, Ohio: Merrill, 1987.

Shulevitz, Uri. *Writing With Pictures: How to Write and Illustrate Children's Books.* New York: Watson-Guptill, 1985.

Sutherland, Zena and Hearne, Betsy. "In Search of the Perfect Picture Book Definition." In *Jump Over the Moon: Selected Professional Readings,* edited by Pamela Barron and Jennifer Burley. New York: Holt, Rinehart and Winston, 1984.

Sutherland, Zena and Arbuthnot, May Hill. *Children and Books.* Glenview, Ill.: Scott, Foresman, 1986.

Thomas, Joyce. "The Tales of the Brothers Grimm: In the Black Forest."

in *Touchstones: Reflections on the Best in Children's Literature,* Vol. Two, edited by Perry Nodelman. Purdue University: Children's Literature Association, 1987, pp. 104-117.

Thompson, Stith. *The Folktale.* New York: Dryden, 1946.

Children's Books Mentioned in the Chapter

Alexander, Lloyd. *The Book of Three.* New York: Holt, Rinehart and Winston, 1964.

Anderson, Margaret. *The Mists of Time.* New York: Knopf, 1984.

Babbitt, Natalie. *Tuck Everlasting.* New York: Farrar, Straus & Giroux, 1975.

Bauer, Marion Dane. *On My Honor.* New York: Clarion, 1986.

Blumberg, Rhoda. *Commodore Perry in the Land of the Shogun.* New York: Lothrop, Lee & Shepard, 1985.

Bryan, Ashley. *The Cat's Purr.* New York: Atheneum, 1985.

Carroll, Lewis. *Alice's Adventures in Wonderland.* New York: Macmillan, 1865, Knopf, 1984.

Christopher, John. *The White Mountains.* New York: Macmillan, 1967.

Cleary, Beverly. *Dear Mr. Henshaw.* New York: Morrow, 1983.

Cooper, Susan. *The Dark Is Rising.* New York: Atheneum, 1973.

The Grey King. New York: Atheneum, 1975.

D'Aulaire, Ingri, and D'Aulaire, Edgar Parin. *Book of Greek Myths.* New York: Doubleday, 1962.

Gag, Wanda. *Millions of Cats.* New York: Coward-McCann, 1928, 1956.

Gish, Lillian. *An Actor's Life for Me!* As told to Selma G. Lanes. New York: Viking Kestrel, 1987.

Grahame, Kenneth. *The Wind in the Willows.* New York: Scribner's, 1908, 1940.

Greenaway, Kate. *A Apple Pie.* Secaucus, N.J.: Castle, 1979 (A facsimile edition).

Grimm, Wilhelm and Grimm, Jakob. *Household Tales.* New York: Schocken Books, 1973.

He, Liyi. *The Spring of Butterflies and other Folktales of China's Minority Peoples.* New York: Lothrop, Lee & Shepard, 1985.

Jacques, Brian. *Redwall.* New York: Putnam, 1986.

Jagendorf, M.A. and Boggs, R.S. *The King of the Mountains: A Treasury of Latin American Folk Stories.* New York: Vanguard, 1960.

Lauber, Patricia. *Dinosaurs Walked Here and Other Stories Fossils Tell.* New York: Bradbury. 1987.

LeGuin, Ursula K. A *Wizard of Earthsea.* Boston: Parnassus, 1968.

L'Engle, Madeleine. A *Wrinkle in Time.* New York: Farrar, Straus & Giroux, 1962.

Lewis, C.S. *The Lion, the Witch and the Wardrobe.* New York: Macmillan, 1950.

Lunn, Janet. *The Root Cellar.* New York: Scribner's, 1983.

Mazer, Norma Fox. *After the Rain.* New York: Morrow, 1987.

McCully, Emily Arnold. *Picnic.* New York: Harper & Row, 1984.

McKinley, Robin. *The Blue Sword.* New York: Greenwillow, 1982.
  The Hero and the Crown. New York: Greenwillow, 1984.

Norton, Mary. *The Borrowers.* New York: Harcourt Brace Jovanovich, 1952.

Paulsen, Gary. H*atchet.* New York: Bradbury, 1987.

Pyle, Howard. *The Story of King Arthur and His Knights.* New York: Scribner's, 1903.

Ransome, Arthur. *Old Peter's Russian Tales.* London: Jonathan Cape, 1916, 1985.

Scheer, Julian. *Rain Makes Applesauce.* New York: Holiday, 1964.

Sendak, Maurice. *Where the Wild Things Are.* New York: Harper & Row, 1963.

Tolkien, J.R.R. *The Hobbit.* Boston: Houghton Mifflin, 1938.

Van Allsburg, Chris. *The Z Was Zapped.* Boston: Houghton Mifflin, 1987.

White, E.B. *Charlotte's Web.* New York: Harper & Row, 1952.

Yorinks, Arthur. *Hey, Al.* New York: Farrar, Straus & Giroux, 1986.

Part II

Perspectives on Evaluation and Selection in Children's Literature

There are so many books and not nearly enough time to enjoy them all. One primary concern shared by all people who work with children and books is how to evaluate and select quality books appropriate for their young audiences.

Part II focuses on various aspects of evaluation and selection and offers in each chapter many helpful suggestions for making informed, intelligent decisions about selecting books not only for general classroom or library use but also for specific situations.

In Chapter 5, Anita Silvey provides an insightful overview of the reviewing process and offers readers some suggested characteristics of good reviewers as well as a series of questions for thoroughly evaluating books. These questions and guidelines, however, are not meant to replace how readers feel individually about books they review. Rather, they can help articulate deeply felt likes and dislikes and move beyond "It's good because I like it."

As Jane Yolen pointed out in Chapter 1, books tend to reflect the society of which they are a part. Until relatively recently, it was rare to find representatives of any other group than white Protestants in books. Fortunately, as society has begun to value diversity as a positive component of our national heritage, this is reflected by the growing body of literature that recognizes and respects differences of color, religion, and national origin. In chapter six Masha Kabakow Rudman discusses the need for a collection of books that includes specific heritages as well as books that reflect universal values and as wide a range of the population as possible. This chapter provides an extensive annotated bibliography of multicultural books aimed at dispelling stereotypes.

Censorship is also a reflection of our society, and is an issue that all educators will invariably face at some time in their careers. Educators should, therefore, have well-defined selection policies as well as examine their attitudes toward the community's role in selection of library books and instructional materials. In Chapter 7, librarian and author Barbara Feldstein offers valuable guidelines for using the selection process as a means of diffusing censorship.

5

Evaluation and Criticism: The Quest for Quality in Children's Books

Anita Silvey

A few years ago, a group of friends spent an evening speculating about the nature of the world when computers could do all the work and humans would have unlimited free time. As most of the assembled group were artists, several said, "Wonderful, everyone could produce more art." I had an instant image of the human race free to read children's books at leisure and free to discuss them at length. A few days later as I was looking over Frances Clarke Sayers' *Summoned by Books* (1965), I was thrilled to see the second paragraph of that glorious speech, "Lose Not the Nightingale": "If there be some such 'heaven of all my wish,' two lively spirits are sitting together there, under some celestial apple tree, talking about children's books and reading." She also envisioned paradise as some grand marathon book discussion and evaluation session.

Think of it. The possibilities are endless. To have a chance to talk to Lewis Carroll and George MacDonald about their books and their works in progress. To argue with Anne Carroll Moore, who did not approve of *Charlotte's Web* (1952), about it. Or even better, to watch Anne Carroll Moore and E.B. White discuss *Charlotte's Web*. The thought of having unlimited time to read, unlimited access to books, and an endless number of intelligent people to talk to seems very much like heaven. That's just what it seems like—heaven; something that we will wait to do until computers or this earthly life liberate us because in busy library systems and busy schools with innumerable demands on our time, we view the evaluation of material, reading and thinking about books as a luxury. Book evaluation is not a luxury but a necessity. As a necessity, we need to understand how to deal with book evaluation here on earth.

The Challenge of the Reviewer

Those of us who work with criticism and books know all too well that nothing is more difficult to sum up and put into words than the elusive process of reviewing or evaluating children's books. About twenty years ago, Paul Heins, the fourth editor of *The Horn Book Magazine,* wrote: "the reviewing and criticism of children's literature is more complex and fraught with misconceptions than any other kind of reviewing and criticism." This state of affairs has not changed in twenty years. Very little literature exists in the children's book field about reviewing and evaluation. People can easily write interesting and humorous pieces about all the things that go wrong in reviewing and evaluation, and it is quite easy to unearth many children's book reviews manque—evaluations that miss the mark. One of my favorites is by that master of literary criticism, Henry James, on Louisa May Alcott's *Eight Cousins.* He felt that she gave children poor entertainment and poor instruction, "no glow and no fairies; it is all prose and . . . rather vulgar prose." Although it is easy to look at what can, and has, gone wrong in children's book evaluation, it is a bit more difficult to talk about how we can be accurate and fair in our evaluations. Still, in this chapter, I will try to examine the process of how one goes about reviewing or evaluating titles, what kinds of questions one should ask about a book when one is engaged in the process, and why children's book evaluation is so important in the first place.

The evaluation and criticism of books for children is, of course, not simply a modern concern. Search for quality in children's books has been a constant adult preoccupation for hundreds of years. In America even the dour Puritan literature, so dogmatic and didactic by contemporary standards, was scrutinized by adults in that society to determine whether or not it would effectively lead young minds to God. During the eighteenth and nineteenth centuries, adults believed that the best children's literature helped children conform to the mores of society. These early moralists and high-minded critics like Sarah Trimmer raged against fairy tales in particular and other kinds of literature that were seen as corrupting young minds. In America, during the twentieth century a vast number of librarians, critics, and publications like *The Horn Book Magazine* have attempted to pursue that elusive goal of determining which of the hundreds and thousands of books published for children are the best.

Children's book evaluation, criticism, and reviewing depends on the idea that adults—with the appropriate sensibilities, taste and appropriate contact with children—can, in fact, make reasoned and enlightened decisions about what books are best for them to read. Part of the rationale for this concern is that childhood is a period limited in time. What children read in that time period is of extreme importance. In childhood reading has its most profound impact on our lives. As Graham Greene wrote in *The Lost Childhood and Other Essays* (1951),

> Perhaps it is only in childhood that books have any deep influence on our lives . . . in childhood all books are books of divination, telling us about the future, and like the fortune-teller who sees a long journey in the cards or death by water, they influence the future. I suppose that is why books excited us so much. What do we ever get nowadays from reading to equal the excitement and the revelation of those first fourteen years?

Fourteen years is not a very long time in which to impart to children all of the knowledge and information they need, all of the beauty and insight.

The Power of Literature

One needs only to scan adult literature to find numerous compelling examples of the effect of reading in childhood on adults in later years. The following paragraphs are by two different writers with two extraordinarily different backgrounds, yet the content of the two statements is amazingly similar.

> I had read *A Tale of Two Cities* and found it up to my standards as a romantic novel. She opened the first page and I heard poetry for the first time in my life.... Her voice slid in and curved down through and over the words. She was nearly singing. I wanted to look at the pages. Were they the same that I had read? Or were there notes, music, lined on the pages. as in a hymn book? Her sounds began cascading gently.... I have tried often to search behind the sophistication of years for the enchantment I so easily found in those gifts. The essence escapes but its aura remains. To be allowed, no, invited into the private lives of strangers, and to share their joys and fears, was a chance to exchange the Southern bitter wormwood for a cup of mead with Beowulf or a hot cup of tea and milk with Oliver Twist.

> My love for the alphabet, which endures, grew out of reciting it but, before that, out of seeing the letters on the page. In my own story books before I could read them for myself, I fell in love with various winding, enchanted-looking initials drawn by Walter Crane at the heads of fairy

tales .... When the day came, years later, for me to see the Book of Kells, all the wizardry of letter, initial, and word swept over me a thousand times over, and the illumination, the gold, seemed a part of the word's beauty and holiness that had been there from the start.

The first quote, from *I Know Why the Caged Bird Sings* (1970), tells of the encounter with books that emotionally saved a raped, deserted Southern black child, Maya Angelou. The second, from *One Writer's Beginnings* (1983), shows how the love of books was instilled in that most gracious and elegant of our contemporary writers, Eudora Welty. Both of these paragraphs demonstrate that what children read can have a tremendous and lasting impact upon them for all of their lives.

Adult Responsibility

The second argument for adult evaluation and intervention in children's reading centers on our general role as caretakers of children. As adults it is our responsibility to ensure that children have the appropriate nutrition, exercise, and physical care, and to take care of the intellectual development of children when it comes to reading. Even though children might well want to exist only on a diet of junk food, as adults we make sure they have nutritious meals. Even if children would like to read only junk novels, it is equally important for us as adults to see to it that they have well-balanced reading fare. Probably the most frequently quoted statement by advocates of adult intervention in books for children is from Walter de la Mare's *Bells and Grass* (1963): "I know well that only the rarest kind of best in anything can be good enough for the young." Others maintain that what we are looking for is the "right book for the right child." Most who spend time with the variety of children's books believe, however, that we have some responsibility to the next generation to pass on to them and locate for them the best in books—to find books that would nourish their minds and souls.

If it is important, then, to evaluate books for children, how does one go about the process? For me that process begins, almost without exception, as a solitary endeavor. I tend to love the most and get the most excited about those books that I discover on my own away from the prying eyes of anyone else. But books are new for all critics and children when we find them. It is easy to identify with a young girl in the Boston Public Library who was overheard saying, "Look, here's a new book by Louisa May Alcott, *Little Men* (1911)."Books are new to us and exciting when we find them. After that initial discovery and reading, the process of evaluation grows more complex. I read, think about the book, and read again.

Then comes a discussion stage when I talk about, argue about, and present my reactions to other people. During this stage the hardest part of the process comes for me and I imagine for other highly opinionated individuals: I have to listen—to opinions that differ from my own, to the way someone else might analyze a work of literature or a picture book, or to the many different ways the same book can be approached by many different people. If anyone wants to become a better critic or reviewer tomorrow than they are today, they must be able to listen. After listening comes rethinking, reconsidering, and often using the book with children to elicit their opinions.

Finally, after all this process comes rereading, rethinking, and that final and most difficult stage of committing opinions to paper. For all of the glamour of reviewing, many unglamorous moments occur when you are staring at a blank piece of paper or a blank computer screen early in the morning and wondering how you are ever going to arrive at anything important to say about the book.

As this description indicates, intelligent evaluation of children's books takes a great deal of time. Far too often, we shortchange the process; we try to arrive at instant decisions and immediate reactions to books. We try to be instant critics. Long periods of time are crucial for the process. As Chekhov said, "What is needed is constant work, day and night. Constant reading, study, will."

Qualities of a Reviewer

There are many qualities that need to be brought to the reviewing and evaluating process. Most fine reviewers and fine reviews exhibit eleven characteristics that are quite easy to identify.

1. *A sense of children, their needs, and how they respond to books.* We are, after all, engaged in a peculiar pursuit. Most children's literature is written by adults, published by adults, and selected and reviewed by adults. The child or children, however, stand as the ultimate test of any book. We need to ask ourselves constantly, "Will children, or a child, understand and appreciate this book? Does this author have something to say to a child?"

2. *A sense of enthusiasm and passion for the material.* In evaluating books for children, who are not by and large cynical or pessimistic, there is no room for being jaded. A good book review should make you want to read the book and use it with children. Although certain famous, or more accurately infamous, reviews—such as Dorothy Parker's review of *The House at Pooh Corner,* "Tonstant weader froed up"—are certainly

amusing, I do not think we should aspire to them. Good reviewers, using those fine words from Helen Garner, should aim to "light a torch, not wield a sword."

3.   *A sense of respect for the creator of a book and for the creation process.* Good reviewers are interested in determining what the author or illustrator has actually set out to do and in evaluating how well he or she has done it. In "The Art of Fiction" (1948) Henry James says that fiction is a tower with a thousand windows; at every window stands a writer. Obviously, the vision is going to be different from every window. The critic cannot make a judgment about where the writer's eyes should look or what they should have seen. This principle is one of the most frequently violated in children's book reviewing. There is an amazing tendency on the part of the reviewer to play author and editor rather than to review the book that is in front of them. This tendency to play editor was one of my own besetting sins as a young reviewer. I actually wrote in *The Horn Book Magazine,* in a review of Almedingen's *Anna,* "Pallid in comparison with some of the great heroines of Russian fiction—women of mettle like Natasha of *War and Peace*—Anna, at least has a certain charming simplicity:" A senior reviewer pointed out that possibly the author had not wanted or needed to create *War and Peace,* or Natasha for that matter, for young readers. We should not in reviews talk about the book that might have been; we simply need to do justice and to be completely fair to one book—the one that has actually been created.

4.   *A sense of style.* Good reviewers have their own sense of style and write readable and enjoyable reviews.

5.   *Sense enough to avoid preconceptions, adages, and old saws.* Good reviewers are not concerned with fitting a book into their particular theory of children's literature. On occasion, authors of books can get away with their adages and old saws, but it is not a privilege we have as reviewers. As John Updike says in *Picked-Up Pieces:* "Do not imagine yourself a caretaker of any tradition, an enforcer of any party standard, a warrior in any ideological battle, or a correction's officer of any kind."

6.   *A sense of humility.* To make sure that I maintain my humility, I keep next to my desk two classic *Horn Book* manque. The first is a review by Ruth Hill Viguers, third editor of *The Horn Book,* in which she says, "Children, however, do not enjoy cynicism. I doubt *Harriet the Spy's* appeal to many of them." The other is

by Anne Carroll Moore; its opening salvo sets the tone for a long, essentially negative review: "I may as well confess that I find E.B. White's *Charlotte's Web* hard to take from so masterly a hand." Reviewers do the best job they can, make the best judgments they can, but they need always to remember that they can make mistakes, be aware that they are fallible, and be willing to reevaluate books.

7. *A sense of history of the genre in which they are reviewing, a knowledge of past books of the author or illustrator, and an ability to make comparisons in a review.*

8. *A sense of balance or proportion between plot and critical commentary.* This varies from book to book: good reviewers tell you what a book is about and why they think it succeeds or fails so that as a reader you have some idea of their critical perspective.

9. *A sense of your audience.* You have to know who your readers are, what they know about books, what they need to know about books, and what similar points of reference you actually have.

10. *A sense of contemporary adult literature, art, film, and theater and an historical perspective on these forms.* Every now and then I am amused by those who see a particular children's book as on the cutting edge of art. Children's books are rarely on the cutting edge of anything, but we need to see them in the wider context of adult literature and art to understand this.

11. A sense of humor. Last, and most important, this is one of the qualities most lacking in children's book reviewing. Children's books are a great deal of fun. Children's book reviews are often very dull. Whether they are funny in print or not, however, children's book reviewers need a sense of humor so they can evaluate the material they read.

Questions for the Reviewer to Consider

If these are the qualities that one brings to book evaluation, what questions do you ask when engaged in evaluation? Usually when we encounter discussions about reviewing and evaluation, textbooks will list questions to be asked of the different genres so we can look at a list of different questions for picture books, novels, nonfiction, science fiction, and poetry. I think that the process is a different one, however. There are basically in children's book evaluation and reviewing, four categories of questions that we should be asking of all the different genres: (1) literary and artistic questions, (2) pragmatic questions, (3) philosophical questions, and (4) probably in children's book evaluation one of the most important categories, personal questions. Depending on your orientation to children's books and for what reason or what children you are selecting books, a group of these questions will emerge as more important than the others. For literary purists, for example, the question of whether or not a book has an index is a relatively unimportant one; for a school librarian with a limited budget to build a small collection, such a question may be the most important to consider. For those building church libraries, quite often the moral and philosophical implications of a book weigh more heavily than any other considerations. For many review journals like *The Horn Book Magazine,* all discussions basically begin with literary and artistic questions; the other categories of question are often crucial, but they are weighed in relation to the literary and artistic merit of a book. What, then, are examples of these kinds of questions? The following are examples only, and the list is by no means exhaustive.

Literary Questions

Do the characters change in a believable way in the process of the narrative?

Does the author convey an intensity of feeling, a truth of emotion?

Does the story have an understandable conflict or resolution?

How well is place or setting conveyed?

How lively or funny is the book?

Are the characters so well developed that we know them completely? The completeness of the characters is one of the most satisfying elements in fiction. As E.M. Forster tells us in *Aspects of the Novel* (1927), we can never understand anyone in real life as totally as we know the truly well-created characters in fiction.

Is the point of view consistent? If there are shifts in this point of view, are they believable? Is the first-person narrator capable of knowing everything he or she is telling you?

Does everything in the book fit, or are there extraneous bits that detract from the way the book works?

How distinctive is the style of writing? Does the author possess what John Cheever calls "singularity" of vision?

Is the plot well-constructed and believable?

Are the characters free of stereotypes? This question is also pragmatic and philosophical, but it is first of all a literary one for the simple reason that stereotyped characters are simply bad characters.

Does the dialogue flow naturally? Is it consistent with the age and background of the child?

How well does the author do what he or she sets out to do?

Does the story contain anachronisms?

Do the events in the plot follow one another in a logical progression?

Is the book interesting? This question is equally important for children's or adult literature. We cannot confine our search to worthy literature that will bore a child to tears, but we need to search for something alive and interesting that will keep the child excited about the reading process. As Henry James states in "The Art of Fiction", "The only obligation to which in advance we may hold a novel . . . is that it be interesting . . . . The ways in which it is at liberty to accomplish this result (of interesting us) strike me as innumerable."

Is the use of language, rhythm, imagery, and diction appropriate and coherent with other choices made by the writer?

How enjoyable is the book? This question is particularly important if you believe that one of the primary purposes of books for children is simply entertainment.

Does the book simplify and make available a complex experience for its readers?

As the book unfolds, is there a sense of mystery, of what will happen next?

Is there some aspect of the characterization, plot, theme or style that is unusual in treatment or that adds to the overall effectiveness of the book?

Artistic Questions

Is the illustrator technically adept? In other words, how well does the illustrator draw? This seems to be one of the most overlooked questions in picture-book evaluation.

How skillful is the use of color?

How much control does the artist have over composition and picture space?

How well-designed are all the elements of the book—endpapers, typeface, placement of art?

Do the illustrations convey the appropriate emotional content for this particular story?

How good is the illustrator at creating mood and atmosphere?

How lively and animated is the artwork?

Are the words and images integrated, mutually dependent, and worthy of each other? Do art and text possess an underlying unity?

Pragmatic Questions

Is there an original source from which the material was taken? Do the variations improve or distract?

Is the material current or will it soon be obsolete?

Is there an apparent bias of the author that alters the way the material is presented?

Are the photos, maps, illustrations, and diagrams carefully placed and labeled?

Is the material covered in the book only of temporary interest or does it have enduring elements?

Is the book user friendly? Does it have an index, table of contents, and other sources so that a child can explore the subject further?

Is the material accurate?

How well does the book compare to others like it or on the same subject?

Is the presentation suitable for the intended audience or the intended age range?

How useful will the book be and will it fit specifically into the curriculum?

Does the book explore a problem area that needs to be introduced to children?

Does the material have a coherent and logical organization?

Will the paper and binding hold up or disintegrate during repeated usage?

Philosophical Questions

Will the book enrich a child's life? Enlarge a child's world?

What is the pervasive theme? What philosophical message is the book conveying to the child?

Does the author have something to say to a child?

How profound is the morality?

Does the book convey a sense of respect for all human beings—for all races, sexes, religions, nationalities, and social classes?

Does the book allow a child to share in human emotion?

Does the book make the ordinary extraordinary?

Does the book convey a sense of hope? Actually, this is one of the old saws in children's books. It is my personal belief that an author can write a superb book for children—for instance, Robert Cormier's *The Chocolate War* (1986)—and have something to say of great importance to children without attempting to impart hope to them. There are other critics and writers, however, who believe that hope is essential to books of lasting merit for children and young adults.

Does the book convey a sense of wonder, awe, or excitement about life?

Does the book respect the audience or is it patronizing or condescending to children?

Personal Questions

Does this book appeal to the child in me?

How comfortable will I be reading this book to a particular child or giving this book to children?

Do I want to return to this book, to look at it again, to read it again?

Am I excited about sharing this book with children or a particular child that I know?

Are there aspects of the author's implied morality or of the various characters' morality that disturb me? Often critics in the children's book field spend a great deal of time trying to unearth literary flaws in a book when what they are really responding to is a difference in their world view and the one shown by the author.

Why do I personally love, like, hate, or feel indifferent to this book?

It could be argued that the entire history of children's book evaluation and criticism has simply been composed of long periods of time when the philosophical questions were the most important—how will these books affect the undeveloped morals and attitudes of children?—alternating with periods when literary and artistic questions were the most important—how crucial will this book be in developing the mind of a child and his or her literary and artistic sensibilities?

This list of questions is merely a starting point for evaluation. Since no two books are alike, no single approach to book evaluation can be used again and again. There simply is no cookie cutter that one can apply to book evaluation. As Lillian H. Smith states in *The Unreluctant Years (1967):*

> The ability to distinguish a good book from a poor one, to know when the spirit of literature is present and when it is not, requires the sensitive feeling and reasoning of the reader....There is no formula we can apply which will infallibly tell us whether what we are reading is good or bad. Familiarity with and understanding of the books which have been proved to have permanent value will give a bedrock of reasoning and feeling which one can work from, and go back to, in the evaluating of contemporary writing for children.

Ultimately, all great evaluation comes from the fusing of all of these questions in some combination. That personal response to books—"I love it; it's mine; it was written for my library; it was written for a child I know; it was written personally for me"—must be combined with literary and artistic knowledge. Otherwise personal passion only sheds more heat than light on any discussion. On the other hand, any approach that aims at a checklist of criteria or pragmatic questions, without that personal and philosophical love of books, is equally deficient. I believe it is precisely in looking at a book with flaws that personal response becomes the most important element in evaluation. Take Herman Melville's *Moby Dick* (1985), possibly one of the poorest technical masterpieces of literature. Perspectives change, as do details of plot. Voice changes occur in the same paragraph, and Melville discusses interminably everything from the fins on the whale to the teeth of the whale. For all its imperfections and for all its flaws, however, the book remains extraordinarily powerful. The same could be said for *A Wrinkle in Time (1962)*, the *Narnia* books, many of Cynthia Voigt's deservedly popular titles, many fine first and second novels like Brock Cole's *The Goats* and Chris Crutcher's *Stotan!* (1986), and countless children's classics. The most frequent, inane critical comment that I encounter is basically, "I have found a literary, artistic, or pragmatic flaw in this book, and now I can dismiss the book." By this thinking we end up selecting books that do nothing wrong and, by the way, do nothing much right either. Simply spotting technical difficulties is in no way true evaluation. When we are engaged in evaluation, we must combine all four categories of questions in some fashion that is appropriate for the book being examined.

How Can Reviewers Prepare?

How does anyone learn to do this? There is only one tried and true way to gain the skills of good book discussion and good book reviewing: practice. Critical skills are not acquired in a course; they are not perfected in classrooms. They come by doing, over and over again—by checking your impressions with others, by looking at how children respond to books over time, by committing yourself verbally or in print and then by watching what happens to that book that you think is a masterpiece or sometimes, just as important, that book you judge to be a failure. In the process we take risks as children's book editors take risks; we must decide where we stand on a book and then try to determine by talking to others, by using the book with children, by reading it again and again, how good our critical opinions actually are. At *The Horn Book,* of course, we take our critical risks in print, where thousands read what is written and can agree or disagree. The process of taking such risks is no less important in local discussion groups, local library systems, local teachers' groups, or on local awards committees. You just have the advantage in these groups of being able to make errors in judgment a little less publicly.

From the description so far, it would seem that book evaluation is fairly arduous, and the time and thought involved immense.

Why Bother?

Why, then, do evaluators and reviewers of children's books go to all this trouble? Why do children's book professionals take all of this time? We do so, I believe, because we know the profound effect that such evaluation has upon the nature of the books published and the quality of the artists and illustrators attracted to children's books. We will get, in future years, just about as good books for children as we demand, and this has always been the case.

For years I sat in editorial meetings in a Boston publishing house, planning future publications and the future of an author's or illustrator's career. Each time we did so we sat with the review file, which included every printed review from any library system, snippet of information, letter, or feedback we had had on a previous book.

We also brought to that meeting all the comments that seemed to bear on the case that we had heard at the American Library Association, the International Reading Association, the American Booksellers Association, or any local school or library discussion groups. It was frankly quite often the case that the printed review from a local library system, school district, or independent bookseller or the well-chosen comments of an interested reader weighed more heavily than the national reviews in the decision-making process. They were the key to going back to the author and directing the work, discussing what books should be published next. These meetings were also often the cause for a manuscript that was already in the house to be accepted, because knowledgeable people wanted a particular kind of book. Those who know and care about children's books, who work with books and children, should be able to tell the publishing community in as articulate terms as possible, in ways that they will truly respect, what they feel about books. Without good book discussion, without such critical exchanges, we will not have the books we would like to talk about in paradise.

Without good book discussion, we will also not encourage the authors and illustrators whom we admire to grow and create even better books for children. Because books of quality for children are so crucial, we need to attract to the occupation of writing or illustrating children's and young adult books the most talented, intelligent, and caring individuals possible. When one of the graduates of the Iowa School of

Writing, Bruce Brooks, came to write young adult novels, he was completely unaware of the children's and young adult field in general. Since the publication of his first young adult book, he has talked about his joy in discovering in this field people who loved and cared about literature, who could talk about what he was doing as a writer, and who could understand his craft. For not only has Bruce Brooks gained by winning awards for his first novel, *The Moves Make the Man* (1984), but those who love children's and young adult literature have gained a writer of incredible talent, who now believes that young adult books are an outlet for that talent and for the kind of fiction he would like to write. If we had waited until we got to heaven to talk about books, we would not have Bruce Brooks or David Macaulay or Chris Van Allsburg or Lois Lowry, to name only a few people who have been persuaded to turn their hand to creating books for children and young adults. What they found was a responsive young audience to read their books, and equally important they found a committed, thoughtful professional group of librarians, teachers, booksellers, and critics who were concerned with excellence, the quality of writing and of art, and the craft of these creators.

In an article "Review the Reviewers?" in the March 1986 issue of *School Library Journal*, Avi wrote about reviewing and talked about how important the evaluation, good or bad, of his books by professionals has been for him as a writer. As a creative person he has always needed feedback from those who know children's books, from those who can intelligently talk about it, and from those he respects. If we are not willing in this earthly paradise to spend time giving that kind of feedback to the writers and illustrators whose work we admire, we are going to have to sit in that great book discussion in the sky without their titles to discuss, and that will be a great loss indeed. The evaluation of children's books is, without a doubt, one of the most important tasks undertaken by professionals in the children's book field. Virginia Woolf once wrote:

> I have sometimes dreamt, at least, that when the Day of Judgment dawns and the great conquerors and lawyers and statesmen come to receive their rewards—their crowns, their laurels, their names carved indelibly upon imperishable marble—the Almighty will turn to Peter and will say, not without a certain envy when he sees us coming with our books under our arms, 'Look, these need no reward. We have nothing to give them here. They have loved reading.'

The love of reading children's books, the ability to talk about them, and the joy in having the critical vocabulary to do so are earthly, not heavenly rewards. When it comes to children's books, book discussion, and evaluation, we need to pursue them with vigor here on earth — heaven cannot wait.

References

Angelou, Maya, *I Know Why the Caged Bird Sings*, New York: Random House, 1970.

Cameron, Eleanor, *The Green and Burning Tree: On the Writing and Enjoyment of Children's Books*, Boston: Atlantic-Little Brown, 1969.

De la Mare, Walter, *Bells and Grass*, New York: Viking, 1963.

Egoff, Sheila, G.T. Stubbs, and L.F. Ashley, Editors, *Only Connect: Readings on Children's Literature*, Second Edition, New York: Oxford University Press, 1980.

Forster, E.M., *Aspects of the Novel*, New York: Harcourt, Brace, 1927.

Kamerman, Sylvia, Editor, *Book Reviewing*, The Writer, 1978.

Sayers, Frances Clarke, *Summoned By Books: Essays and Speeches*, New York: Viking, 1965.

Smith, Lillian H., *The Unreluctant Years*, New York: Viking, 1967.

Welty, Eudora, *One Writer's Beginnings*, Cambridge, MA: Harvard University Press, 1983.

6

Multicultural Children's Literature: The Search for Universals

Masha Kabakow Rudman

The need for multicultural education has become more and more apparent as America moves away from the notion of a melting pot toward the idea of parallel cultures comprising a mosaic or salad bowl of different groups, customs, ethnicities, religions, and heritages. Each group has within it many diverse aspects, and everyone is the richer for sharing in an understanding of the variety and engaging in dialogue with people different from themselves. Schools have added this understanding to their curricula and publishers have enthusiastically responded to the many talented authors and illustrators who are, at last, beginning to present special insights about their own heritages to the reading public. An added incentive is the demographic information from the national studies on trends in population: By the last quarter of the twenty-first century, people of color will constitute the majority in America. Latinos are fast growing as a group, as are Asians. But numbers aside, it is important that people value people, and that even without the pressure of numbers, people should learn to live with each other respectfully and appreciatively.

Professionals in the field of children's literature have long advocated the inclusion of multicultural issues into classrooms. Violet Harris has edited *Teaching Multicultural Literature in Grades K-8*, a volume giving strategies for classroom use, discussions about the literature, and the politics of multiculturalism. *Children's Literature: An Issues Approach* has, since its first edition in 1976, included criteria for excellence in children's literature about different populations and heritages, as well as annotated listings of recommended books. Rudine Sims Bishop's column in *The Horn Book* reports on current multicultural children's book titles and her *Shadow and Substance* provides light on books about African Americans. Beverly Slapin and Doris Seale have contributed invaluable insights about Native Peoples' perspective in *Through Indian Eyes*. R.R Bowker has published a comprehensive annotated bibliography on literature pertaining to many different groups in *Our Family, Our Friends, Our World* by Lyn Miller-Lachmann. Each publisher of children's books now prints a separate catalogue of titles that contribute to an understanding of multiculturalism.

All of the above resources are valuable for any teacher, librarian, or parent interested in helping children understand the particular flavors and essences of individual groups. Children may also see in these works the similarities between and among groups as well as the factors that distinguish them, one from the other. Similarities and differences are important to note and appreciate. All of us need mirrors to reflect our own idiosyncracies, characteristics, interactions, and feelings. We also need windows to help us look out at the world and open our perspectives and horizons so that we continue to appreciate new ideas and experiences. Thus an exposure to many books reflecting many different peoples is crucial.

Multiculturalism, however, consists of more than valuing diversity. It also brings with it the obligation to reject stereotyping. A study that highlights differences without helping people see commonalities is insufficient if the aim is to help people create unity from diversity. Sometimes a focus on contrasts heightens a situation of inequity and injustice; sometimes it leads to casting people in rigid roles without regard to their distinct individuality aside from their ethnicity. It is therefore wise to balance studies disparate or parallel groups with a conscious attempt to dispel rigid boundaries of class, culture, religion and ethnicity and look for universal expressions of emotion and attitude. This is especially important if people from certain groups have been typecast in young people's minds. Children's books can help to dissipate these images that conflict with a healthy society's functions.

This chapter focuses on the similarities that people share across cultures, classes, and geographical boundaries. The bulk of the chapter contains an annotated bibliography of books reflecting universal human emotions, experiences, and needs, and that present these with a special sensitivity to avoiding stereotypes. For the most part, the books reflect middle class America but include rather than exclude characters who are not Caucasian. Too often in American children's literature, non-

Caucasian characters have appeared only when there is a problem, the setting is urban, or the message has been one that pertains only to the specific cultural practices of the group. The impression has often been given that if a story is about a family that is well off economically, contains two parents, or is engaged in everyday activities, the characters are depicted as Caucasian. The acknowledged standard has been that of the white Protestant middle class. This bibliography aims to help change the image of white people as the only legitimate participants in middle class society. Working class people will also be included in the bibliography, and they too will represent many hues and backgrounds. The aim here is to reconstitute the image of America in children's literature so that it is representative of the range of people engaging in everyday activities previously reserved to one segment of the population.

We are now in a new golden age of publishing where we are blessed with a veritable cornucopia of books. Poetry, nonfiction, folklore, fantasy, picture books, chapter books and novels may now be found that express deep human emotions and experience without stereotypic conventions of race, gender, or class and without suggesting that everyone blend into the same appearance or behavior. Criteria for selection include demonstrated respect for the characters and culture by making the illustrations authentic (not cartoonlike or basic Caucasian faces tinted in different colors), presentation of situations that ring true rather than being forced, and avoidance of treating non-Caucasian characters as quaint objects of wonder or uniformly persecuted and deprived. An indication should be provided that the characters live in a multicultural world. Literary criteria should apply in all cases. That is, the book's language should be well crafted and appropriate to the audience as well as to the culture of the characters; the story should be engaging and move the reader along with each page; the plot, characterization, and setting should be well developed; the style should be engaging and consistent. Stereotypic or cliche portrayals and situations should be absent from all good literature.

The following annotated bibliography is a selected list of current books that teachers, librarians, and parents may acquire in order to balance a collection so as to help young readers understand that this world is, indeed, multicultural. The flavors of each culture enhance and enrich us while at the same time affirm that we are all members of one human family.

Annotated Bibliography

ADDY, SHARON HART. *A Visit With Great-Grandma.* Illus. by Lydia Halverson. Niles, Illinois: Whitman, 1989. (Ages 5-8.)
The story celebrates both heritage (in this case, Czechoslovakian) and the relationship of a young girl to her great-grandmother. Even though her great-grandmother knows very little English and Barbara cannot speak her great-grandmother's language, the two communicate through traditional food, looking at pictures, and, above all, loving each other.

ADA, ALMA FLOR. *The Gold Coin.* Illus. by Neil Waldman. NY: Atheneum, 1991. (Ages 5-9.)
A strong, kind old woman helps transform a miserable, twisted, nasty thief into a healthy man who appreciates honest labor and the beauty of the natural world. The story is told in non-didactic language, and the values of kindness and collaboration shine through.

ADOFF, ARNOLD. *All the Colors of the Race.* Illus. by John Steptoe. NY: Lothrop, Lee & Shepherd, 1982. (Ages 5-up.)
Celebration, compassion, self-pride, and understanding mark the poetry and illustrations in this beautiful book. Readers can empathize, learn, and appreciate the images of life and people that are presented here through the deceptively simple poems.

ADOFF, ARNOLD. *Hard to Be Six.* Illus. by Cheryl Hanna. NY: Morrow, 1991. (Ages 5-6.)
Narrated in verse by the six-year-old boy in this loving and close-knit biracial family, the story tells of his frustrations at not being able to do all of the things his capable ten-year-old sister can do. His sister is very understanding of his feelings. Every member of his family tries to assure him of his worth. It is finally his grandmother who helps him the most, by reminding him of his deceased grandfather who believed in taking time slowly, making life count, and passing love on. The illustrations are realistically drawn close-ups of each family member, creating a pictorial album to accompany the story.

ADOFF, ARNOLD. *In for Winter, Out for Spring.* Illus. by Jerry Pinkney. San Diego: HBJ, 1991. (Ages 6-10.)
Poems celebrating a child's good feelings about herself and her family include everyday events within a framework of the changing seasons. The family illustrated here is African American. They represent all loving, active, respectful families while at the same time retaining their special individual personalities and characteristics. The illustrations convey the joy and liveliness of the seasons and the people.

ADOFF, ARNOLD. *Sports Pages*. Illus. by Steve Kuzma. NY: Harper, 1986.(Ages 9-12.)
Representing both male and female athletes, these thirty-seven poems depict the universal feelings of triumph and defeat in sports. Each poem reveals the momentary thoughts of the athletes in action or at rest dreaming. The impressionistic drawings complement the rhythmic verse.

AGARD, JOHN (compiler.) *Life Doesn't Frighten Me At All*. NY: Holt, 1989. (Ages 12-up.)
Poet John Agard has compiled this anthology for teens according to the philosophy that "poets come from all sorts of cultures and are inspired by all sorts of things." Some of the poems are written by well-known writers such as W.B. Yeats and Nikki Giovanni, but most were written by a wide range of people. There's even a poem written by Nelson Mandela's daughter Zinzi when she was twelve. The poets' cultures are as diverse as their occupations. Every part of the world is represented in this eclectic but unified collection.

AKSAKOV, SERGEI, TRANSLATED BY ISADORA LEVIN. *The Scarlet Flower: A Russian Folktale*. Illus. by Boris Diodorov. NY: HBJ, 1991. (Ages 10-12.)
A "Beauty and the Beast" variant, lavish in its language and illustrations. A comparative study of any fairy tale including many cultures and countries will yield high dividends in terms of universals and differences.

ALBERT, BURTON. *Where Does the Trail Lead?* Illus. by Brian Pinkney. NY: Simon & Schuster, 1991. (Ages 5-8.)
A young African-American boy explores a trail that takes him through fields, along the edge of the sea, across dunes, down an old train track, and even to a "ghost town of shanties." His journey that begins in the morning ends in the twilight at a family campfire on the beach. Brian Pinkney's scratchboard illustrations capture and enhance the flavor of the text.

ALMONTE, PAUL, and DESMOND, THERESA. *The Facts About Interracial Marriage*. NY: Crestwood House, 1992. (Ages 9-12.)
An informational book detailing the problems and ways of coping with societal prejudice against interracial marriages. A number of case studies are provided. The writing is straightforward and non-judgmental.

ALIKI. *I'm Growing.* Illus. by the author. NY: HarperCollins, 1992. (Ages 4-6.)
A "Let's-Read-and-Find-Out" science book that is illustrated with examples of children from several heritages, and an indication of a thriving multicultural community. The major character in the book is a child of color. Many different sorts of people, old, young, fat, thin, tall, and short are included.

ALLISON, DIANE WORFOLK. *This Is the Key to the Kingdom.* Illus. by the author. Boston: Little Brown, 1992. (Ages 5-8.)
A rendering of the traditional chant that introduces the reader to a young African American girl who lives in the inner city and whose imagination takes her to wondrous far-off places of warmth and opulence. When she returns to reality she manages to make someone else's life a little warmer and happier. The child is not an object of pity; she serves as an excellent model for coping with hard reality in an unusual way. The universals here are imagination, coping with difficult circumstances, and the power of children to make adults happier.

ASHABRANNER, BRENT and MELISSA. *Into A Strange Land.* NY: Putnam, 1987. (Ages 12-up.)
Stories of young refugees, mostly Vietnamese and Cambodian, who escaped from situations of incredible hardship and threat to come to havens in America. The authors explain how foster families are selected and how adjustments are made so that the young people can have stable environments and access to educational programs. The refugee experience is a dramatic universal of current history.

BAER, EDITH. *This is the Way We Go to School.* Illus. by Steve Bjorkman. NY: Scholastic, 1990. (Ages 5-8.)
Rhymed verse introduces readers to many different modes of transportation children all over the world use to go to school. Twenty-two examples are included of children with authentically chosen names and their unique method of getting to school. Included in the back of the book is an index of where each child is from plus a map of the world labeled with the specific countries. The illustrations add flavor to the text plus turn the story into a guessing game of each child's location.

BANG, MOLLY. *Ten, Nine, Eight.* Illus. by the author. NY: Greenwillow, 1983. (Ages 4-6.)
A counting book that counts down from ten, describing things children do before going to bed. The characters are an African-American girl and her loving, attentive father. Counting books as well as alphabet books can serve as stimuli for children to make their own versions, using their own heritage or interests as a springboard.

BARKER, MARJORIE. *Magical Hands*. Illus. by Yoshi. Saxonville, MA: Picture Book Studio, 1989. (Ages 7-10.)
A rare book celebrating the nurturing spirit and a respect for people's aesthetic needs. The four characters are middle aged working class men who meet for lunch every day. William, the cooper, sees to it that each of his three friends, two storekeepers and a baker, get their wishes for their birthdays. He thinks he has gone undetected, but on his birthday all of his wishes come true. The sense of love and caring is strengthened by the luminously textured illustrations.

BARRETT, JOYCE DURHAM. *Willie's Not the Hugging Kind*. Illus. by Pat Cummings. NY: Harper and Row, 1989. (Ages 5-8.)
Willie, a young African-American boy, makes it known to his family that he's not the "hugging kind." Although Willie secretly craves the hugs he received when he was younger, he feels pressured by his friend Jo-Jo, who thinks hugging is silly. When Willie begins to hug inanimate objects to replace human hugs, he realizes that he needs someone who will hug back. This story depicts the nurturing male viewpoint as well as the universal need for children to show and receive affection. The illustrations greatly add to the story line, revealing the characters' emotions in an endearing way.

BERRY, JAMES. *When I Dance*. Illus. by Karen Barbour. NY: HBJ, 1988. (Ages 10-up.)
Fifty-nine poems celebrating daily life in London and the Caribbean. Although these are very different settings, a link is made between the urban and rural locations by similar characters such as street merchants, as well as through universal themes of love, loneliness, work, and friendship.

BETHANCOURT, T. ERNESTO. *The Me Inside of Me*. Minneapolis: Lerner Publications, 1985. (Ages 10-12.)
Social pressures, class boundaries, and self-identity are explored in the story of seventeen-year-old Alfredo Flores. Alfredo is a young, middle-class man of Latino heritage who unexpectedly becomes very wealthy. He quickly finds himself in the fast lane of the rich and must adjust to his new status and identity. What Alfredo learns in the end is that money and prestige cannot bring happiness and fulfillment in life; it comes only through discovering the "me inside of me". In Alfredo's case, he rediscovers pride and respect for his Latino heritage.

BRADMAN, TONY and EILEEN BROWNE. *Wait and See*. Illus. by Eileen Browne. NY: Oxford, 1987. (Ages 5-8.)

Two sets of pictures on the same page depict simultaneous events of Jo and her biracial family. When Jo and her mom decide to go shopping in their profusely multicultural neighborhood, Jo's dad offers to stay home and cook lunch. Jo plans to spend her money on something good to eat but decides to wait and see what Dad is making. Meanwhile Dad is portrayed in the second set of pictures. They run into a few obstacles, including the dog eating Dad's prepared lunch, but all is resolved through Jo's generosity. The story and pictures reflect the warmth and joyfulness of a multicultural community.

BRYAN, ASHLEY. *Lion and the Ostrich Chicks.* Illus. by the author. NY: Atheneum, 1986. (Ages 7-10.)
Lively retellings of four tales from the Masai, Bushmen, Hausa, and Angolan peoples. The prose is musical in its movement and the illustrations complement the text admirably. A collection of folktales is a valuable addition to any library, providing a context for comparisons.

BUNTING, EVE. *Fly Away Home.* Illus. by Ronald Himler. NY: Clarion, 1991. (Ages 7-10.)
A poignant look at homelessness through the eyes of a child. Andrew and his dad live in airport terminals as an alternative to the streets. They have friends, the Medinas (7-yr-old Denny, his mom, and his grandmother), who are also homeless. Although they are safe for now, Andrew longs to have a real home. It is only when he sees a bird trapped in the terminal who manages to free itself and fly away, that he begins to have hope of flying away also. The fact that homelessness can happen to anyone is realistically supported by depicting Andrew and his dad as Caucasian.

BUNTING, EVE. *Summer Wheels.* Illus. by Thomas B. Allen. San Diego: HBJ, 1992. (Ages 7-10.)
The bicycle man is an important helper in the multiracial neighborhood. He fixes bicycles and lends them to the children free of charge. His rules are strict, and he also teaches the children responsibility. Even tough kids who may not be trusted by others blossom under his consistent and nurturing involvement.

BUNTING, EVE. *The Wall.* Illus. by Ronald Himler. NY: Clarion, 1990. (Ages 5-9.)
Captured in this story is the devastating loss that war brings to all people as a little boy and his father visit the Vietnam Veterans' Memorial to view their beloved grandfather's name. It takes a while for the father to find the name but when he does, his fingers cannot leave it. His young son feels honored yet saddened that his grandfather's name is listed. The

illustrations convey the powerful emotion that this monument brings to its observers, especially those who have lost loved ones in the war.

CAMERON, ANN. *The Stories Julian Tells*. Illus. by Ann Strugnell. NY: Knopf, 1981. (Ages 7-10.) also *More Stories Julian Tells* (1986) *Julian, Secret Agent* (1988) and *Julian, Dream Doctor* (1990)
This series of volumes introduces the reader to a loving, joyful family consisting of Julian, his younger brother Huey, and their parents. The father provides a model as a caring, consistent, firm parent who finds the time and energy to cook and to intervene wisely in his sons' disputes. Julian is bright and imaginative and manages, with his parents' help, to extricate himself from thorny situations. Julian and his brother have some altercations, but for the most part are good company for each other. The fact that the family is African American is a bonus.

CAMERON, ANN. *The Most Beautiful Place in the World*. Illus. by Thomas B. Allen. NY: Alfred Knopf, 1988. (Ages 9-11.)
Seven-year-old Juan works hard shining shoes to help support his grandmother whom he loves and respects very much, yet he secretly yearns to go to school. When he finally gets enough courage to ask his grandmother, she instructs him to stand up for what he wants and always to walk tall. Although the setting is Guatemala, the application of this sort of intergenerational love could transform any place into "the most beautiful place in the world."

CARLSTROM, NANCY WHITE. *Light: Stories of a Small Kindness*. Illus. by Lisa Desimini. Boston: Little, 1990. (Ages 9-12.)
Seven stories from several different cultural setting (Haiti, Mexico, New York City, and Guatemala) describe small kindnesses and mystical events. The universal aspects of faith, determination, and confronting adversity affirm the human spirit.

CARLSON, LORI M. AND CYNTHIA L. VENTURA, EDS. *Where Angels Glide at Dawn*. Illus. by Jose Ortega. NY: Lippincott, 1990. (Ages 10-up.)
A collection of different sorts of stories from South America, Cuba, and Puerto Rico. Each one is different in genre and tone. However, each captures some element of the past and some of the flavor of its nation of origin.

CHBOSKY, STACY. *Who Owns the Sun?* Illus. by the author. Kansas City: Landmark Editions, Inc., 1988. (Ages 9-12.)
The young author won a writing award for this story. An African-American child who, upon learning that he and his family are slaves, demands to know why one human being can own another. Sensitively

and poetically expressed, this story explores the universal yearning for freedom.

CLIFTON, LUCILLE. *Everett Anderson's Year.* Illus. by Ann Grifalconi. NY: Henry Holt, 1974. (Ages 5-8.)
The story follows seven-year-old Everett throughout his year, in which every month holds something new. From seasons to holidays to beginning school, Everett's calendar is full of learning and growing. All of the Everett Anderson books hold universal values and truths. All are expressed in verse that conveys depth of emotion and astute observations. Others in this fine series include *Some of the Days of Everett Anderson,* which introduces the six-year-old boy to us in all his exuberance and with some of his sorrows and fears; *Everett Anderson's 1-2-3,* in which he adjusts to a new daddy; *Everett Anderson's Friend,* where he learns that girls can be good friends; *Everett Anderson's Goodbye,* in which he endures and copes with the death of his father; and *Everett Anderson's Nine-Month Long* in which he responds to the birth of a baby sister.

CLIFTON, LUCILLE. *Three Wishes.* Illus. by Michael Hays. NY: Bantam, revised edition, 1992. (Ages 5-8.)
Told in the cadences of black English, the story builds on the classic tales of three wishes and how they are spent or misspent. In this version, Lena finds a penny with her birthday on it and knows that she is now entitled to three wishes. Her wishes don't change her life, but they all come true, and the reader is invited to speculate about whether or not magic was involved. Readers may want to engage in the game of "If I had three wishes I'd..."

COHEN, NEIL. *Jackie Joyner-Kersee.* Illus. by Brad Hamann. Boston: Time, 1992. (Ages 10-12.)
A biography of a remarkable athlete "up close and personal." Stereotypes of prominent sports figures are contradicted in this fact-filled book.

COREY, DOROTHY. *Will There Be a Lap For Me?* Illus. by Nancy Poydar. Morton Grove, Illinois: Whitman, 1992. (Ages 7-9.)
Kyle loves to sit in his mother's lap; it is his favorite place to be. But when his mom becomes pregnant, Kyle's special place becomes smaller and smaller until all he can do is snuggle next to her. He is impatient, but knows that he must wait until his baby brother is born to regain his place on his mother's lap. The family is African American. All readers, no matter what their background, can empathize with Kyle.

DAY, DAVID. *The Sleeper*. Illus. by Mark Entwisle. Nashville: Ideals Children's Books, 1990. (Ages 8-10.)
Although based on ancient folklore, this adaptation of a Chinese fairy tale contains many modern themes such as the importance of literacy and the valuable contributions of children to society. The fantastical and symbolic journey of Wu Wing Wong, a young monk responsible for transporting the last of the kingdom's books to the evil Emperor to be destroyed, is suspenseful and filled with many surprises. Everything is resolved in the end by Wu's efforts and dedication, including the cessation of a two-hundred-year war. The language and illustrations are poetic with an understated tone.

DELACRE, LULU. *Arroz Con Leche*. Illus. by the author. NY: Scholastic, 1989. (Ages 5-8.)
This collection of Latin American songs and chants in Spanish is accompanied by English translations, musical scores, and colorful ethnic illustrations. The countries represented are Puerto Rico, Mexico, and Argentina, with a variety of themes such as work, love, marriage, and songs about animals. Occasional footnotes describing games that go with the songs provide good information. Children can be invited to add sections to this book, based on their own family heritage of songs and chants.

DOLPHIN, LAURIE. *Georgia to Georgia: Making Friends in the U.S.S.R.* Photographs by E. Alan McGee. NY: Tambourine, 1991. (Ages 8-10.)
A special trans-Atlantic link exists between children of Atlanta, Georgia, and Soviet Georgia through the work of Project Peace Tree. By communicating and sharing daily customs, hobbies, and dreams, these children have experienced and discovered the many similarities among people. One such relationship between two boys, Joe Schulten and Misha Matiashveli, is explored here through wonderful photography and Joe's own narrative of his trip to the Soviet state. A good model for forming international friendships.

DOOLEY, NORAH. *Everybody Cooks Rice*. Illus. by Peter J. Thornton. Minneapolis: Carolrhoda, 1991. (Ages 6-8.)
The picture here is of a multicultural, interfaith, harmonious neighborhood, where all of the families are industrious, loving, and open-hearted. Despite the idyllic setting and characters, the story conveys enough of a realistic flavor to make it pleasant and informative. Food is an excellent metaphor for a multicultural world, with enough commonalities to understand the universal needs and enough differences to convey many flavors. A bonus at the end of the book is the inclusion of eight rice recipes from all over the world.

DRAGONWAGON, CRESCENT. *Half A Moon and One Whole Star.* Illus. by Jerry Pinkney. NY: Macmillan, 1990. (Ages 6-10.)
An African-American girl dreams of the woods around her house, jazz music from downtown, bakers and sailors, her parents, and what she will do in the summer sun when she wakes. The images reflect important parts of her life. Children may want to narrate and illustrate their own dreams in response to this story. The soothing, rhymed text is accompanied by colorful watercolor illustrations.

DRAGONWAGON, CRESCENT. *Home Place.* Illus. by Jerry Pinkney. NY: MacMillan, 1990. (Ages 8-12.)
A young hiker comes upon relics in the woods such as a doll's arm and glass marble, and from them invents a story of an African American family living on this site in the past. The dialect and detailed descriptions of the home, characters, and food are vivid. The author uses nature as a medium to pull the two worlds together. The illustrations add feeling to the text, capturing the essence of the young girl's day dream.

ESBENSEN, BARBARA. *Who Shrank My Grandmother's House? Poems of Discovery.* Illus. by Eric Beddows. NY: HarperCollins, 1992. (Ages 7-12.)
A collection of poems brilliantly written from a child's perspective of "life's little wonders." Universal topics of weather, color, time, seasons, and even pencils are personified with occasional questions posed such as "What if..." and "Why does..." A book that all ages can enjoy for its creative representation of ordinary events.

FALWELL, CATHRYN. *Shape Space.* Illus. by the author. NY: Clarion, 1992. (Ages 4-7.)
Pictured here is a lively African-American dancer who plays with all types of colorful geometrical shapes she finds in a toy box. The different shapes are triangles, semicircles, rectangles, circles, and squares that the girl forms into toys, clothing, a playmate, and a village. A creative way to explore the concept of shapes. Too often concept books exclude any group but Caucasians. This one is a good balancing addition to a library.

FERRIS, JERI. *What Are You Figuring Now?.* Illus. by Amy Johnson. Minneapolis: Carolrhoda, 1988. (Ages 8-10.)
A true account based on the life of a very talented and innovative man, Benjamin Banneker. As a free black man living in the mid-1700s, Banneker accomplished major feats such as astronomy, surveying, mathematics, and owning and managing his own farm. He was known and respected by George Washington and Thomas Jefferson for his ingenuity and perseverance. The author has created a comprehensive biography of an amazing man who defies stereotypes.

FINGER, CHARLES. *Tales from Silver Lands.* Illus. by Paul Honore. NY: Doubleday 1924. (Ages 10-up.)
Woodcuts enrich the text of this excellent collection of tales from South and Central America. The stories are well told and can easily be related to folk tales from other countries in terms of theme and values. Included are creation tales, witches, enchantments, wicked stepmothers, noble commoners, loving siblings, wishes that go awry, and the valuing of courage, kindness, and loyalty.

FLORIAN, DOUGLAS. *City Street.* Illus. by the author. NY: Greenwillow, 1990. (Ages 3-5.)
A sparse text made up of rhyming phrases accompanies the active, colorful illustrations of what takes place on a city street at various times of the day and night. City dwellers will see familiar sights and rural readers can be introduced to the complexity and multicultural makeup of the city in a positive way. The stereotype of the city as ghetto and crime-ridden fearsome place is contradicted.

FLOURNEY, VALERIE. *The Best Time of Day.* Illus. by George Ford. NY: Random House, 1979. (Ages 5-8.)
William's day is very busy. From cleaning his room, playing with his friends, making his own lunch, and grocery shopping with mom, he is on the go from morning to night. But he always has time for his favorite part of the day, when his daddy comes home from work. Although published some time ago, the story of a competent child in an African-American family is timely and provides a good model.

FREEDMAN, RUSSELL. *Children of the Wild West.* NY: Clarion. 1983. (Ages 12-up.)
This detailed photographic history with accompanying text of the nineteenth-century American West spotlights children of pioneer families as well as Native American boys and girls. Described are the journeys westward, settling down, frontier schools, and a poignant look at the injustices wrought on the American Indians, especially the children sent to boarding schools disrespectful of their culture. The remarkable photographs alone speak the history of this time period. The combination of text and photos helps dispel many stereotypes.

FREEDMAN, RUSSELL. *Lincoln. A Photobiography..* NY: Clarion, 1987. (Ages 12-up.)
This Newbery Award-winning work of non-fiction describes a great leader and humanitarian and the critical role he played during the most traumatic period in American history. Accompanying the text are vivid

photographs of the war and other events such as Lincoln's nationwide funeral procession. In addition, there is a sample of quotes from letters and speeches of the President, including the words from his second Inaugural Address, which sum up his lifetime stance: "With malice toward none; with charity for all."

FRIEDMAN, INA R. *How My Parents Learned to Eat.* Illus. by Allen Say. Boston: Houghton Mifflin, 1984. (Ages 5-8.)
A naive but engaging story of how the narrator's parents, one Japanese and one American, learned to adapt to each other's ways. No small matter is the cultural pattern of customs that accompanies eating. In this story, the two young lovers try very hard to please each other.

GARNE, S.T. *One White Sail.* Illus. by Lisa Etre. NY: Green Tiger, 1992. (Ages 3-6.)
Watercolors and rhymed verse fill this Caribbean counting book from one to ten. The illustrations represent the islands' people, occupations, homes, and, since water is such an important factor, their boats. Counting books are excellent devices for inviting children to contribute their own ingredients and can often represent different cultures.

GAY, KATHLYN. *The Rainbow Effect: Interracial Families.* NY: Franklin Watts, 1987. (Ages 12-up.)
A very personal and comprehensive look at multiracial families. Through interviews with many different families, the author has pieced together very relevant issues such as interaction within the families; dealing with outside attitudes, prejudices, and discrimination; acceptance within the community; and the experiences of biracial and mixed children. Many photographs of these families accompany the text.

GERAS, ADELE. *My Grandmother's Stories.* Illus. by Jael Jordan. NY: Knopf, 1990. (Ages 9-12.)
As with most folktales, the lessons and themes are universal, but the individual tales retain their own flavor. The author is a talented writer, combining the personality of the modern day grandmother telling the tales with the messages of the tales themselves.

GERSTEIN, MORDICAI. *The Mountains of Tibet.* Illus. by the author. NY: Harper and Row, 1987. (Ages 7-10.)
After living a long and contented life a dying woodcutter is given the choice of becoming part of heaven or being reincarnated. Thus begins a series of choices of what the man will become in his new life. He finally decides to live on the same planet, in the same country, and in the same

area he has already lived. The one difference is that he now wants to return as a female rather than a male. The story emphasizes the cyclical nature of life. The little girl who is born has the same affinity for kite flying that the woodcutter did as a young boy. The illustrations affirm the cyclical message of the text.

GINSBURG, MIRRA. *The Twelve Clever Brothers and Other Fools*. Illus. by Charles Mikolaycak. NY: Lippincott, 1979. (Ages 7-10.)
From these tales the understanding emerges that every culture has its share of fools and tricksters. The collection also demonstrates how varied the Russian people are, with the tales from such differing sources as Armenian, Veps, Chuvash, Tatar, Latvian, Moldavian, and Assyrian peoples.

GOLD, SHARLYA, and CASPI, MISHAEL MASWARI. *The Answered Prayer, and Other Yemenite Folktales*. Illus. by Marjory Wunsch. Philadelphia: The Jewish Publication Society, 1990. (Ages 8-up.)
This book captures tales that might otherwise have been lost because of the lack of a written tradition in the Yemenite community. The stories echo themes from other cultures yet retain a distinctive flavor. The names of the characters are different from the more familiar European names, and the stories provide a background for learning more about Jewish Yemenite heritage.

GORDON, RUTH I. *Time Is the Longest Distance*. NY: A Charlotte Zolotow Book, 1991. (Ages 12-up.)
An international anthology of selected poems (all English translations) dealing with the universal constancy of time. Featured works include Yiddish, Hebrew, French, Italian, Chinese, Japanese, American, German, Spanish, Russian, and Persian heritages.

GRAY, NIGEL. *A Balloon for Grandad*. Illus. by Jane Ray. NY: Orchard, 1988. (Ages 5-8.)
Only the illustrations inform the reader that Sam is a biracial child. When Sam's balloon floats off into the sky, his father consoles the child by helping him imagine the journey of the balloon to Sam's grandfather's island home, where the grandfather will receive the balloon and know that it is a gift and a message of love from Sam.

GREENE, CAROL. *Caring For Our People*. Hillside, NJ: Enslow, 1991. (Ages 5-8.)
Environmentalism and human ecology are global issues today and have been helping in binding nations together with the goal of preserving the

earth. People have begun to realize that all humans are interdependent and must cooperate for survival. Presented in simple terminology, this book explains why people are important, the consequences of our actions, and how children can help. Photographs represent many different ethnicities and cultures.

GREENFIELD, ELOISE. *Honey, I Love.* Illus. by Leo and Diane Dillon. NY: Harper & Row, 1978. (Ages 5-up.)
A book of poems told from the perspective of a young African-American girl whose boundless spirit and embracing of life permeate the pages. From an accounting of all that she loves in this world to an appreciation of being a writer, to a touching memory of a neighbor who died, the poems convey many universals not confined to childhood or to any group but nevertheless wonderfully reflective of her heritage.

GRIFALCONI, ANN. *Osa's Pride.* Illus. by the author. Boston: Little Brown, 1990. (Ages 5-8.)
Jewel-like colors illuminate the text in this third book in the series of stories about the village of round and square houses. In this story, Osa's grandmother helps Osa to see how her behavior has driven away her friends, and she sets Osa on the right trail to regain her peace of mind. The grandmother is wise and understanding, and Osa is receptive to her advice. Also see *The Village of Round and Square Houses* (1986) and *Darkness and the Butterfly* (1987.)

GROSS, RUTH BELOV. *You Don't Need Words!: A Book About Ways People Talk Without Words.* Illus. by Susannah Ryan. NY: Scholastic, 1991. (Ages 5-9.)
A comprehensive overview of the multiple ways people express meaning without words. Some methods explored are sign language, body language, facial expressions, pantomime, and picture writing using familiar symbols. Emphasis is placed on sign language for people who are deaf, and sign and picture writing of some Native Americans. Every page contains illustrations representing different forms of non-verbal communication.

GRUNSELL, ANGELA. *Let's Talk About Racism.* NY: Watts, 1991. (Ages 9-12.) Taking an honest look at racism, the book defines such words as racism, prejudice, stereotype, and apartheid. The author uses both historical references and an up-to-date accounting of how racism affects individuals, countries, and the entire world. The pictures are multicultural in content. Racism is discussed as a world-wide problem, not just a black/white issue.

GUTHRIE, DONNA. *A Rose for Abby.* Illus. by Dennis Hockerman. Nashville: Abingdon 1988. (Ages 5-8.)
Rose learns what homelessness is by looking out the window one day. Wanting to help, she pulls out a hat and pair of gloves from the lost and found box at church and gives them to the old woman she sees searching through garbage cans and sleeping in boxes. Then she thinks of a special way everyone on the street can help the homeless. The illustrations respectfully add to the sensitive text.

HABER, LOUIS. *Black Pioneers of Science and Invention.* San Diego: HBJ, 1970. (Ages 10-14.)
A profile of African American men and their lasting contributions. Each chapter begins with a biographical account and proceeds with a detailed description of the invention. Included in the work are Benjamin Banneker, George Washington Carver, Granville T. Woods, Garrett A. Morgan, David Hale Williams, Jan Earnst Matzeliger, Charles Richard Drew, and others.

HALL, MAHJI. *"T" is for terrific.* Design by Deb Figen. Seattle: Open Hand, 1989. (Ages 5-10.)
Written by a talented elementary school student, this Spanish and English alphabet book uses words that begin with the same first letter such as "guitarra" and "guitar." Included in the back of the book is a pronunciation guide for both English and Spanish words, a helpful method of comparing the similarities between the languages.

HALLORAN, PHYLLIS. *Oh Brother! Oh Sister!.* Illus. by Kathryn E. Shoemaker. St. Louis, MO: Milliken, 1989. (Ages 4-6.)
Although this book is theoretically a part of a basal reading series by Milliken, it stands on its own as literature. The brief, simple (but not simplistic) poems illustrated with pictures that depict children of all heritages and conditions of ability address many aspects of sibling interactions without judgment or didacticism. New siblings, father-son relations, rivalry, birth order, and teasing are but a few of the issues uncovered here. The book is sensitive and endearing.

HAMILTON, VIRGINIA. *The Bells of Christmas.* Illus. by Lambert Davis. N Y: HBJ, 1989. (Ages 8-10.)
An African-American family in 1890 anticipates and enjoys Christmas. The father is disabled by a leg injury. The family is self-sufficient: the mother is a seamstress and the father is a very capable woodcarver and carpenter who does not let his disability hinder his productivity. The picture of African Americans before the twentieth century helps to dispel

stereotypes and provides a solid ground for multicultural understanding.

HAMILTON, VIRGINIA. *The Dark Way*. Illus. by Lambert Davis. San Diego: HBJ, 1990. (Ages 10-up.)
Universal to the human condition is the need to create stories of the supernatural. Tales of darkness, death, and spirits fulfill the fear of the unknown as well as help to explain phenomena and order the environment. It is the aim of the author that this collection of folktales on the supernatural from cultures around the world will entertain this need. Many of these stories are transcribed from the oral tradition and come complete with eerie black and white sketches.

HAMILTON, VIRGINIA. *In the Beginning*. Illus. by Barry Moser. San Diego: HBJ, 1988. (Ages 12-up.)
A collection of twenty-five creation stories from around the world. This universal theme is one that has always fascinated humans. The variety of interpretations presented here provides a tapestry of beliefs and cultures. The vision of this book is to describe how all humankind creates myths to explain and give purpose to their lives.

HANSEN, JOYCE. *The Gift-Giver*. NY: Clarion, 1980. (Ages 8-11.)
Although the setting and characters are decidedly African-American, the universal qualities of kindness, self-esteem, and friendship all come into play. Amir is a unique literary figure who is larger than life and who makes an impact on his friends (notably Doris) and on the environment. In the sequel, *Yellow Bird and Me* (1986), Doris misses Amir so much that she has difficulty functioning. Because of Amir's urging, Doris learns to help Yellow Bird, a boy with learning disabilities, in a way that also helps her to know and like herself better and to be more liked by her peers.

HASKINS, JIM. *Against All Opposition: Black Explorers in America*. NY: Walker, 1992. (Ages 12-15.)
A comprehensive profile of African-American explorers whose names have generally been suppressed in history books. In addition to adding to young readers' store of knowledge, this book helps dissolve stereotypes, and provides a counter to inaccurate history.

HAVILL, JUANITA. *Jamaica's Find*. Illus. by Anne Sibley O'Brien. NY: Scholastic, 1986. (Ages 5-7.)
Jamaica, an African-American girl, finds a stuffed dog when playing in the park. She becomes instantly attached to the toy but knows in her heart that she must return it to the lost and found so the rightful owner

can enjoy it. When she does find the owner and sees how happy Kristin is to get her dog back, Jamaica is happier than ever. A story about children learning the lesson "It's better to give than to receive." The interracial friendship that is formed is comfortable and unpretentious.

HAYES, SARAH. *Happy Christmas Gemma.* Illus. by Jan Ormerod. NY: Lothrop, Lee & Shepard, 1986. (Ages 4-6.)
The illustrations provide the special quality of joyousness and mutual acceptance that this book conveys. Narrated by the older brother, the focus is on his and Gemma's relationship. There is no rivalry, but there certainly is the sense of how the older brother and baby sister differ in their responses and abilities. This African-American family celebrates Christmas like many other middle class Christian families.

HEIDE, FLORENCE PERRY. *The Day of Ahmed's Secret.* Illus. by Ted Lewin. NY: Lothrop, Lee & Shepard, 1990. (Ages 6-9.)
The reader journeys with Ahmed, a young boy in Egypt, as he delivers gas canisters and meets vendors. He keeps telling the reader that he has a secret. When the day ends, Ahmed returns to his home and family and shares his joyful secret: he has learned to write his name. This is a heart warming story that is not only culturally rich but also universal in its implications about such important issues as self-confidence, responsibility, and pride.

HELGADOTTIR, GUDRUN. *Flumbra.* Illus. by Brian Pilkington. Minneapolis: Carolrhoda, 1986. (Ages 8-10.)
Building on Icelandic folklore and the connection between supernatural traditions and the harsh environment of the country, the author has created a humorous tale of the giant Flumbra. After falling hopelessly in love with an ugly, lazy giant who lives far away, Flumbra decides to make the trek to see him. Her journey causes the ground to shake and disturb the people, especially when she finally meets her giant. On her next visit Flumbra doesn't arrive before daybreak and turns to stone. This tale humanizes giants, who are traditionally portrayed as evil, threatening beings. Children may study the folklore of giants from around the world and compare them.

HELLER, LINDA. *The Castle on Hester Street.* Illus. by the autor. Phila: The Jewish Publication Society of America, 1982. (Ages 5-8.)
Julie's grandfather regales her with stories he has invented about the past and his youthful adventures. After each of these tales Julie's grandmother sets the record straight with what really happened. Woven into the family's bantering is an appreciation of the hardships this

immigrant couple encountered in Europe and as newcomers to the land of their choice.

HILL, KIRKPATRICK. *Toughboy and Sister.* NY: Margaret K. McElderry, 1990. (Ages 8-12.)
The story details how Toughboy, an eleven-year-old Athabascan boy, and his younger sister survive at an isolated campsite near the Yukon River. Their mother died the past autumn; their father, an alcoholic, had brought them to the camp to spend the summer with them and then died upon his return from an alcoholic binge. The meticulous details of how the pair survive and the underlying information about modern, changing Athabascan life enrich the story. The children's feelings toward each other and their mutual contributions to coping with their desperate situation make for a survival tale with universal implications.

HOBERMAN, MARY ANN. *Fathers, Mothers, Sisters, Brothers: a Collection of Family Poems.* Illus. by Marilyn Hafner. Boston: Joy Street, 1991. (Ages 7-10.)
Poetic reflections, sometimes funny, sometimes serious, on family gatherings, sibling relations, feelings about adoption, divorce, individual family members, and being an only child ("An only child is always first!"). The book voices a child's view in a tone that is light but accurate. People of all colors are represented in the illustrations as well as the poems.

HOOKS, WILLIAM H. *Moss Gown.* Illus. by Donald Carrick. NY: Clarion Books, 1987. (Ages 8-11.)
A southern version of a tale with antecedents from *King Lear* and *Cinderella.* When Candace is banished by her father after failing to flatter him as much as her deceitful sisters, she wanders in the woods, acquires a magic gossamer gown from a beautiful black magical woman, meets a charming young prince, and is reunited with her father, after helping him to understand how much she has always loved him. An explanation of the tale's multiple sources is given in the back. The pictures are multiethnic.

HOPKINS, LEE BENNETT. *Through Our Eyes.* Illus. by Jeffery Dunn. Boston: Little Brown, 1992. (Ages 4-7.)
A special collection of poems and photographs describing the experiences of children growing up in the 1990s. Poems dealing with identity formation, peer pressure, sibling interaction, biracial children, abandonment, and the latch-key child are explored. Some poets featured are Myra Cohn Livingston, Lee Bennet Hopkins, Langston Hughes, and Ruth Krauss. Children of many different heritages are represented in the photographs.

HORT, LENNY. *How Many Stars in the Sky?*. Illus. by James E. Ransome. NY: Tambourine, 1991. (Ages 5-8.)
An African American boy and his father share a magical night together. They each find it difficult to sleep because the mother is away on a business trip. When the boy wants to count the number of stars in the sky his father takes him on a drive to where they can see the stars and count them. They both acknowledge that the mother would know about the number of stars. Stereotypes are blasted, but above all a sense of a loving family is strongly conveyed.

HOWARD, ELIZABETH FITZGERALD. *Aunt Flossie's Hats (and Crab Cakes Later.)* Illus. by James Ransome. NY: Clarion, 1991. (Ages 5-8.)
Aunt Flossie has a tale for each one of her hats, which come in all shapes, colors, and styles. They represent special memories in Aunt Flossie's life such as a great fire experienced in her childhood, the day the soldiers came home from World War I, and a walk in the park with her nieces. The characters are African American and demonstrate the joy of inter-generational love and sharing. Beautifully illustrated with oil paints on canvas, the economically comfortable family as well as the Baltimore of the mid-twentieth century vividly emerge.

HOWARD, ELIZABETH FITZGERALD. *The Train To Lulu's.* Illus. by Robert Casilla. NY: Bradbury, 1988. (Ages 5-8.)
The watercolor paintings capture the tones and shadings of the events as well as the feelings of the characters in this reminiscence of the first time Beppy and her sister Babs rode alone on a train. They go from Boston to Baltimore to spend the summer with their Aunt Lulu. The simple text details the specifics of the ride and conveys to the reader the warm relationship between the sisters as well as the secure and loving involvement of the entire family.

HUGHES, SHIRLEY. *Wheels.* Illus. by the author. NY: Lothrop, Lee & Shepard, 1991. (Ages 8-10.)
Carlos wants a new bike. His mom, however, cannot afford an expensive bike with her salary at the bakery. Carlos tries to hide his disappoint-ment on his birthday when he does not receive a bike. However, everything brightens when Carlos's older brother gives him a surprise gift of a go-cart that he constructed himself. This is a story of love and cooperation in families. Children of many ethnicities are represented in the illustrations.

JENNESS, AYLETTE. *Families: A Celebration of Diversity, Commitment, and Love.* Illus. with photographs by the author. Boston: Houghton

Mifflin, 1990. (Ages 8-up.)
Black and white photos accompany the words of seventeen children talking about their diverse families. (The book began as an interactive photographic exhibit in the Boston Children's Museum.) Each of the children pictured here lives in a different family constellation. Represented are single parents, gay and lesbian parents, several cultures, families with adopted and foster children as well as biological children, only-children, families with many children, and blended families.

JOHNSON, ANGELA. *Tell Me A Story, Mama.* Illus. by David Soman. NY: Orchard, 1989. (Ages 5-8.)
A simple and genuine account demonstrating how loving is the act of engaging in story. The child knows very well what stories she wants and her clever and nurturing mother permits the child to contribute most of the details of the story while at the same time maintaining the interaction with her own well-placed comments. The illustrations of African American family add to the value of the book.

JOHNSON, ANGELA. *When I Am Old With You.* Illus. by David Soman. NY: Orchard 1990. (Ages 5-8.)
In a rapturous daydream, a young boy imagines himself old alongside his beloved grandfather, with both of them enjoying activities that they already engage in or could easily do. This is an exercise in the art of the possible. The partnership of this author and illustrator is a felicitous one. The characters are depicted as African American.

JOOSE, BARBARA M. *Mama. Do You Love Me?.* Illus. by Barbara Lavallee. San Francisco, CA: Chronicle, 1991. (Ages 2-6.)
An imaginative child challenges her mother's ability to demonstrate unconditional love, and the mother succeeds admirably in doing so. Even when her daughter's fantasy turns the child into a ferocious bear, the mother is able to see the child within the bear. The Alaskan setting and the vocabulary of the Inuit people heightens the effect of the book. The stylized, expressive illustrations convey an authentic picture of an Alaskan village.

KLASS, SHEILA SOLOMON. *Kool Ada.* NY: Scholastic, 1991. (Ages 10-12.)
Ada Garland, a troubled and angry sixth-grader from the Appalachian Mountains, has come to live with her aunt in Chicago after both her parents die. Adjusting to city life, the tall buildings, the feeling of being crowded, street fighting, people selling drugs, and kids at school picking on her because she is different, is hard at first and her immediate impulse is to fight back. It is only through the kindness, honesty, love,

and perseverance of her African-American teacher, Ms. Walker, that Ada confronts the war within herself and learns to think before she acts. The picture here is realistic: Not everyone becomes friends in the end. Ada has found a lifelong friend in her teacher, and she and her aunt will survive.

KNIGHT, MARY BURNS. *Talking Walls.* Illus. by Anne Sibley O'Brien. Gardiner, ME: Tilbury House, 1992. (Ages 6-10.)
Walls tell the history of people all over the world. The Great Wall of China, The Lascaux Cave, Mahabalipuram's Animal Walls, the Vietnam Veterans Memorial, the Berlin Wall, and many more are described. The beautifully illustrated book examines the history, purposes, and meaning of the walls to each culture. Appended is a complete index of each wall's history as well as a labeled world map.

KUKLIN, SUSAN. *How My Family Lives in America.* NY: Bradbury, 1992. (Ages 6-9.)
Sanu, Eric, and April—three children with multiethnic backgrounds—tell of their daily routines and special celebrations, unique to their individual heritages. A common medium of food is used throughout the book which includes recipes in the back. Wonderful use is made of photography to capture the flavor of each child's culture.

LANKFORD, MARY D. *Hopscotch Around the World.* Illus. by Karen Milone. NY: Morrow, 1992. (Ages 8-12.)
A very interesting look at different variations of the game of hopscotch throughout the world. Included with each description are directions and a full-page illustration of children playing the game. Games are described from seventeen countries, including Aruba, Bolivia, Trinidad, Nigeria, India, Honduras, Great Britain, El Salvador, and France.

LEINER, KATHERINE. *Both My Parents Work.* Illus. by Steve Sax. NY: Franklin Watts, 1986. (Ages 6-8.)
Some of the examples included in this book are positive and harmonious; others show the discord and loneliness children experience when both parents are away. The book is particularly apt today with the changing economy and the numbers of women now in the work force. Families from many heritages and occupations are represented.

LENSKI, LOIS. *Sing A Song of People.* Illus. by Giles Laroche. Boston, MA: Little, Brown, 1987 (newest edition) copyright 1965. (Ages 4-6.)
A simple poem about the variety of people seen in a large city. The depiction of people of all shades of color, ages and conditions of ability,

engaging in many different activities makes this an excellent addition to any library. It graphically and positively demonstrates the multiethnic and multicultural urban world.

LEVINE, ELLEN. *I Hate English.* Illus. by Steve Bjorkman. NY: Scholastic, 1989. (Ages 6-8.)
Language is often a key factor in defining one's heritage. It can be a traumatic experience at any age to learn a second language out of necessity when there is a fear of losing one's special identity and becoming mainstreamed. This is how Mei Mei feels in this story when she must learn English at school. Finally, through a caring teacher, she realizes the benefits of being bilingual and knows that she can still maintain her Chinese heritage.

LEWIS, RICHARD. *In the Night, Still Dark.* Illus. by Ed Young. NY: Atheneum, 1988. (Ages 9-12.)
This poetic, secular version of a Hawaiian Creation myth is a shortened variation of *The Kumulipo* from Maria Leach's *In the Beginning: Creation Myths Around the World.* This is a wonderful conceptual look at evolution through paintings, beginning from the deep of the night into the light of the new day. As with folk and fairy tales, myths invite multicultural comparisons.

LOH, MORAG. *Tucking Mommy In.* Illus. by Donna Rawlins. NY: Orchard, 1987. (Ages 4-7.)
Two little girls tell the bedtime story one night so that their mother can rest. They then lead their sleepy mom to her bed and tuck her in. They are rightfully proud of their behavior, and their father affirms his appreciation when he comes home from work. The illustrations depict a family of color, perhaps Asian, underscoring the fact that not only white, middle class families are loving and considerate of each other.

LOUIE, AI-LING. *Yeh Shen: A Chinese Cinderella.* Illus. by Ed Young. NY: Philomel, 1982. (Ages 7-10.)
This first known *Cinderella* variant comes complete with a wicked stepmother and one nasty stepsister. The magical intervener is a fish, and then an old man. The outcome is the same: Yeh Shen marries the prince. The values expressed here are those of loyalty, inventiveness, and assertiveness. The illustrations make the book magical. The stereotype of European beauty is dispelled.

MARTIN, BILL JR.; ARCHAMBAULT, JOHN. *Here Are My Hands.* Illus. by Ted Rand. NY: Henry Holt, 1985. (Ages 3-5.)

All children everywhere can celebrate their different body parts. This concept book demonstrates this through illustrations of children of diverse ethnicities. Each points out a special part of their body and what they use it for, such as "Here are my cheeks for kissing and blushing."

MELTZER, MILTON. *The Amazing Potato.* NY: HarperCollins, 1992. (Ages 8-12.)
A look at the value of the potato throughout history. In a chronological approach, the author presents eye-opening facts and myths about this amazing vegetable beginning with the Spanish conquistadors to the Irish famine to McDonald's french fries and every country and people that rely on the potato. The author's meticulous research provides a fine model for students to try to do similar investigations.

MELTZER, MILTON (editor). *The American Promise: Voices of a Changing Nation.* NY: Bantam, 1990. (Ages 12-up.)
Arranged by themes rather than chronologically, this provocative look at American history from 1945 to the present seeks to draw connections and show the immense and profound changes that have occurred in the last half of the decade. Content discussed ranges from the Women's Equal Right's Movement, the Environmental Movement, changes in Eastern Europe since the Cold War, and the declining economy in the United States.

MERRIAM, EVE. *Daddies at Work.* Illus. by Eugenie Fernandes. NY: Simon and Schuster, 1989. (Ages 4-7.)
See also *Mommies at Work*, 1989. Two books that help children to understand that mothers and fathers come in all sizes, shapes and colors, and do all sorts of work. The idea here is to avoid stereotypes, and the author and illustrator succeed admirably.

MILLS, LAUREN. *The Rag Coat.* Boston: Little Brown, 1991. (Ages 8-18.)
Minna's new coat is very special to her since it is made from rags, each piece having a history all its own. Made for her by the kind-hearted Quilting Mothers from her small mining town in the Appalachian region, Minna greatly appreciates their sacrifice to allow her to attend school with the approach of winter. Although the first reaction of the other children is negative and they make fun of her, Minna finds the strength to face them and share with them each piece of history in her rag coat. A very endearing story of a child's inner strength, even through difficult times, and the love that often exists within small communities.

MITCHELL, ADRIAN. (ed.) *Strawberry Drums*. Illus. by Frances Lloyd. NY: Delacorte, 1989. (Ages 9-up.)
The poems were selected because "they are bright and sweet like strawberries. And all of them have a beat like drums." The variety includes poems of the West Indies, Native Americans, English, and America's midwest. A section is included encouraging children to write their own poetry and giving them some hints for doing so. The poems are light and free of conflict.

MOHR, NICHOLASA. *Going Home*. NY: Bantam, 1989. (Ages 10-12.)
There is a misconception that prejudice against groups only happens in the United States. Felita, a twelve-year-old girl of Puerto Rican heritage living in New York City, experiences hostility when she visits Puerto Rico one summer. Confused about why she is not welcomed she longs to go home to her family and friends. Through perseverance, she finally makes friends and brings home with her a different perspective of her native land as well as a better sense of her own identity.

MOLLEL, TOLOWA M. *The Orphan Boy*. Illus. by Paul Morin. NY: Clarion, 1990. (Ages 6-10.)
This Maasai story from the author's homeland echoes many myths that affirm the importance of keeping one's word and overcoming one's own curiosity. The story is also one that explains the existence of the planet, Venus. Some other universal themes include the craving of an adult for a child of his own and the inevitable separation of the child from the parent when the time has come. The illustrations shimmer with inner light and demonstrate the artist's familiarity with the pasturelands of Tanzania as well as his respect for the culture of the people.

MORRIS, ANN. *Bread Bread Bread*. Illus. by Ken Heyman. NY: Scholastic, 1989. (Ages 4-9.)
Breads from many different cultures and countries are pictured. Whether it is fat, skinny, round, or with a hole, bread is a favorite and nutritious food everywhere. An index is included with twenty-nine ways people eat bread all over the world. Other books in this series having the same format and including information about many cultures include *Hats Hats Hats* (1989), *Loving* (1990), and *On the Go* (1990), about how people all over the world travel to where they are going. The photographic arrangement in each book leaves a lasting impression of the similarities of people rather than the differences and the author provides an excellent model for children to design their own integrated studies of other universal topics.

MYERS, WALTER DEAN. *The Mouse Rap.* NY: Harper and Row, 1990. (Ages 9-12.)
Mouse is ambivalent about whether or not he wants his long-absent father to return to their family. He has adjusted to the fact that he and his mother are a family entity, and now his father wants to return. In addition to capturing voices and cadences of young people in this Harlem neighborhood, Myers also reflects the complexity of the parents' relationship. The plot gets complicated with a story of hidden loot and a dance contest that somehow turns into a career for one of the young men, but it's light and fun, and along the way readers can appreciate the tempo, language, and style of the teenagers in this community.

NIXON, JOAN LOWERY. *Land of Hope.* NY: Bantam, 1992. (Ages 9-12.)
Rebekah, Rose, and Kristin come from different countries, cultures, and religions, but they become friends on the ship coming to Ellis Island. Rebekah and her family are the main characters in this volume, but the immigrants all share the same sorts of aspirations and tribulations. Modern day immigrants, too, are experiencing the losses and challenges of these early twentieth century immigrants.

NYE, NAOMI SHIHAB (editor). *This Same Sky: A Collection of Poems from around the World.* NY: Macmillan, 1992. (Ages 12-up.)
About 161 poems by poets from around the world demonstrating universal emotions are included. The map, indexes, and notes on the poets provide information for further exploration. The variety of poetic style adds to the value of the book.

OCHS, CAROL PATRIDGE. When I'm Alone. Illus. by Vicki Jo Redenbaugh. Minneapolis: Carolrhoda, 1993. (Ages 4-6.)
A high-spirited, African American girl explains in verse, incidentally counting from ten to one, how numerous animals (aardvarks, lions, turtles, camels and hippos among them) have created the horrible mess in her room. Here is an example of the depiction of a child who, in less multicultural times, would have been a Caucasian boy. It is good to have this sort of balancing, entertaining literature.

PALMER, EZRA. *Everything You Need to Know About Discrimination.* NY: Rosen, 1990. (Ages 8-10.)
This book is filled with information about various types of discrimination (religious, gender, racial, age, and condition of ability). Some history and definitions are also supplied, along with anecdotes about what people did when they found themselves victims of discrimination.

PELLEGRINI, NINA. *Families Are Different*. Illus. by the author. NY: Holiday House, 1991. (Ages 5-up.)
A wonderfully diverse look at all types of families and the love that "glues them together." The families range from multiracial, adopted, one-parent, two-parent, and divorced. The illustrations make the story come alive.

RAYNOR, DORKA. *My Friends Live in Many Places*. Chicago: Whitman, 1980. (Ages 6-10.)
Pictures of people from many places around the world playing, mourning, studying, working, celebrating, and eating. Although there are few photos from South America or Africa and none from Australia or the Arctic regions, if care is taken to supply additional resources, the excellent quality of the photos and the variety of lifestyles shown can add to children's understanding of unity in diversity.

ROHMER, HARRIET, ADAPTER. TRANSLATED INTO SPANISH BY ALMA FLOR ADA AND ROSALMA ZUBIZARRETA. *The Legend of Food Mountain*. Illus. by Graciela Carrillo. San Francisco: Children's Book Press, 1982. (Ages 8-10.)
A mythic reminder that food and its sources must be respected by people. This story, in Spanish and English, is derived from Aztec legends and tells of the bringing of food to the ancient people by Quetzalcoatl, with the help of a giant red ant and despite the intervention of the rain dwarfs.

ROSEN, MICHAEL (editor.) *Home*. NY: A Charlotte Zolotow Book, 1992, (Ages 7-9.)
Thirty well-known authors and illustrators of children's books share their special personal images of what home means to them.

ROSEN, MICHAEL. *South and North. East and West: The Oxfam Book of Children's Stories*. Cambridge, MA: Candlewick, 1992. (Ages 8-10.)
A distinguished collection of stories from around the world illustrated by many famous artists. Many of the stories are traditional folktales. Some of the countries represented are Korea, Cyprus, the Dominican Republic, and Bangladesh.

ROSENBERG, MAXINE B. *Living in Two Worlds*. Illus. by George Ancona. NY: Lothrop, Lee & Shepard, 1986. (Ages 8-10.)
Wonderful black-and-white photos illumine the text with images of children and their parents representing a number of different racial backgrounds. The explanations of race and descriptions of each family member in these interracial families focus only on the positive aspects of being biracial.

SAN SOUCI, ROBERT D. *Larger Than Life*. Illus. by Andrew Glass. NY: Doubleday, 1991. (Ages 7-10.)
John Henry, Old Stormalong, Slue-Foot Sue, Pecos Bill, Strap Buckner, and Paul Bunyan figure in these tall tales of larger-than-life American folk heroes. A discussion of characteristics the heroes share and which of these remain positive values today may be beneficial to children.

SAN SOUCI, ROBERT D. *Short and Shivery*. Illus. by Katherine Coville. NY: Doubleday, 1987. (Ages 9-12.)
Terrifying tales from Native American, Russian, Appalachian, British, French Canadian, Orkney Islands, Jewish, Japanese, German, Costa Rican, Norse, African, New England, California, New Mexico, and Shetland Islands sources.

SAN SOUCI, ROBERT D. *The Talking Eggs*. Illus. by Jerry Pinkney. NY: Scholastic, 1989. (Ages 6-8.)
Like other folktales, this story of two sisters—one bad, one good, with the mother favoring the bad child—contains a tapestry of details and a number of archetypal incidents. Obedience and generosity are the virtues to be admired. The Creole setting and contemporary realistic artwork (which earned the book a Caldecott Honor) distinguish this version from its European counterparts. Children may enjoy seeing a number of versions of the tale and comparing them. (Try comparing it with "Mother Hulda" from Grim.)

SCHWARTZ, ALVIN. *And the Green Grass Grew All Around: Folk Poetry from Everyone*. Illus. by Sue Truesdell. NY: HarperCollins, 1992. (Ages 5-up.)
More than 250 poems and chants transmitted via the oral tradition through the ages and across many cultures. The commentary interspersed with the rhymes adds to readers' appreciation.

SHANNON, GEORGE. *Stories to Solve: Folktales from Around the World*. Illus. by Peter Sis. NY: Beech Tree, 1985. (Ages 8-10.) see also *More Stories to Solve: Fifteen Favorite Folktales From Around the World* (1989).
The very brief tales collected here all end with problems for readers to solve. For example, in a story where there is a test to discover which flower is real among many artificial ones, the reader is invited to guess how King Solomon did it. (He opened a window and let a bee fly in.) The tales are from many different origins.

SHELBY, ANNE. *Potluck*. Illus. by Irene Trivas. NY: Orchard, 1991. (Ages 4-7.)
A rollicking alphabet book is the context for a multicultural feast, with

each item especially chosen by a child to contribute a variety of ethnic and culinary flavors ("Ben brought bagels" and "The triplets turned up with tacos"). Not all ethnic groups are represented, but the book provides a model for young readers to replicate and build upon.

SIMON, NORHA. *All Kinds of Families*. Illus. by Joe Lasker. Niles, Illinois: Whitman, 1976. (Ages 4-7.)
The book celebrates the concept of family as people who belong together for one reason or another. The illustrations represent people of all ages, colors, economic conditions, and geographic locations. The family is described as "a strong, invisible circle."

SINGER, MARILYN. *Nine O'Clock Lullaby*. Illus. by Frane Lessac. NY: HarperCollins, 1991. (Ages 4-8.)
Brightly colored pictures alive with movement illustrate various cultures and geographic locations around the world at a given moment in time: 9 p.m. in Brooklyn, N.Y., p.m. in Puerto Rico; 2 a.m. in someone's pantry somewhere in England, 3 a.m. in Zaire and Switzerland, and so on, until we are back in Brooklyn at 9 p.m. Although Brooklyn, Sydney, Nome, and Los Angeles are the only cities mentioned, it is to the author's credit that she does not simply name the continents. The illustrations capture a flavor of each location.

SOTO, GARY. *Baseball in April*. San Diego: Harcourt Brace Jovanovich, 1990. (Ages 12-up.)
A collection of 11 realistic short stories featuring young Latinos in California. The themes are growing up, determination, honesty, education, and hard work. The stories are well written and contain humor. Except for the characters' names and the occasional insertion of Spanish into the dialogue, the characters could be from any culture.

STEPTOE, JOHN. *Mufaro's Beautiful Daughters*. Illus. by the author. NY: Lothrop, Lee & Shepard, 1987. (ages 8-10.)
An African *Cinderella* variant. Two sisters—both beautiful, one selfish and mean-spirited, the other kind and loving—vie for the hand of the King. The illustrations are glorious. The lesson learned is that kindness and cooperation pay off. Incidentally, the message is communicated that the beauty of these two women is palpable and not European in standard.

STOLZ, MARY. *Storm in the Night*. Illus. by Pat Cummings. NY: Harper Row, 1988. (Ages 5-8.)
Thomas and his grandfather weather a fierce storm by watching it from

their front porch and telling stories. The grandfather helps Thomas acknowledge his feelings when he tells of the time when he was a boy and was afraid of a storm. The characters are African American. The situation and feelings are universal. Further adventures of the loving pair may be found in *Go Fish* (1991).

TAYLOR, MILDRED D. *The Gold Cadillac*. Illus. by Michael Hays. NY: Dial, 1987. (Ages 9-12.)
A trip south that begins as a prideful family journey encounters disaster in the form of bigotry, but the family remains strong and surmounts the ugliness.

TAYLOR, MILDRED D. *The Road to Memphis*. NY: Dial, 1990. (Ages 10-up.)
A sixth book in the series about the Logan family that dramatically and authentically conveys a sense of the struggles and passion of this African American family in Mississippi during the time of the Great Depression. The other books are *Song of the Trees* (1975), *Roll of Thunder, Hear My Cry*. (1976), *Let the Circle Be Unbroken* (1981), *The Friendship* (1987) and *Mississippi Bridge* (1990). This latest volume takes place in 1941 and includes a romantic interlude for Cassie, now grown up. The series blasts the passive, downtrodden stereotype and sustains a strong message of strength, togetherness, intelligence, and determination.

THOMAS, JOYCE CAROL (ED.). *A Gathering of Flowers: Stories about Being Young in America*. NY: Harper & Row, 1990. (Ages 12-up.)
Stories by such competent authors as Maxine Hong Kingston, Jeanne Wakatsuki Houston, Joyce Carol Thomas, Kevin Kyung, and Gary Soto all relating some aspect of growing up in a particular community in America. Each of the stories reflects the author's own background and heritage.

WADE, BARRIE. *Little Monster*. Illus. by Katinka Kew. NY: Lothrop, Lee & Shepard, 1990. (Ages 4-7.)
Mandy grows tired of hearing her mother tell everyone how perfect Mandy is. She envies her little brother's mischievous exploits. For a full day Mandy becomes a little monster and thoroughly enjoys infuriating her parents. At the end of that day this African American close-knit family are all able to laugh about it, and her parents assure Mandy that they love her no matter what.

WALTER, MILDRED PITTS. *Mariah Keeps Cool*. NY: Bradbury, 1990. (Ages 8-10.)
Mariah's half-sister, Denise, comes to stay and Mariah and her sister

Lynn must help Denise to adjust to a new way of behaving. The family's rules make sense, and Lynn responds well to the loving family structure. *Mariah Loves Rock* (1988) introduced this lively character to reading audiences. The family is African American; the interactions and concerns are universal.

WILLIAMS, VERA. *A Chair for My Mother.* Illus. by the author. NY: Morrow, 1982. (Ages 5-8.)
Also see *Something Special for Me* (1983) and *Music, Music for Everyone* (1984). This working class family consists of a child, her mother, and her grandmother. In each of these three books, although they are struggling economically, the family members manage to find some selfless but realistic way of making each other happy.

WILLIAMS, VERA B. *"More More More," Said the Baby.* Illus. by the author. NY: Greenwillow, 1990. (Ages 4-6.)
A love-filled, rollicking set of three episodes in the lives of three different families from varied heritages, all consisting of making babies gurgle with delight and beg for more of the same.

WILSON, BETH P. *Jenny.* Illus. by Dolores Johnson. NY: Macmillan, 1990. (Ages 5-8.)
Jenny is reminiscent of the young narrator in Eloise Greenfield's *Honey I Love*. She is endearing, honest, in love with herself and the world, and generous in sharing her feelings about her parents' divorce, her relationships with her teacher, friends, and family members, her fears, and her pleasures. The flavor of her loving African American family communicates well through the format of brief poetic messages.

WINGET, MARY (editor). *Vegetarian Cooking Around the World.* Illus. by Robert L. and Diane Wolfe. Minneapolis: Lerner, 1992. (Ages 9-up.)
Food is an excellent medium for learning about and experiencing different traditions of people around the world. This series of cook books provides recipes from many different countries with maps, a glossary of specific cooking utensils, terms, and special ingredients. Some other cuisines in the series are African, Australian, Caribbean, Chinese, French, German, Greek, Hungarian, Indian, Israeli, Italian, Japanese, Korean, Lebanese, Mexican, Norwegian, Polish, Russian, Spanish, Thai, and Vietnamese. Readers may compare the different foods, noting the similarities and differences, speculating on why certain foods are so popular, and researching more information about each group represented.

YOLEN, JANE (editor). *Favorite Folktales from around the World.* NY: Pantheon, 1986. (Ages 10-up.)
More than forty cultures are represented in this excellent volume of 160 tales categorized in batches such as "Tricksters, Rogues and Cheats," "Heroes: Likely and Unlikely," "Shape Shifters," "Death and the World's End," and nine other sections of equally intriguing topics.

YOLEN, JANE. *The Lullabye Songbook.* Illus. by Charles Mikolaycak. Music arr. by Adam Stemple. San Diego: HBJ, 1986. (Ages 7-12.)
A collection from many cultures attesting to the fact that the universal ingredients of repetition, nonsense, and rhythmic melodies exist in lullabies around the world.

References and Selected Resources

BISHOP, RUDINE SIMS. "Books from Parallel Cultures: New African-American Voices" in *The Horn Book,* vol 1xviii, no 5, September/October, 1992. pp 616-620.

HARRIS, VIOLET. (ed.) *Teaching Multicultural Literature in Grades K-8.* Norwood, MA: Christopher Gordon, 1992.

LINDGREN, MERRI V. (ed.) *The Multicolored Mirror: Cultural Substance in Literature for Children and Young Adults.* Fort Atkinson, Wisconsin: Highsmith Press, 1991.

MANNA, ANTHONY L. AND CAROLYN S. BRODIE, (eds.) *Many Faces, Many Voices: Multicultural Literary Experiences for Youth.* Fort Atkinson, Wisconsin: Highsmith press, 1992.

MILLER-LACHMANN, LYN. *Our Family, Our Friends, Our World.* New Providence, NJ: R.R. Bowker, 1992.

RUDMAN, MASHA KABAKOW. *Children's Literature: An issues Approach.* 3rd edition. NY: Longman, 1993.

SIMS, RUDINE. *Shadow and Substance: Afro-American Experience in Contemporary Children's Fiction.* NCTE, 1982.

SLAPIN, BEVERLY and SEALE, DORIS. *Through Indian Eyes: The Native Experience in Books for Children.* Philadelphia: New Society, 1992.

7

Selection as a Means of Diffusing Censorship

Barbara Feldstein

The problem of censorship has plagued our country from its earliest beginnings to the present day with an ebb and flow of both rigid and liberalizing trends. Since the Supreme Court decision of 1973 that handed down a new set of guidelines enabling states to ban books, magazines, plays, and motion pictures offensive to local standards, there has been an increasing number of attempts to remove material from schools and libraries. This trend makes it imperative that educators in the public sector define their selection policy and reexamine their attitudes toward the community's role in selection of library books and instructional materials.

Who Are the Censors?

Censors can be viewed as those who wish to intercede between the creator and the consumer in the hopes of preventing other consumers from access to the ideas of the creator. There is no definitive way of predicting who these censors might be or what they might find offensive. Censors can be individuals who believe fervently in a particular ideal or who are offended by a specific concept; or they can be groups of people who feel compelled to work in the interests of society as they perceive it. These groups can represent religious sects as well as political views from both the left and the right wing. The major targets for censors are as follows:

1. *Political views that differ from that of the censor.* This is often interpreted as disrespect for authority. This is reflected in the furor following the publication of *Sylvester and the Magic Pebble* (1969) by William Steig in which, although all the characters were animals, the portrayal of policemen as pigs was seen as objectionable.

2. *Treatment of minorities in a multiethnic society.* This concern is based on the fact that there has been a limited portrayal of minorities and these portrayals are often stereotypical. There were objections to the illustrations in *The Five Chinese Brothers* (1938) by Claire Bishop because all the characters looked exactly alike and their appearances were reduced to the common stereotypical denominators of bilious yellow skin, slit and slanted eyes, queues and coolie clothes; furthermore, the people were depicted as a vindictive mob devoid of human compassion.

3. *Stereotyped roles of women portrayed in ways differing from modern feminists' point of view.* Over the past twenty years, no doubt as a result of the efforts of the feminist groups, there has been an increase in the number of positive role models in children's literature. Nonetheless, there are still objections to passive female characters who do not take control over their own destiny.

4. *Problems of contemporary society such as violence, drugs or permissive sex.* It is in this category that groups such as the Moral Majority have exerted the most influence and have been successful in preventing books by authors such as Judy Blume from reaching children.

5. *Unacceptable language.* Again, political or religious groups have taken it upon themselves to determine what is acceptable for all children.

Reactions to Censorship

Some publishers, anticipating possible controversy, have themselves become censors. In the article "Some Thoughts on Censorship" (*Top of the News*, Winter, 1983, p. 146), Betty Miles indicated that a school book club refused to publish her book *The Trouble With Thirteen* (1983) because she would not change the word "sexy" to "snazzy." Recently there have been increasing numbers of objections to materials based on religious grounds. This is reflected in the insistence that creationism be taught as part of the curriculum and in opposition to the growth of secular humanism.

All too often the initial response of the professional educator to inquiry about material is defensive and confrontational. This adversarial stance can transform a parent genuinely concerned about the effect of a particular book on his or her child into an angry militant. The educator must ask, "Does this parent have a right to question material used in the classroom? How would I react if my child were exposed to material I believed to be biased?"

Censorship vs. Selection

Very often the difference between book selection and censorship is in the eye of the beholder—if I'm doing it, it's selection; if you're doing it, it's censorship. It is important to examine the differences carefully. Realistic constraints of space and money force the professionals to make choices of which materials to purchase. The collections in the schools and libraries reflect the values of the community. These values must be weighed when purchases are considered; however, this does not preclude the selection of materials that might provoke the prevailing attitudes.

It is at this point that the Library Bill of Rights, especially its support of the obligation to present "all points of view on current and historical issues" is useful. Professionals benefit from an overview of what materials are available. They can then select from them those items that best portray a variety of ideas and concepts. They must be prepared to defend those choices. Selection is predicated on *inclusion,* while censorship emphasizes *exclusion.* Censors prevent others from exposure to material the censor has determined to be detrimental. Selectors provide a variety of material so that users are forced to weigh differing thoughts and reach a conclusion for themselves. Censors limit the material provided so that users will conclude that the values and ideas of the censors are the only valid ones.

While the selector is an "aye" sayer, the censor is a "nay" sayer. That is not to suggest that selectors do not say "no" to some materials. Obviously they do, but that rejection is based on assessing the work in its entirety. The selector views the work as a whole; the censor tends to look at the work narrowly, determining that a work is objectionable based on a particular passage or concept. A selector might disapprove of a specific passage and then determine that the positive impact of the work as a whole outweighs the questionable sections. A censor reacts in a more limited way—if there is an objectionable word, passage or concept, the work as a whole is discarded. Both the censor and the selector have individual points of view. The selector seeks to be aware of and sensitive to his or her own bias and does not allow that bias to prevent the purchase of material representing diverse opinions. The censor seeks to eliminate opposing positions and supports the exclusive dissemination of his or her point of view.

When people have a strong sense of values, there is a natural tendency to proselytize. Therefore, professionals must periodically reexamine their own attitudes and behavior and be sure they have not crossed the fine line, becoming more a censor than a selector.

Dealing with Concerns

When a concern about material is voiced, the educator should adjust the style and substance of response based on whether it is a concerned parent asking a legitimate question or whether it is a political group lobbying for a particular point of view. The concerns of an individual can probably be addressed on a one to one basis. When a group is taking a stand, it is advisable to seek the assistance of agencies whose function it is to deal with censorship issues. *Censorship, A Guide for Teachers, Librarians and Others Concerned With Intellectual Freedom* (1976) by Lou Willett Stanek is a source for materials and agencies that are available if controversy should arise.[1]

If we accept that the community does have a legitimate role in selection, the next step is to establish a formal statement of policy regarding the selection of library and instructional materials and the method for requesting review of material. This statement should (1) specify the general policy of the instructional unit, (2) contain specific selection criteria, (3) delegate responsibility for selection to designated staff members, and (4) specify procedures for challenging specific titles. A sample public school library materials-selection policy is appended at the end of this chapter.

Once a policy has been established and is in place, the educator can proceed with developing professional techniques that might prevent censorship confrontations. First of all, the person selecting materials should examine his or her professional responsibilities and personal style of response. He or she must have familiarity with what is available already in the classroom, school, or library. He or she must make decisions about which books to purchase based on the needs of the curriculum and the community. As has been indicated earlier, if money and space were not the object, the issue of censorship would be less acute; one would simply have almost everything available. Since this is never the case, the teacher or librarian must use resources to best meet the needs of the community. He or she must learn to avoid defensiveness and, finally, must develop the ability to understand and be sensitive to diversity of opinion.

Before Questions Arise: Reviewing Books

Although the community does have the right to question, the ultimate responsibility for book selection rests in the hands of the professional, be it librarian, teacher, or reading specialist who examines a variety of reviews and uses these reviews in determining which materials to purchase. However, it is vital that this person read as many of the books as possible. One of the most important roles of a reading professional is to introduce a wide range of literature to children and to stimulate a desire to read. The enthusiasm for literature is contagious, but this enthusiasm can only come from a genuine knowledge of the books. Furthermore, one can not rely exclusively on reviews in making selection decisions. Occasionally a book will receive rave reviews but the librarian, upon close reading of the text, may determine it is unsuitable for her community. For example, *Space Station Seventh Grade* (1982) by Jerry Spinelli received a starred review in the *School Library Journal* (October, 1982, p. 156) and was suggested for children in grades four through seven. Although it is not recommended to pull sentences out of context, sometimes specific passages can have a negative effect on the work as a whole. In this book one character talks about the weird stuff they (Jews) do. The character specifically lists some Jewish foods and the practice of wearing "little beanies in church—which they go to on Saturdays." The character says that Jews are terrified of pigs and think that pork is poisonous, but concludes that "Jews know how to live" (p. 17). There are also derogatory references to Italians and black people. This character says that black people are likely to be carrying knives (p. 134). Some readers might object to such words as "faggot face" (p. 22) and "pussy" (p. 38). Here is an example when a selector might reject a book because although some of the concerns and misconceptions of adolescence are presented in a light and funny way, the overall quality of the book is not high enough to offset the one-dimensional characters and the questionable ethnic and sexual humor.

Sometimes the reading of the book requires close examination of the illustrations as well as the text. In The *Adventures of Isabel* by Ogden Nash (1963), illustrated by Walter Lorraine, the verse that deals with the troublesome doctor has a picture of Isabel being examined by a doctor with negroid characteristics. On the next page where Isabel is "cured"; the doctor is white. These few examples are intended to emphasize the importance of having the person responsible for selection read as many of the books as possible.

Responding to Concerns

When a parent questions a book, particularly one with which the educator is familiar, there is often a tendency to react defensively. Rather than really listening to the complaint, the educator might be tempted to counter with all the reasons why that book was selected. The discussion becomes confrontational rather than problem solving.

One parent came into the child's school library very angry that her fourth grade child had read *The Outsiders* (1967) by S.E. Hinton. She felt that the book was very violent and demanded that it be removed from the library. Having spent a good deal of thought on how to avoid adversarial situations, the librarian encouraged the parent to sit down, have a cup of coffee, and describe specifically what was objectionable. The librarian agreed that this was not a book appropriate for most fourth graders, but would the parent agree that it would be acceptable for some sixth graders? Since the library had open stacks and since volunteers staffed the circulation desk, could the parent suggest any method for preventing young children from borrowing books possibly more suitable for older children? The tone of the dialogue diffused the parent's hostility, and she left satisfied that she had had an opportunity to express her valid point of view. In discussion with parents, it is important to point out the appropriateness of their being involved in what their own children are reading but the inappropriateness of their making decisions for other children.

Learning not to be defensive is one of the maturing processes that most teachers and librarians must undergo. Another sign of maturity is the recognition that we do not have all the answers. Young people often see things simplistically—issues are reduced to black and white. As we get older, and perhaps wiser, we become aware of various interpretations. This does not mean to imply that difficult decisions should be avoided, but rather all aspects of an argument should be respectfully considered before the decision is reached.

One librarian read *Sadako and the Thousand Paper Cranes* (1977) by Eleanor Coerr to fifth and sixth graders. The principal questioned the appropriateness of this book, wondering whether the children were mature enough to understand. The book initiates a discussion of nuclear war. Sadako died of leukemia resulting from the dropping of the atomic bomb. The author's intention seems to be to move children so deeply that they, as adults, would do whatever they could to avert such a catastrophe. Were we asking children to cope with feelings that even we adults find difficult? The librarian countered with the opinion that the book was appropriate since the children were already familiar with aspects of World War II and that although the book is sad, the reader is left with some hope. By making her story known and by erecting a statue of Sadako as a symbol of peace, the author and Sadako's peers hope to alter the future. Children reading the book can feel empowered knowing that it was young people who were the force behind the monument's construction. The librarian decided to continue to read this book to the students but to be particularly sensitive to any concerns and ideas expressed by the young listeners.[2]

Presenting various points of view

With the growing emphasis on whole language and literature based instruction, teachers have an increased responsibility to see to it that the books they select for classroom reading reflect a wide variety of points of view and represent diverse religious, ethnic, racial and cultural groups. Having students read books that include female and minority characters as role models is an important way to broaden their attitudes and to develop their respect for human differences. Books that might be used to generate discussion include Avi's *Nothing but the Truth* and *The True Confessions of Charlotte Doyle,* which both deal with the concept of truth; Babbitt's *Tuck Everlasting,* which causes readers to reconsider their attitudes toward death; Reeder's *Shades of Gray,* which causes readers to reconsider the notion of a hero; O'Dell's *Sing Down the Moon,* which uncovers the hardships of Native Americans; and Taylor's *Mississippi Bridge,* which provides a look at the treatment of African Americans.

Discussions following the sharing of a provocative book or discussions relating to current affairs present teachers with a difficult task. Teachers must work at having meaningful, thought provoking conversations that cause their students to consider the issues, but at the same time teachers must try not to impose their own values and opinions on their students. This becomes very difficult when the issues discussed are particularly meaningful for the teacher; for example, classrooms were the scene for many discussions following the trial of the police officers accused of the Rodney King beating. In one school, there was a fifth grade teacher who was appalled by the fact that these officers were acquitted. Down the hall, there was another fifth grade teacher who, although repulsed by the scenes of the beating, felt that due process had been served and that it was necessary to abide by the court's ruling. It is hoped that the breadth of the discussion was not adversely affected by the beliefs of the teachers.

In a public school setting, the classroom teacher should not let strong personal feelings about controversial topics interfere with class discussion. A teacher's role is to facilitate a discussion, to act as a devil's advocate so that the students are able to develop their own opinions about controversial issues based on discovering pertinent information and hearing various viewpoints. A discussion about a controversial topic in which the teacher expresses his or her own personal feelings will not be open and it will inhibit the students from testing their opinions.

The issue of capital punishment is often brought up in upper elementary classes. When it is mentioned, the teacher's responsibility is to present both sides of the issue. For example, of a student says, "I think if someone kills someone else, that person should be killed." The teacher should not respond, "You're right. I agree," but rather the teacher should pose questions that would encourage the class to think about the statement "What if the person who was put to death was not really guilty?" "Do you think we should ever forgive someone for murder and allow them to live?" "Will the execution of a murderer stop others from murdering?" "Will the execution of the murderer bring back the victim?" Another student might initiate a discussion by saying, "I think people can be rehabilitated and should not be sentenced to death." Once again, the teacher should not agree but rather ask the student and the class, "If the person killed someone in your family, would you feel the same way?" "What if this person killed more than one person?" "If criminals knew they wouldn't die if they killed someone, do you think it would make a difference?" In this discussion the teacher is a facilitator who is helping the students appreciate the complexities of the topic and learn that they have a responsibility to hear both sides of an issue before forming an opinion. Furthermore, the teacher should suggest that the students investigate the topic further, helping them locate articles that would support or refute their positions and aiding them in developing strategies to evaluate the newly acquired information. It is also hoped that the teacher can indicate that one's attitudes about a variety of issues are not written in stone but are subject to change over time.

When teachers are consciously aware of the influence they have on students and therefore make a concerted effort to provide multiple points of view, they are doing much to prevent angry concerns from would-be censors.

Encouraging Critical Thinking

Once the adults have become aware of their responsibility in book selection and sensitive to their response to inquiry, they can explore instructional techniques that will enable children to think critically and evaluate material for themselves. As early as kindergarten, children should be exposed to open-ended questions following the sharing of a book. In most stories, there is a problem that has to be solved. Children can be asked to state the problem and its resolution. Can they think of alternative solutions? Have they ever had a similar problem? How was it solved? Also, in most stories, the main character changes. How did that character change? What caused the change? In what ways are the children like fictional characters? As the instructor continues to pose interesting, thought provoking questions to which there is not a prescribed response, the children continue to participate in animated, thoughtful discussion.

One reading specialist was disturbed by the book *Nightmares: Poems to Trouble Your Sleep* (1976) by Jack Prelutsky. Although it was regarded by the American Library Association as a notable book, the specialist thought it was especially gory and might be disturbing to some readers. She shared it with some fifth and sixth graders and asked for their reactions to it. They loved it! When the specialist voiced her concerns, they responded with "You seem to be losing your sense of humor. This is a funny book." When asked if it were possible that it might be frightening for some readers and indeed might produce nightmares, the children's response was that those children who were easily scared would not select the book. Both the title and the cover illustration prepared the reader for what was inside. The children's arguments were so cogent that not only did the specialist keep the book, it became a Halloween tradition. When students are involved in an honest interchange where their opinions are valued, they will often surprise adults with their insight, knowledge, and sensitivity.

Several years ago the Council on Interracial Books for Children (1841 Broadway, New York, NY 10023) prepared a pamphlet, *10 Quick Ways to Analyze Children's Books for Racism and Sexism*. The following guidelines were offered. (1) Check the illustrations: Look for stereotypes. Look for tokenism. Who is doing what? (2) Check the story line. What are the standards for success, what is the resolution of the problems, and what is the role of women? (3) Look at the lifestyles. (4) Weigh the relationships between people. (5) Note the heroes and heroines. (6) Consider the effects on a child's self-image. Are norms established that limit the child's aspirations and selfconcepts? (7) Consider the author's or illustrator's background. (8) Check out the author's perspective. (9) Watch for loaded words. (10) Look at the copyright date.

Providing the children with some guidance in helping them to identify incidents of racism and sexism is more successful than trying to shield them from such incidents. In the book *Indian Summer* (1968) by F.N. Monjo, a group of Indians, who are trying to lure the children into the woods so they can scalp them, are outwitted by a woman and her children. Readers should be encouraged to ask themselves how the Indians are portrayed. Is there any indication of why the Indians are fighting? While reading *Charlie and the Chocolate Factory* (1964) by Roald Dahl, the children can be encouraged to question the depiction of the Oompa-Loompas, the little black men from Africa who have rhythm and love working and living in the underground factory. In a more recent book by Alice and Martin Provensen, *Shaker Lane* (1987), the changes in a community are presented. A piece of land was sold and a group of relatively poor people lived on it. They accumulated lots of junk and were sloppy. When land developers forced them to leave, there was no mention of where they were going or any hint of the possible hardship of their relocation. Readers should be encouraged to question and discuss this depiction of poverty.

A few years ago there were requests and even demands made by some feminist groups that fairy tales be removed from library shelves. Rather than banning these books, a wide variety from many different cultures and providing many perspectives should be made available. Children should be instructed that fairy tales, in the folklore tradition, have been handed down from generation to generation orally in order to transmit the values of a culture. In all fairy tales, good is rewarded and evil is punished. One quickly notices that physical beauty is regarded as a virtue worthy of reward. Readers should be encouraged to consider whether physical attractiveness is a virtue. How do different cultures describe attractiveness? Fairy tales such as James Riordan's *Woman in the Moon and Other Tales of Forgotten Heroines* (1985), Rosemary Minard's *Womenfolk and Fairy Tales* (1975), Alison Lurie's *Clever Gretchen and Other Forgotten Folk Tales* (1980), and Ethel Johnson Phelps' *Maid of the North: Feminist Folktales from Around the World* (1981), in which the female is successful more because of her wit or courage than her appearance, should be introduced.

In addition to becoming sensitive to issues of racism and sexism, children need to learn how to distinguish between fact and opinion and how to evaluate information. With these objectives in mind, the following project was presented to a fifth grade class. Each student was to select one topic and read three articles on that topic in three different encyclopedias. After reading the articles and taking appropriate notes, the students were asked to write a position paper in which each child indicated which encyclopedia was best and which was worst. The position had to be substantiated with specific examples from the articles. Since this was a difficult project, it was introduced with a modeling technique. The teacher did with the class exactly what each child was to do individually. He read three different articles about General Custer. A few of the children read related articles on native Americans and discovered that the word "battle" was used when the white men were victorious but "massacre" was used when the native Americans won. Although not all the children reached this level of sophistication, they all profited from a genuine investigation in which they were responsible for making a decision and substantiating that decision with specific examples. The more we provide children with learning experiences in which they must weigh information and make meaningful decisions, the less we will have to intervene in what they are reading or viewing.

Keeping the Community Aware and Involved

The tasks of an educator have increased so much in recent years that it is understandable that keeping the community aware of what is happening in the schools has not been a first priority. All too often this type of communication is seen as a public relations gimmick and not worthy of the time it requires. This is unfortunate. If the community were informed of curriculum issues, educational objectives, recommended materials, and so forth, the likelihood is that they would be more vocal in their support. Outstanding events are occurring in the schools of which the community is totally unaware. Rather than waiting for negative comments and reacting to them, educators should find ways of reporting to the district and of encouraging constructive dialogue. In keeping with this idea of involving the community, the following are specific suggestions that have been found successful.

There was no established sex education course in the school. Several faculty members and the school librarian noticed that the children were exhibiting interest in this topic and felt they should have access to information. It was decided that sex education books should be purchased and made available on open shelves in the library. Through the school newsletter, the parent community was informed of this proposal, and parents were requested to volunteer to serve on the committee that would aid in the selection of the books. A group of books that had been favorably reviewed were gathered. The parent committee, chaired by a librarian, read the books, discussed them, and recommended which ones to purchase. Since these discussions occurred before the era of AIDS, that topic was not an issue. The major source of disagreement centered on the subject of masturbation. After lengthy conversation, the majority recommended the books, which were then purchased and placed on the shelves. Knowing that a group of parents had been involved in the process seemed to avert controversy. It is not recommended that all issues that might produce controversy be handled by a committee, but, in some instances, this preventative approach is useful. The professionals established the policy; the community aided in implementation.

Another way of avoiding confrontation with the community is to establish channels of communication that build confidence and trust. In one community a group of parents expressed interest in children's literature to their librarian. A parent book discussion group was formed in which parents would read the books in advance of the meetings, which were held about once a month. The books were discussed in the same way adult books would be discussed. Although the books chosen by the librarian to be read and discussed represented primarily current, well-written literature, this vehicle of book discussion could be used to examine titles that are potentially controversial. The parents were not only stimulated and provoked by the discussions, they developed a greater appreciation for current literature and no longer argued that the reading program be devoted exclusively to "classics." During the course of discussion, the parents often indicated curiosity about how their children would respond to a particular idea or passage. Since these meetings were held in the library during school hours, children often overheard the conversation. They later commented on the same books to the librarian. This mutual interest in the reaction of adults and children prompted the establishment of a parent/child book discussion group.

The parent/sixth grade child book group that evolved from this initial group has been in existence for the past six years. The group meets in the evening, one a month, and discusses a commonly read book. The major purpose of these meetings is to enhance communication between parents and children. The librarian recommends the books and is particularly interested in books that treat such themes as peer pressure, friendship, parent/child relations, and problems involved with growing up.

About five years ago it seemed everyone was talking about the problem of drugs in the schools. The librarian had read Alice Childress' *A Hero Ain't Nothin' But a Sandwich* (1973) and although she had not purchased it, thinking it was better suited to an older audience than an elementary school library, she suggested that the parent/child group read it. Upon second reading, she was surprised by the frequency of the words that many people label obscene. With some trepidation, she began the discussion by sharing her concern that the language might have offended some of the readers. She was quite blunt. "I had forgotten that the word 'fuck' seemed to appear on every other page. I am sorry if you were offended." By recognizing the language problem she acknowledged the criticisms of some of the participants and demonstrated a regard for their opinions. The discussion was then able to move on to the substantive issues presented powerfully in the book. It is not suggested that a book potentially as divisive as this be the first one introduced, but it does demonstrate that once a mutually respectful climate has been established, controversial matters can be explored.

Summary

It is important to construct a framework for establishing a selection policy and a method of dealing with challenges to that policy. There is a need for continual professional growth that involves an awareness of the responsibilities regarding book selection and of the sensitivity required in dealing with the community. As professionals, we have the training and experience to make decisions. We must not abdicate our responsibilities, yet we must avoid the appearance of an omniscient arrogance that precludes honest inquiry. On the other hand, when we perceive an attempt to threaten our students' freedom to read, we must be prepared to fight to defend the principle of free expression and free access to ideas. Instructional techniques that enable children to examine and evaluate material for themselves should be introduced. Finally, interaction with the community that seeks to inform as well as to foster trust and confidence should be established. With this combination of professional behavior children will learn to better select, critique, appreciate, and love literature.

Library Materials Selection Policy Sample

I. General Policy

The primary object of the public school libraries is to implement, enrich, and support the educational program of the schools. In doing so, the library collection strives to provide a wide range of materials on all levels of difficulty, with diversity of appeal and different points of view.

To help students and teachers develop a critical awareness of the problems and issues in our rapidly changing world, materials presenting all aspects of these problems and issues will be included—the unpopular as well as the popular, the questionable as well as the accepted, the minority as well as the majority opinions.

The development of an individual's taste, judgment, critical capacity, and lifelong reading habit is to be encouraged; to that end a considerable range of materials must be included in the library collection. Recreational reading, listening, and viewing contribute to this growth; therefore, items for this purpose will be available along with those that are supportive of curricular activities.

Specific responsibilities of the school library:
1. To provide materials that will enrich and support the curriculum, taking into consideration the varied interests, abilities, and maturity levels of the pupils served.
2. To provide materials that will stimulate growth in factual knowledge, literary appreciation, aesthetic values, and ethical standards.
3. To provide a background of information that will enable pupils to make intelligent judgments in their daily lives.
4. To provide materials on opposing sides of controversial issues so that young citizens may develop, under guidance, the practice of critical analysis of all media.

5.   To provide materials representative of the many religious, ethnic, racial, and cultural groups that portray the roles of their contributions in the development of America.
6.   To place principle above personal opinion and reason above prejudice in the selection of materials of the highest quality in order to assure a comprehensive collection appropriate for the users of the library.
7.   To develop the lifelong habit of reading that fosters freedom in the exchange of ideas.

II. Responsibility for Selection of Materials

The actual selection of materials is the responsibility of professional, trained personnel on the library staff who know the courses of study, the methods of teaching, and the individual differences of the pupils. The librarians will choose materials that are keyed to the interests and needs of the students and faculty and that will open up possibilities in cultural, social, and economic fields. In this task, the librarians will be aided by purchase suggestions from administrators, faculty, students, and parents. The individual school librarian is responsible for the final evaluation and selection of materials for her or his school.

III. Criteria for Selection of Materials

Criteria for the selection of materials are consistent with the guidelines for materials and selection noted above and are based on the needs of the individual school as determined from a knowledge of the curriculum, requests of administrators and teachers, and the needs of individual students as determined from a knowledge of children and youth and the requests of parents and students.

Materials for purchase are considered on the basis of overall purpose, factual accuracy, authoritativeness, timelessness or permanence, importance of the subject matter, quality, balance, readability, format, availability, and price.

IV. Procedures for Selection of Materials

In selecting materials for purchase, the librarian consults reputable, professionally prepared selection aids. Additional suggestions are obtained from faculty members, librarians, book exhibits, professional meetings and courses, and book lists from other school systems.

In specific areas, the librarian follows these procedures:

1.   Gift materials are judged by basic selection standards and are accepted or rejected by these standards.

2. Worn or missing standard items are replaced periodically,
3. Out-of date or no longer useful materials are withdrawn from the collection.

V. Challenged Materials

Despite the care taken to select materials of excellence for student and teacher use, objections to a selection are sometimes made to the public. In such instances, the principles of the freedom to read and the professional responsibility of the staff must be defended rather than the materials.

If a complaint is made, the procedures are as follows:

1. The complainant will file her or his objections in writing on the Citizen's Request for Re-evaluation of Library Materials form (beginning on page 154).
2. The complainant is directed to mail the completed form to the coordinator of library services.
3. The material in question shall be reviewed by a committee of eight, composed of: coordinator of library services, librarian from school involved, principal from school involved, assistant superintendent for program, district program coordinator, parent representative appointed by school PTA, school librarian from system, and teacher from school involved.

The review committee shall function at the call of the coordinator of library services upon receipt of a complaint. The material shall be considered with the specific objections in mind. The majority and minority report of this committee's findings are submitted directly to the superintendent, who will in turn submit them to the school committee and file them in the school and administration offices.

The review of questioned materials shall be treated objectively and as an important matter. Every opportunity shall be afforded those persons or groups questioning school materials to meet with the committee and to present their opinions.

Instructions to Evaluating Committee

Bear in mind the principles of the freedom to learn and to read and base your decisions on these broad principles rather than on defense of individual materials. Freedom of inquiry is vital to education in a democracy.

Study thoroughly all materials referred to you and read available reviews. The general acceptance of the materials should be checked by consulting standard evaluation aids and local holdings in other schools.

Passages or parts should not be pulled out of context. The values and faults should not be weighed against each other; rather opinions must be based on the material as a whole.

The best interests of the students, the curriculum, the school and the community shall be of paramount consideration.

Citizen's Request Form for Re-Evaluation of Library Materials[3]

Initiated by _____

Telephone _____

Representing:

Self _____ Organization or group _____
(Name)

School _____

MATERIAL QUESTIONED:

Book: Author_____ Title _____

     Publisher _____ Copyright date _____

AV Material: Kinds of media_____
(film, filmstrip, record, etc.)

Title _____

Other Material: Identify _____

Please respond to the following questions. If sufficient space is not provided, please use additional sheet of paper.

1. Have you seen or read this material in its entirety? _____

_____

2. To what do you object? Please cite specific passages, pages, etc. _____

_____

3. What do you believe is the main idea of this material? _____

_____

4. What do you feel might result from use of this material? _____

_____

5. What reviews of this material have you read?_____

_____

7. For what other age group might this be suitable?_____

_____

8. What action do you recommend that the school take on this material? _____

_____

9. In its place, which work of equal literary quality do you recommend that would convey as valuable a picture and perspective of a subject treated? _____

_____

_____   _____

Date   Signature

References

1. Stanek, Lou Willett. *Censorship, A Guide for Teachers, Librarians and Others Concerned with Intellectual Freedom.* New York: Dell, 1976.

2. Cochran, N. and Feldstein, B. "A Learning Experience" *Newton Voices.* Newton Public Schools, 1987.

3. The library material selection policy is rooted in and supportive of the following documents:

   Academic Freedom in the Secondary Schools. New York: American Civil Liberties Union, 1968.

   The Students' Right to Read. Urbana, IL: National Council of Teachers of English, 1962.

   Intellectual Freedom Documents of the American Library Association, Chicago, IL, 1974.

   Library Materials Selection Policy of the Public Schools of Brookline, Massachusetts, 1973.

Titles used in parent book discussion groups

Alexander, Lloyd. *The Book of Three.* New York: Holt, Rinehart, and Winston, 1964.

Babbitt, Natalie. *Kneeknock Rise.* New York: Farrar, Straus & Giroux, 1970.

Blume, Judy. *Are You There, God? It's Me, Margaret.* New York: Bradbury, 1970.

Cleaver, Vera and Bill. *Ellen Grae.* Illustrated by Ellen Raskin. New York: Lippincott, 1967.

Collier, James and Christopher. *My Brother Sam Is Dead.* New York: Four Winds, 1974.

Holman, Felice. *Slake's Limbo.* New York: Scribner's, 1974.

Hunter, Mollie. *A Stranger Came Ashore.* New York: Harper & Row, 1975.

Lowry, Lois. *A Summer to Die.* Boston: Houghton Mifflin, 1977.

O'Dell, Scott. *Sing Down the Moon.* Boston: Houghton Mifflin, 1977.

Paterson, Katherine. *Bridge to Terabithia.* Illustrated by Donna Diamond. New York: Crowell, 1977.

Snyder, Zilpha Keatley. *Below the Root.* New York: Atheneum, 1975.

Titles used in parent/child book discussion groups

Alexander, Lloyd. *Westmark.* New York: Dutton, 1981.

Babbitt, Natalie. *Tuck Everlasting.* New York: Farrar, Straus & Giroux, 1975.

Blume, Judy. Tiger Eyes. New York: Bradbury, 1982.

Bosse, Malcolm. The *79 Squares.* New York: Crowell, 1979.

Degens, T. *Game on Thatcher Island.* New York: Viking, 1977.

Greene, Constance. *Getting Nowhere.* New York: Viking, 1977.

Konigsburg, E.L. *Throwing Shadows.* New York: Atheneum, 1979.

Paterson, Katherine. *The Great Gilly Hopkins.* New York: Crowell, 1978.

Speare, Elizabeth George. *The Sign of the Beaver.* Boston: Houghton Mifflin, 1984.

Taylor, Mildred. *Roll of Thunder, Hear My Cry.* New York: Dial, 1976.

Voigt, Cynthia. *A Solitary Blue.* New York: Random House, 1983.

Works Mentioned in the Chapter

Titles used in parent book discussion groups.

Titles used in parent/child discussion groups.

Alexander, Lloyd. *The Book of Three.* New York: Holt, 1964.

Alexander, Lloyd. *Westmark.* New York: Dutton, 1981.

American Civil Liberties Union. *Academic Freedom in the Secondary Schools.* New York: ACLU, 1968.

Avi. *Nothing but the Truth.* Orchard, 1991.

Avi. *The True Confessions of Charlotte Doyle.* Orchard, 1990.

Babbitt, Natalie. *Kneeknock Rise.* New York: Farrar, Strauss & Giroux, 1970.

Babbitt, Natalie. *Tuck Everlasting.* New York: Farrar, Strauss & Giroux, 1975.

Bishop, Claire. *The Five Chinese Brothers.* Illustrated by Kurt Wiese. New York: Coward, 1938.

Blume, Judy. *Tiger Eyes.* New York: Bradbury, 1982.

Blume, Judy. *Are You There, God? It's Me, Margaret.* New York: Bradbury, 1970.

Bosse, Malcolm. *The Seventy-nine Squares.* New York: Crowell, 1979.

Childress, Alice. *A Hero Ain't Nothin' But a Sandwich.* New York: Coward, 1973.

Cleaver, Vera and Bill. *Ellen Grae.* Illustrated by Ellen Raskin. New York: Lippincott, 1967.

Cochran, N. and Feldstein, Barbara. *"A Learning Experience"* in *Newton Voices.* Newton, MA: Newton Public Schools, 1987.

Coerr, Eleanor. *Sadako and the Thousand Paper Cranes.* Illustrated by Ronald Himler. New York: Putnam, 1977.

Collier, James Lincoln and Christopher. *My Brother Sam is Dead.* New York: Four Winds Press, 1974.

Council on Interracial Books for Children. *Ten Quick Ways to Analyze Children's Books for Racism and Sexism.* New York: CIBC, 1975.

Dahl, Roald. *Charlie and the Chocolate Factory.* Illustrated by Joseph Schindelman. New York: Bantam, 1964.

Degens, T. *The Game on Thatcher Island.* New York: Viking. 1977.

Greene, Constance. *Getting Nowhere.* New York: Viking, 1977.

Hinton, S.E. *The Outsiders.* New York: Viking, 1967.

Holman, Felice. *Slake's Limbo.* New York: Scribner's. 1974.

Hunter, Mollie. *A Stranger Came Ashore.* New York: Harper & Row. 1975.

Konigsburg, E.L. *Throwing Shadows.* New York: Atheneum, 1979.

Lowry Lois. *A Summer to Die.* Boston: Houghton Mifflin, 1977.

Lurie, Alison. *Clever Gretchen and Other Forgotten Folktales.* Illustrated by Margot Tomes. New York: Crowell, 1980.

Miles, Betty. "Some Thoughts on Censorship" in *Top of the News.* Winter, 1983, p.146.

Miles, Betty. *The Trouble with Thirteen.* New York: Knopf, 1979.

Minard, Rosemary. *Womenfolk and Fairy Tales.* Illustrated by Suzanna Klein. Boston: Houghton Mifflin, 1975.

Monjo, F.N. *Indian Summer.* Illustrated by Anita Lobel. New York: Harper & Row, 1968.

Nash, Ogden. *The Adventures of Isabel.* Illustrated by Walter Lorraine. Boston: Little, Brown. 1963.

National Council of Teachers of English. *The Students' Right to Read.* Urbana, IL: NCTE, 1962.

O'Dell, Scott. *Sing Down the Moon.* Boston: Houghton Mifflin, 1977.

Paterson, Katherine. *The Great Gilly Hopkins.* New York: Crowell, 1978.

Paterson, Katherine. *Bridge to Terabithia.* Illustrated by Donna Diamond. New York: Crowell, 1977.

Phelps, Ethel Johnson. *Maid of the North: Feminist Folktales from Around the World.* Illustrated by Lloyd Bloom. New York: Holt, Rinehart and Winston, 1981.

Prelutsky, Jack. *Nightmares: Poems to Trouble Your Sleep.* Illustrated by Arnold Lobel. New York: Greenwillow, 1976.

Provensen, Alice and Martin. *Shaker Lane.* New York: Viking, 1987.

Reeder, Carolyn. *Shades of Gray.* Macmillan, 1989.

Riordan, James. *Woman In the Moon and Other Tales of Forgotten Heroines.* Illustrated by Angela Barrett. New York: Dial, 1985.

Snyder, Zilpha Keatley. *Below the Root.* New York: Atheneum, 1975.

Speare, Elizabeth George. *The Sign of the Beaver.* Boston: Houghton Mifflin, 1984.

Spinelli, Jerry. *Space Station Seventh Grade.* Boston: Little, Brown, 1982.

Stanek, Lou Willett. *Censorship, A Guide for Teachers, Librarians, and Others Concerned with Intellectual Freedom.* New York: Dell, 1976.

Steig, William. *Sylvester and the Magic Pebble.* New York: Simon & Schuster, 1969.

Taylor, Mildred. *Mississippi Bridge.* Dial, 1990.

Taylor, Mildred. *Roll of Thunder, Hear My Cry.* Illustrated by Jerry Pinkney. New York: Dial Press, 1975.

Voigt, Cynthia. *A Solitary Blue.* New York: Atheneum, 1983.

Part III

Literature In and Beyond the Classroom

This section reflects specific concerns of the classroom teacher: How does one apply the literature directly to the classroom outside of readalouds and sustained silent reading? What is the place of poetry in the curriculum, and what are the resources for introducing it to children? How can literature enhance the rest of the curriculum, in particular, the social studies themes and units that help children become citizens of the world? And how can teachers and parents become partners in the process of bringing literature and children together.

There are so many demands on teachers' class time that it is difficult to consider their doing more, and many people consider using literature in the classroom "one more thing to do." Children's literature can open up the whole learning experience for youngsters, with the proper planning. In Chapter 8, Masha Rudman gives readers a useful background summary of reading practices and relates her experiences in setting up a literature-based program in her own classrooms in New York City schools. She also addresses a number of real-life concerns voiced by teachers willing to embark on this new method but unsure of how to measure the approach's effectiveness using traditional means.

In Chapter 9 Lee Bennett Hopkins uses his impressive expertise and talent to place poetry in perspective and provide an excellent base for working with poetry and children in the classroom. In Chapter 10 Jennifer Ladd, a specialist in global education, contributes concrete guidelines for how to select and use children's literature to enhance children's awareness of societal issues.

The job of bringing literature into the lives of children does not solely belong to the teachers. Parents are also a tremendous positive influence. Teachers and parents can forge a strong school-home relationship, and in Chapter 11, Nancy Larrick draws from her own considerable experience to describe a number of practical suggestions for forming and encouraging this crucial alliance.

Childrens Literature in the Reading Program

Masha Kabakow Rudman

Introduction

Any reading program is predicated on a definition of reading. If such a definition includes the making of personal meaning by the reader, and also implies an active involvement of the reader in the process, then the materials of the reading program must incorporate everyday encounters with print (such as labels, signs, newspapers, magazines, menus, advertisements, notes, and letters, the child's own picture-captions and writing, and so forth) and other items containing continuous, meaningful text that make sense to the reader. The importance and appropriateness of using literature, in particular, will be highlighted in this chapter, as will some practical advice about how to implement such a program.

Good literature offers many rewards to readers: knowledge, pleasure, heightened awareness of self and others, deeper appreciation of the world and its visual and cultural treasures, the opportunity for armchair travel, a nurturing of the imagination, an aid to the development of a moral sense, and a greater understanding of what it means to be human. As Donna Norton says in *Through the Eyes of a Child* (1991), "Literature entices, motivates, and instructs. It opens doors of discovery and provides endless hours of adventure and enjoyment" (p. 2). She goes on to say that children benefit developmentally as well by reading and engaging in literature-related activities.

In their fourth edition of *Children's Literature in the Elementary School* (1987), Huck, Hepler, and Hickman define literature as "the imaginative shaping of life and thought into forms and structures of language. The province of literature is the human condition: life with all its feelings, thoughts, and insights. The experience of literature is always two-dimensional, for it involves both the book and the reader" (p.4). This involvement coupled with the quality of the language and the compelling nature of story provide an excellent partnership in the process of helping children learn to read, and to value reading as a lifelong process.

A Literature Approach to Reading

In a literature approach to reading the teacher and the child are partners in a pleasurable endeavor, and the materials are of interest to everyone. Literature uses natural language that is evocative and descriptive. It invites the reader into a world of people who have feelings akin to the reader's as well as people who differ widely from the reader. It provides a mirror of one's behavior and life, and affords a window onto the rest of the world. It introduces and affirms a sense of beauty, models values and behaviors, and instructs and entertains.

A literature approach to reading focuses on stories and nonfiction; biographies and personal accounts; poetry, fairy tales, folklore, and myth. Teachers and administrators are recognizing now that it makes sense to use trade books (children call them "real" books) as the basic materials for a reading program because they are designed to be attractive and engrossing as well as informative.

In providing children access to books of worth and teaching them to select such books for themselves, the classroom teacher can help children take a major step toward becoming enthusiastic lifelong readers. A well-chosen book is one that reflects, responds to and extends the interests, questions, concerns, imagination, and passions of the child. It is a source of solace, excitement, enrichment, and satisfaction.

Evidence of this pleasure and substance can be seen in such books as E.B. White's *Charlotte's Web* (1952), which offers insights on friendship, life and death, tolerance of differences, and growing up. The wisdom of the mother in Margaret Wise Brown's *The Runaway Bunny* (1977) clarifies and comforts; the beauty and personal responsibility of Barbara Cooney's *Miss Rumphius* (1985) inspires. Donald Hall in his *Ox-Cart Man* (1979), and Eric Carle in *The Very Hungry Caterpillar* (1969) convey factual information in aesthetic form; any of Arnold Lobel's work contributes humor and understanding. All testify to the power of literature and its long-lasting effect. When children read these books, and others of equally high quality, they love and look forward to reading. They learn how to read better, for the act of reading is the single best way to become proficient at reading.

Starting at Home

Exposure to literature begins at home. A home environment where books and other printed matter are clearly in evidence and are part of the regular routine of the household, where parents read to their children and enjoy reading themselves is the best indicator of a child's eventual success in school. Babies as young as three months evidence responses to books, and by the age of six months their preferences are clearly discernible, demonstrating that parents can begin very early to introduce literature to their children.

A number of guides have been published to help parents introduce a love of books to their youngsters. Among these are Jim Trelease's *The New Read-Aloud Handbook* (1989), an excellent annotated bibliography, and *For Love of Reading* (1988) by Masha Kabakow Rudman and Anna Markus Pearce, which describes more than a thousand books that are appropriate for pre-reading children. The latter also describes the stages of development that children go through from infancy to age five and emphasizes the importance of the role of the adult in making the child's experience of interacting with books a pleasurable one.

The Path to Reading

Children want to learn to read. Tomie de Paola has poignantly described his passionate desire to read books from the library when he was a little boy (Cullinan, 1987). He was disappointed that he was not given the opportunity to learn to read in kindergarten. In first grade he read the entire preprimel during one weekend, and was rewarded with permission to apply for his very own library card. Thus began his true journey into reading. He is not alone.

Too often adults place obstacles in children's paths that are difficult to overcome. Children are forced to look at print in a meaningless context. They are drilled in bits and pieces of exercises and given paper-and-pencil tests that have little or nothing to do with the sense of reading. Sometimes those children who find it difficult to read out loud are embarrassed by being forced to parade their "errors" in front of their peers in a process of public diagnosis known as "Round-Robin oral reading."

If truth be told, many children learn to read in spite of their program of instruction. As Frank Smith points out in *Reading Without Nonsense* (1985), "All methods of teaching reading can achieve some success, with some children, some of the time." But he goes on to say, "No method succeeds with all children" (p.5). He and many others who have conducted research in this area have come to the conclusion that it is important to make learning to read attractive, accessible, possible, pleasurable, and useful.

Many children, because of their eagerness to learn, persevere and become readers. Others are so disheartened by the lack of meaning in what they read and by the punitive nature of the process that they give up. They view themselves as non-readers, and, often, as failures. Studies have demonstrated that children placed in low reading groups in first grade remain in those low groups throughout their entire academic careers. (Eldredge and Butterfield, 1988.) Unfortunately, this grouping approach over the years has become "the way it's s'posed to be," and some teachers have found it difficult to break away from this traditional format.

Basal Readers: The Traditional Approach to Teaching Reading

For many years controversy has raged over the "best" way to teach reading. The usual instructional format has been that of permanent groups (generally three) of "fast," "average," and "slow" readers. In these groups students are taught to say the words they see on the page by using various mechanical strategies such as sounding-out, looking at spelling similarities or patterns, trying to discover familiar little words inside the big ones, discovering the root of the word and then tackling the prefixes and/or suffixes, using the configuration of the words and letters, and, finally, looking at the context. The materials most frequently used are the basal reader (so called because it is designed to provide a complete and systematic approach to the acquisition of reading skills) and the workbook. Numerous ditto sheets containing practice exercises are also part of this packaged approach.

Especially in books targeted for grades one through three, vocabulary is strictly controlled and language may be somewhat stilted. Children's reading is evaluated through paper and pencil tests supplied by the publisher to coincide with the vocabulary and the scope and sequence of the series. The ongoing evaluation that is incorporated into the instructional sequence consists of a series of workbook exercises and comprehension questions, often focusing on literal recall of the text rather than on higher level thought.

Over the years, the appearance and content of basal readers have changed. Publishers employ reading experts as consultants to help keep up with the changing vocabulary and current research. Basals are far more attractive now, and contain new and more colorful illustrations and a greater variety of genres and story formats. Their enrichment sections have been expanded, and most of them recommend additional materials. But many of the underlying assumptions remain the same as they were in 1920: Teachers and children need someone outside the classroom to select materials for them; vocabulary and skills must be uniformly and sequentially taught; word-calling comes before comprehension, and should be acquired by means of a systematic set of predetermined strategies.

Publishers now are producing basals that contain excepts from children's literature. The detailed guide that covers each of the stories is a comfort to some teachers who are uneasy about the awesome responsibility of helping children learn to read. Ken Goodman pinpoints the practice of adapting the literature in his *New Advocate* article, "Look What They've Done to Judy Blume!: The 'Basalization' of Children's Literature" (Goodman, 1987). Among the many examples he gives is Gerald McDermott's story that had originally begun, "Tasulo was a lowly stonecutter. Each day the sound of his hammer and chisel rang out as he chipped away at the foot of the mountains." It was changed by the publisher to read, "Once there was a strong man. Each morning he went to the mountains. There he dug up stones" (Goodman, p. 38).

Problems in changing from the Basal Reader Approach

It is difficult and frightening to go against a sixty-year old tradition. The fact that grades are awarded as a result of tests, coupled with the concern for "accountability" also exacerbates the problem of moving away from the basal. Many teachers have been uncomfortable with the materials and methods of the basal approach, but they have been fearful that any deviation from these programs would harm the children. Lacking information on an alternative method, some teachers have creatively supplemented and even bypassed the basal, but often they have felt guilty about going against the system. Perhaps more teachers would feel comfortable deviating from the basal if they knew that even though ninety percent of classrooms across the country use basals, fewer than half of these teachers are required to use basals exclusively, and more than sixty percent report that they are encouraged to go beyond the basal. Thus, the practice of using additional mater is more widely sanctioned by administrators than most teachers believe (Turner, 1988).

Criticism of a mechanistic approach to reading is not new. Nineteenth century advocates of a meaningful approach included Horace Mann in the 1840s, and Francis Parker and Joseph Mayer Rice in the 1880s and 1890s. Progressive education, led by John Dewey and William Kilpatrick, was the umbrella for reform of the model of education that relegated the teacher and students to meaningless and disconnected pedagogical practices. But after the turn of the century, and into the 1920s, the effect of the misinterpretation of many of the Progressive education principles, and the emergence of all sorts of "scientific" investigations and revolutions, compounded by the development of the testing practices of some educational psychologists, gave birth to a movement for a more standardized curriculum in reading. The basal readers were born. As Kenneth Goodman et al say in their informative *Report Card on Basal Readers* (1988), "Promoted as the result of scientific study, basal materials promised that all children would learn to read well if teachers and students would simply follow the directions supplied in teachers' manuals" (p. 19).

Escape from Jack and Janet: Alternatives to the Basal

Even with the best intentions, and with an understanding of the principles underlying alternative methods such as the literature, or process-approach to reading, teachers need help in the actual design of such a program. Because most teachers have been instructed in the traditional three-group, skills-based basal reader system, it is difficult to introduce, manage, and sustain a reading approach that is more open-ended and personalized.

Nevertheless, the concept of going beyond the basal has been important for at least forty years. Among the first educational leader to advocate a more personalized and literary approach were Leland Jacobs and Jeanette Veatch. Their work directly affected my own life as an educator. When I was a fledgling teacher in New York City in 1954, I tried dutifully to gather my three groups daily and propel my third graders through Jack and Janet's inanities. But I was bored, my students were bored, and we all vastly preferred the stories I read to them, the stories they invented, and the exciting activities we were engaging in for our social studies units. I felt very guilty about my regularly "forgetting" to have our reading groups.

One day, when our district reading supervisor came to my class for a routine visit, she asked me how my reading program was progressing. I told her the truth. Instead of chastising me she smiled, and asked if I would like to be a pilot teacher for a new program the district was trying, based on the work of Jeanette Veatch, called Individualized Reading. I would, and I did. I learned how to introduce the program to the children, how to help them keep their own records, and how to observe their behavior while reading and discussing their reading. I also learned to conduct reading conferences. The children and I introduced more and more diverse, high-quality children's books into the classroom. We went on more field trips to the local library where we discussed how to select books that we would enjoy and benefit from. The children read and wrote more and more; we produced a class newspaper that became the pride of the school. And I was never again bored by our classroom reading program.

Since the reading program reflected a respect for their interests and needs, my inner city children felt good about themselves, devoured books, and scored well beyond their peers on the mandatory standardized tests. (I did teach them the skills of test-taking as a survival tactic.) A few years later the New York City Board of Education published a Guide called *A Practical Guide to Individualized Reading* (1960), to which teachers like me contributed to help other teachers learn this approach. A number of teachers adopted Individualized Reading, but somehow, in the face of some misunderstanding of its tenets, a lack of systematic instruction across the city's schools, and because teachers are so vulnerable to criticism, the practice was isolated and scattered.

But those teachers who really understood the process did not go back to a sterile program of instruction, and, with the help of more and more researchers, their influence has spread. Parents, teachers, and librarians across the country, and, indeed, throughout the world, are finding that when real reading material, including literature, is the basis for children's reading instruction, and when that instruction respects and stimulates the children's interests and abilities, then the children approach reading as an enjoyable and informative activity, rather than as a chore. Teachers involved in this sort of approach are less likely to be bored themselves, and find that they can function as observers, responders and instructors in helping children to achieve success.

Current research on reading gives us many valuable insights into how children learn. We know that each child is an individual with different learning styles, interests, backgrounds and abilities (Carbo, Dunn and Dunn, 1986). The whole language movement, led by people like Ken and Yetta Goodman and Frank Smith, does not prescribe a particular methodology, but it affirms that children need to engage in meaningful activities with print. This includes the everyday printed materials they encounter, particularly stories and literature.

Given persuasive research evidence of the importance of literature in children's backgrounds, it is understandable that the idea of a literature approach to reading instruction has achieved popular acceptance, if not practice. The combination of the process approach to writing spearheaded by Donald Graves and Lucy Calkins, and the whole language movement led by the Goodmans and Frank Smith has reached elementary school classrooms. The Commissioner of the State of California declared a California Reading Initiative that focuses on the use of literature in classrooms. Several school systems across the country in Ohio, Vermont, Massachusetts, Colorado, New York, Illinois, and Michigan, to mention just a few, have embraced a literature approach. Books describing the theory and practice of whole language are being bought by the thousands by teachers.

Defining Some Terms

Because this approach has a long history and many roots, there are a number of terms that describe it. "Whole language," "individualized reading," "process approach," "literature-based reading instruction," are all terms that are heard at international reading conventions, at gatherings of teachers and curriculum specialists, and are seen increasingly more often in articles and books about reading and writing. What do they mean, and how can teachers sort them out?

Whole Language

Whole language is a philosophy and set of guiding principles that focus on maintaining the wholeness, natural quality, interest, and relevance of language. A whole language approach applies to any aspect of language: reading, writing, listening, speaking, or thinking. It is relevant to the learner's interests and concerns; is at the reader's level of development; is part of a larger construct; is not isolated as a learning event; respects the learner's ownership of his or her own learning; uses materials that have been selected and often created by the learner; contains options for the learner to decide upon; is interesting; is appropriate; and empowers rather than punishes or renders powerless. It is based on the learner's and teacher's strengths and a "can do" assumption rather than a deficit model of learning.

The Process Approach

The process approach to writing, as promulgated by Donald Graves (1983) and his associates and students (such as Lucy Calkins, Jane Hansen, and Nancie Atwell), has convinced many teachers, parents, and children across the country, and, indeed, throughout the world, that a whole language approach to writing enables children to think of themselves as writers and to become remarkably fluent, enthusiastic, effective communicators at a surprisingly early age. It is a movement that ensures children's ownership of their own writing by permitting them to write about their own interests and experiences rather than arbitrarily assigned topics; and encourages a natural and organic evolution into standard structure rather than an over-reliance on the rules of grammar and spelling. It espouses procedures such as partners sharing their writing with each other; one-on-one conferences with the teacher in which the child's work is viewed as worthy of respectful conversation; lots of opportunities for writing; lots of time permitted for writing activities; and writing across the curriculum (the elimination of artificial barriers of subject matter). The principles of the process approach apply as well to reading as they do to writing, as Jane Hansen has demonstrated in her book, *When Writers Read* (1987); and Nancie Atwell in *In* the Middle: *Writing, Reading, and Learning with Adolescents* (1987); Regie Routman in *Transitions: From Literature to Literacy* (1988); and Timothy Shanahan in *Reading and Writing Together: New Perspectives for the Classroom* (1990).

Individualized Reading

Individualized reading predates whole language by some thirty years, and is compatible with its principles. Not a tutorial, not an exclusively recreational reading program, not programmed instruction, and not a *laissez-faire* system, this approach helps teachers to organize an instructional reading program that is based on each child's interests and abilities and builds on strengths. Individualized reading is based on three major features: self-selection of materials by the children, self-pacing and self-evaluation. Jeanette Veatch, one of the major proponents of this program, has written extensively on it over the years. (*Individualized Reading: For Success in Classrooms* [1954], *How to Teach Reading with Children's Books*[1968], *Reading in the Elementary School* [1978]).

The goals are that children will learn how to select appropriate materials for themselves, pace themselves appropriately, and that they will acquire the skills necessary to evaluate their own progress and their own needs, with the help and strategic intervention of the teacher. Sometimes groups of children will want to read the same book. Sometimes the teacher will want to use the same book as the basis for a group's discussion. But for the most part, in this sort of program, it is feasible for children to be reading different books, and still to be able to discuss their reading with each other and with the teacher.

The structure of an individualized reading program is similar to that of the process approach to writing. It is based on the assumptions that children can learn to make appropriate and constructive choices about the materials of their learning. It uses the strategy of a teacher-child reading conference as a vehicle for respectful discussion of the child's reading; it invites children to read about their own interests and experiences rather than arbitrarily assigned topics; it provides a natural and organic evolution into the making of meaning rather than an over-reliance on the rules of phonics.

Essential features of this program include partners sharing their reading with each other and one-on-one conferences with the teacher in which the child's work is viewed as worthy of respectful conversation and attention. The program demands multiple opportunities for reading; lots of time permitted for reading and related activities; the elimination of artificial barriers of subject matter and the use of all sorts of materials available in the child's everyday world, in addition to story and literature.

The term, individualized reading, is no longer in widespread use, but the procedures it introduced makes sense, and can be applied productively in any literature-based program.

Implementing a Literature-based Reading Program

There are many ways to implement such a program. Even in school systems where a basal reader is required, it is acceptable to introduce additional, meaningful materials. Indeed, a number of publishers' manuals recommend book titles to bring into the classroom to supplement the basal. One way of easing into the program is to obtain multiple copies of several books. With the advent of inexpensive paperbacks this is not a difficult task. With multiple copies children can select which book they want to read and both they and the teacher will be assured that there will be a number of people who can discuss the same book. Eventually the teacher and class can move into wider student selection.

Grouping

Teachers may also enter into this program by changing their instructional strategies. Instead of permanent grouping and round-robin oral reading teachers can institute the reading conference, during which the child and teacher talk about the child's reading, listing strengths and deciding together on next steps. Using these decisions teachers can group children who exhibit the same need for a "next step", or for thematic discussions, author investigations, or planning groups for making presentations to the class. In this way the learning is specifically tailored to the demonstrated needs of the children, thus providing for more efficient delivery of instruction.

Peer interaction is an important element of a literature-based reading program. The children engage in projects together and receive appropriate and necessary instruction in small groups on specific aspects of the reading process. They work with partners, listening to each other read, asking each other questions and engaging in conversations about their books.

The Conference

Conferences scheduled weekly with each child in the class for approximately five to ten minutes each seem to work best. Biweekly conferences are possible, but the rule is, the more the better. In the course of the conference, the teacher and child prepare for the rest of the week's activities in reading. It is during the conference that the child exercises the ability to discuss his or her own reading process. This is not an instructional time, but rather is a brief opportunity for diagnosis and design of future learning strategies.

At a conference, for example, after engaging in some conversation about why a child chose a book that turned out to be too difficult or unsatisfying, the teacher and child might decide that the child needs more help in self-selection. The teacher might then schedule a session with this child and others who are ready for such a small group lesson.

Sharing

The child might discuss during conference time how to share the book he or she is reading. This sharing need not be an individual endeavor; children can collaborate on their presentations. These book-sharings help children express themselves, critique books, and "sell" books to their peers.

Children may choose many ways to present their books. Appendix D of *Children's Literature: An Issues Approach* (Rudman, 1993) describes more than fifty activities children may select, and there are countless more that may be found in magazines such as *Teaching preK-8, Learning,* or *Instructor,* and in such books as *Ideas and Insights* (1987), compiled by Dorothy Watson.

Materials

Teachers may begin by asking children what materials they think they can bring into the classroom that will help them learn to read better. The children should be encouraged to suggest as many different kinds of reading materials as possible, and all these suggestions should be accorded respect by the teacher. The teacher should also encourage conversation about why we read, and how often we read outside the classroom. The aim here is to legitimatize reading, and to demonstrate that it is not relegated to the realm of academe, but is, indeed, a life-activity.

Once it has been established that there are many varieties of acceptable printed matter, the children can be invited to bring in materials. They should be encouraged to discuss and bring in the books that they enjoy. If they have few books at home, membership in one of the paperback book clubs such as Scholastic or Trumpet can inexpensively remedy this situation. Subscribing to such a club also provides regular opportunities at ordering-time, when the books arrive, and as children read the books, for the teacher and children to discuss and recommend books to each other. Frequent trips to the school's library, and, perhaps, some field trips to the neighborhood library can provide another source of books.

Selection

A very important whole-class lesson involves the art of selecting books. Children will readily admit that they select books upon the recommendation of a friend, because of a book's attractive cover, illustrations or lack of them, size, shape, thickness, amount of print on a page, size of print, and the relevance or interest of its content. They also discuss their acquaintance with and preference for certain authors, genres, styles, or topics. When they are respected as people who have some control over their selections, they respond enthusiastically and constructively.

Sometimes, in their eagerness to read a book, children may select material that will frustrate them because of the level of difficulty. It is at this point that Jeanette Veatch's "Five finger exercise" can come in handy (pun intended). A child selects a passage of about one hundred words (three to five paragraphs, or a few pages of a picture book) and folds down one finger every time he or she comes to a word or phrase that gets in the way of meaning. Sometimes a child will not know a word, but it won't impede the meaning if the child skips the word. Then the child need not put down a finger. If the child needs to use more than five fingers before coming to the end of the passage, then it is likely that the book will be too difficult. The operating guide here is a ninety-five percent level of ease with the words and structure, similar to "informal reading inventories" but not as elaborate.

Children will not necessarily become proficient immediately at selecting books that interest them and are at their level of development or understanding. But if they know that this sort of selection process is important, and that they are responsible for working at getting better at it, then they will understand questions about their reasons for selecting books and they will respond accordingly. Their memories may need to be refreshed about selection strategies such as defining a purpose for reading a particular piece, ensuring that the book is not too difficult, looking for familiar authors, looking at the blurb on the dust jacket, and asking the opinions of friends now and then, but, in general, this process works quite smoothly.

Other whole-class introductory lessons prove helpful to the smooth workings of a literature-based approach to reading. Conversations about what good readers do and how people know that they are good readers help children to identify their strengths as readers, and also help them to participate in the decision making about what their next steps might be. The more they can articulate what they have learned, the more effective that learning will be. The act of talking about reading helps to cement the learning about reading. It also helps, politically, when, in response to parents' queries, children can say what it is they are learning.

The Teacher's Role

Since this is an instructional program, the teacher's interaction and intervention is critical. Teachers who are uneasy about how to manage the conference and the diagnostic process may wish to make a list, with the children, of those attributes that make a person a good reader. Comprehension will certainly be one of the factors and it is worthwhile to talk at some length about just what this means. Comprehension is more than remembering details. It includes retelling a story, interpreting it, and comparing it to other stories and to one's own experience. It also includes a discussion of how well the story works, if it is stereotypic or appropriate in its perspective, and if the characters ring true. The language of the story can be discussed and evaluated. The author's style can be reflected upon. Children can discuss the pictures and their place in the story. The conversations and interactions among the children are excellent indicators of how well they understand their reading.

Because the teacher is constantly observing and listening to the children in a variety of small group situations, in conferences, and in students' presentations to the rest of the class, it is possible to deliver appropriate instruction. The aim is that no child will endure an unnecessary lesson. The reason for each lesson is that it is an appropriate next step for a few children.

There are many sources of ideas for these lessons. A number of them are listed at the end of the chapter; occasionally some may also be found in teachers' manuals. In this case, the manuals can be helpful in providing appropriate next steps.

The teacher in this program is an instructor, facilitator, co-learner, model, and guide. The teacher also takes every opportunity possible to demonstrate a love of reading. During the daily period of free reading (Sustained Silent Reading) during which time everyone in the classroom reads a book of his or her choice, the teacher should participate actively, taking care not to use this time for catching up on recordkeeping or engaging in housekeeping chores. It is also invaluable for the teacher to read aloud daily and to select a wide range of books from which to read aloud (no matter what the age of the students).

Managing the Program

The schedule can vary from day to day, or it can be regularly preset. Time should be set aside for conferences, reading aloud, sustained silent reading, small group or whole class instruction, and sharing. At any point children should be permitted to read their own books. They may also be given the opportunity to interact with their partners or with other groups of children with whom they are preparing a presentation. Library work and research are important parts of classroom activity and children should be encouraged to use their time in exploration of reference materials.

The children are capable of helping design the schedule and resolving problems that arise. The more they are involved with the management of the program the more they will benefit from it. The more ownership they have in every phase, the better the entire program will work.

Questions and "Yahbuts"

Because I conducted this sort of program for a number of years with children from first grade through sixth, and because I have worked with teachers, helping them to manage such programs for almost thirty years, I have had some experience in dealing with a number of the questions that arise when teachers begin to implement the approach. Some of these questions and answers follow.

What if a child insists on reading only one kind of book when there is the practice of self-selection in the classroom? That is a phenomenon that may occur, but it need not be a problem. After all, how many adults prefer certain genres of books, and read them, almost to the exclusion of anything else? We permit ourselves to read nonfiction, fantasy, books about World War II, mysteries, or biographies, and we respect our own choices. We would probably react negatively to suggestions that we were wasting our time or that we should use our brains to better advantage. And we might not accept well-intentioned recommendations for different reading matter if these suggestions were couched in critical terms.

So, too, teachers would make a big mistake if they ordered students to "Stop reading those crummy books; they'll rot your brain." Whenever we're punitive about an act that we care about, we're not on safe ground. And we do care about reading. If we respond to our students' passions, to the things that pull them, to the things that engross them, we can use these interests and build on them.

On the other hand, we also have a responsibility as teachers to widen our students' world. If a child reads only nonfiction about World War II he or she might be willing to be guided to some of the fictional works about that war. Certainly there is fiction that is written as compellingly, authentically, and truthfully as some of the historical accounts. From there, based on the child's acknowledged interest, the child might be interested in biographies of some of the people who lived through the war, or, perhaps, some high fantasy that involves good and evil, or that contains mythic warfare. Does a child like horror? Perhaps some myths from different cultures would be of interest. Fairy tales from around the world contain many of the elements of today's horror stories, and might be attractive to these readers.

There is an enormous difference between "Don't read that trash." and "Oh, you like that? Well then, you'll probably *love* this." And "You enjoyed that book? I just read an interesting book that is very much like that, only it's about ..." We're not trying to make them stop reading what they love; we're trying to expand their repertoire and to build on their base of interest.

Some people think that they must read a set of specific books or they will die unfulfilled. The sad story is that because we will never be able to read all of the books we want to, we die unfulfilled. Of course we all have our favorites that we think everyone should read, and we become excellent advocates of those books because we got so much from them, but we probably each have a different list. The parent, teacher or librarian may even, on occasion, want to put some different types of books into children's hands in a very directive way, in order to ensure exposure to different authors and varying genres.

Reading aloud is also a potent way of inviting children into books they might not choose on their own. We invite people to expand their world when we read aloud to them, especially if we cultivate our oral reading abilities. It is the teacher's responsibility not only to keep on introducing new and more books to the students but also to teach children how to choose books for themselves. This is an ongoing procedure, and there are several principles that govern the process.

First of all, children should be made aware that there is no such thing as a book that is too easy. Certainly, there are books that are too *empty*. But if a book has substance, it is not too easy for anyone. The stories in Lobel's *Frog and Toad* series (1979-1986), for example, examine philosophical and societal questions in most of the episodes. They can be read and enjoyed at a preschool level, but they can also be appreciated by adults, and by all the ages in between.

There is, on the other hand, such a thing as a book that is too hard. The subject matter or the abstract quality of the ideas may be too difficult for some children. For example, *Alan and Naomi* (1977), by Myron Levoy is a beautifully written book about the effects of the Holocaust on a child, Naomi, and of the attempts of another child, Alan, to help her overcome her trauma. The book addresses many issues and arouses many emotions. It explores anti-semitism, emotional illness, existential questioning, and friendship. It can probably be read and understood by alert fifth-graders and older children, but younger readers would very likely have a hard time with it. There are books on the Holocaust for younger readers, such as Judith Kerr's *When Hitler Stole Pink Rabbit* (1972), that are not as painful or deep, but that are, nevertheless, quality literature.

Other books, such as Julius Lester's *This Strange New Feeling*

(1985), are also appropriate for older readers, and would probably prove somewhat frustrating for younger ones. The subjects of slavery and bigotry are important for readers of all ages to encounter and think about, but for younger readers, Mildred Taylor's *Song of the Trees* (1984), *Roll of Thunder, Hear My Cry* (1976), and *Let the Circle Be Unbroken* (1983), with their equally powerful stories, protagonists who are younger, and less complex language, may make the subject more accessible. Sometimes it is simply the words and sentence structure that are too sophisticated for a young reader, and the child is likely to become frustrated. Children should learn to judge whether or not they can handle the book's level of mechanical difficulty. The teacher can also help advise children about the appropriateness of the book's subject matter.

Children get very good at assessing their ability to handle a book, especially if they are not punished for selecting books that the teacher labels as "too easy," and are not rewarded for choosing books that are too frustrating or demanding. They should be helped to provide challenges for themselves, not in the mechanics of the text, but by being encouraged to ask probing questions of themselves and the author. They should be taught to become active and thoughtful readers rather than mere word-sayers. They need to read and respond, wonder, compare, question, think, and enjoy.

How can I assign a grade to my students' reading if I'm not giving them the basal reader unit tests? The issue of grading a child's reading is a difficult one in any case. In a basal program a teacher often finds that a child who is reading well, is articulate, and who demonstrates an understanding of the material may not necessarily do well on the paper-and-pencil tests. It is to be hoped that the teacher takes this into consideration when assigning a grade to the child. In the best of circumstances, a child is not graded, but is, rather, a partner in an agreed-upon assessment plan. If a grade must be imposed, then it is best for teachers, administrators, children, and parents to decide ahead of time what criteria will be applied for judging the children's reading achievement. Such factors as engaging in the reading, time spent, amount read, sharing-projects completed, understanding demonstrated, and improvement shown during conferences and through portfolios of work might be considered. Evaluation has three functions in any educational program:

1. It is used as a means of designing curriculum. The conference is an excellent evaluation (diagnostic) strategy for this purpose.
2. Evaluation often serves as a way of reporting to parents, supervisors and administrators, and community, what is going on in

the classroom that is worthy of note, as well as how well the children are progressing. Bulletin boards, invitations to the community to be present at dramatic presentations and other sharing of the children's reading, collections of the children's work, journals that indicate the ongoing dialogue the children have with each other and with the teacher about their reading, records that the children keep on their reading, and records that the teacher keeps on the children's reading are all legitimate and informative strategies for this function of evaluation.

3. Evaluation tells us what worked, how well we did, how well the children did, and how well we met external expectations. This is the most problematic aspect of evaluation. It is value-laden; it can be ambiguous; and it certainly can be tension-provoking. Do we judge our own and our students' success by how hard we worked? Is effort the criterion? Do we judge by some normative standard of ability? How do we decide on what norms to use? What relationship do these norms have to our own curriculum and goals? If there is a predetermined standard, then we can help our children to meet this standard, and make certain that they know that it may be outside the palpable evidence of their real achievement.

The point is, that no matter what hoops we must jump through to maintain our survival, there are always the factors of the children's own work and the real business of the classroom to consider. Any substantive assessment should be a collaborative effort with the children and their parents, and everyone involved should be aware of the criteria and goals driving the outcome.

In fact, children will probably achieve the same scores on tests that they would have, had they been subjected to the basal reader. A few sessions on how to take standardized tests will probably increase their scores, but they need to know that standardized tests have no relationship to real reading. (See the chapter on test-taking in Lee and Rudman, *Leading to Reading*, 1984.) If you must, give the children the basal unit tests. They will probably be able to handle them quite well.

Recognize, however, that any grade is an artificial imposition. The notes you take during conference time and after small group instructional sessions, the logs and portfolios the children maintain that keep track of their reading, conversations you have with your students, and the daily demonstrations of their ability will be the best indicators of success.

How can I be sure that my students are gaining all of the necessary skills of reading if I don't use a basal? The assumption here is that reading is composed of a heap of skills common to everyone and measurable in isolation. In fact, skilled readers become more skillful through the act of reading. Yes, intervention and guidance are helpful, but these cannot be managed well outside the context of a child who is reading and responding to his or her own personal interaction with the text. The best way to see if a child is a skilled reader is to observe the child reading and reacting to the reading, and to see what use the child makes of reading.

Reading viewed holistically can provide evidence of a child's abilities. Children who are selecting good material, understanding what they read, discussing it intelligently, and sharing it with their peers are probably in no danger of missing out on necessary "skills."

What about phonics? Not every child needs direct or extensive phonics instruction. It is only after a child understands that reading is the construction of meaning from print that phonics can be helpful. After all, If you saw a line of print that read: "Indim stroud glenched frack lollibly." you would be able to say the words, but you would not understand what they meant. This is not reading; this is word calling. Children must learn that until and unless print makes sense, it is not reading. Therefore I strongly urge that you not begin with, "Sound it out." Rather, say "What makes sense here?" Then, after speculating and suggesting what makes sense, a child might use the clue of the first or last letter as a further check on the word. Graphophonemic cueing is one of the three systems all good readers use (syntactic and semantic are the other two) but the semantic should come first.

I can't possibly read every book each child reads if I permit everyone to be reading something different. How can I handle all those books? If you haven't read a book, then, when you ask a child to tell you about it, you will really be interested in the answer, and you will not have a preconceived notion of what that answer will be. You can probably detect illogic or confusion. Then you can invite the child to show you the evidence of his or her response. Or you can ask if anyone else has read the same book, and recommend a conversation among those children.

If the child is inventing a story out of whole cloth, first of all, that demonstrates a talent for story-making that is to be commended. Second, it is a signal to you that this child has some need to play a certain kind of game, and that is useful diagnostic information for you. The conference is NOT a test. It is an opportunity to collect information and to engage in literary conversation. If a child perceives this as a threat, then there are activities that can be done to transform the situation into one that is more conducive to learning.

Another advantage to the teacher's not having read every book is that it provides occasions for the child to be an influence on the teacher and entice the teacher into wanting to read the book.

I'm just not comfortable with the idea of self-selection. I like literature, and I think I could find some novels and some other sorts of books that I could get to know well and could use with my children. By all means, start with your selecting several books and inviting your students to select one that attracts them. You may wind up with three groups again, but at least these will be groups that have, in some measure, exercised their own choice. The groups will last only as long as the book discussion lasts, and the children will have the opportunity afterward to hear about the other books. It is important here to avoid a sense of top, middle and low groups. Encourage the "best" readers to join a group reading an "easy" book so that you can demonstrate how to probe the depths and intricacies of a book with simple text.

How do I help children probe the depths and intricacies of a book with simple text? Let's go back to *Frog and Toad Are Friends,* by Arnold Lobel. On one level, it can probably be read by a second-grader. There is an episode in this book called "The Swim." In this story Frog and Toad go swimming. Toad requests that Frog hide his eyes while Toad puts on a funny-looking bathing suit. Frog obliges, and the two friends swim happily for a while. A number of animals (among them a turtle, some dragon flies, a mouse, a snake) congregate on the river bank, impervious to Frog's plea that they honor Toad's request to leave. When Toad emerges, dripping, from the river, all of the animals, including Frog, laugh at him. Toad asks Frog why he is laughing, and Frog tells him it is because he *does* look funny in his bathing suit. Toad says, "I told you so.", picks up his clothes, and goes home. That is the end of the story.

Low-level questioning would ask children to "Name the animals on the riverbank." and "Tell in what order they appeared." Who cares? It makes no difference to the story. One of the problems with these types of questions is that they too often have little relationship to the sense of the story, or send the child looking for a particular word or sentence without much thought required. In discussing this story children may want to invent the dialogue that Frog and Toad would have the next day. Since the author has not supplied us with any more details, it is up to the reader to use what he or she knows about Frog's and Toad's character, how they have resolved differences before this, and, in general, how friendship works.

Children might also want to debate Toad's reaction. Was he angry? hurt? self-righteous? resigned? I know that after I read this story for the first time, I needed comforting. The children assured me that the two friends would make up. They informed me that "Everyone gets laughed at sometimes." They also criticized Toad for making such a fuss about his bathing suit, which, they were convinced, his mother made him wear.

They reasoned that, since there was another story following "The Swim" that the friendship would be sustained. If this story were the last one in the book, they might not be so sure. In any case, the story stimulates prediction, analysis, construction of several scenarios, criticism, and discussion. And children above second grade would not be offended if they were invited to engage in genuine conversation about the story, even though the words are easy to read.

How do we motivate reluctant readers to read literature? At least, in a basal, they're forced to read a certain amount. This is one of the best features of a literature-based reading program. Children read more, and are happier about it than in any other sort of program. The high quality of the books, language, pictures, and the opportunity to make some decisions for themselves, as well as the fact that this is "real" reading, and they know it, provide intrinsic motivation. The sharing part of the program also helps interest children in the books that their peers are reading. They gain respect and confidence in themselves and in their peers. They are no longer placed in ability groups, but interact with other groups of children on tasks that make sense. The fact that they can go at their own pace also adds to the enjoyment and popularity of the program.

If I'm having conferences one-on-one with children, or teaching small groups, what are the other children doing? What happens to discipline? It turns out that discipline is no problem in this program. The children know just what they should be doing, and they do it. They don't engage in meaningless exercises that have to be graded by the teacher; they are interacting with peers, reading the books of their choice, reading aloud or listening to a partner read, working on their sharing, writing in their logs, or doing research. Because they share the responsibility for the success of the program they rarely sabotage it.

If each child is reading a different book, how can they have discussions with each other? One group might want to talk about the interesting characters they're reading about, and what makes them interesting. Another group might be able to discuss the settings of the various stories, and the part the setting plays in conveying the sense of the book. Still another group might get together because they are reading a particular type of book, such as horse stories, mysteries, or books about divorce, and they might want to compare and contrast how the authors handle different aspects of these common elements.

Every folk or fairy tale has several versions, and the differences are often remarkable. For example, several children might be reading different stories of "Cinderella", which has more than a thousand variants. Among them is *Yeh Shen* (1982) by Ai Ling Louie, with illustrations by Ed Young. How does this oldest of Cinderellas compare with those that followed? How do the different elements affect the impact of the story? This sort of discussion can get children who might not ordinarily be attracted to fantasy or folktales to become interested in the intriguing differences among them.

This may be all well and good for advanced readers, but how about beginning readers and children in need of remediation? It is precisely the beginning reader and the child who has been labeled a "remedial" reader who need this program the most. It is essential that children understand from the start that reading has meaning. It is also essential that children view reading as pleasurable rather than punitive, and that they be permitted to build upon their successes rather than focus on their failures.

Wordless picture books can help children use books to foster their story-telling skills. (A list of some wordless books is located at the end of this chapter.) If their words are written down, they can probably reconstruct their own stories using the pictures as clues. They can certainly draw their own pictures and have captions written for these pictures. They can then read their captions again and again. There are many books that are beautifully illustrated and respectfully written, even though they are simple to read. There are also cassette-book packages where professional actors read the storybook aloud. Many children find that they can read along after they have heard the stories a number of times. Children can make these learning packages of their own once they have mastered a story. Then their cassette can be used by a peer. Thus children can aid in instructing each other, even when they have not ever thought of themselves before as the "best" readers.

Summary

We are advocating a reading program that focuses on meaning, helps children learn to select their own materials, and apply them to their learning across the curriculum. These materials should be varied, but should always reflect the child's interests and needs, and should make sense in and of themselves. When literature is used as the base of a reading program, and when the teacher and child engage in respectful and interesting conversations about the literature, then children will come to books with joy and with a sense of wonder.

As Marcia Burchby eloquently states in her article, "Literature and Whole Language," in *The New Advocate* (Spring, 1988),

> Teaching reading in a way that will democratically empower students means going well beyond the basals. It means being concerned with children having power over words, rather than words having power over them. (p. 118)

References and Selected Resources

Armstrong, Joyce Carroll. *Picture Books: Integrated Teaching, Writing. Listening, Speaking, Viewing, and Thinking.* Englewood, CO: Teacher Ideas Press, 1991.

Atwell, Nancie. *In the Middle: Writing, Reading, and Learning with Adolescents.* Portsmouth, NH: Boynton/Cook Publishers, 1987.

Barchers, Suzanne L. *Creating and Managing the Literature Classroom.* Englewood, CO: Teacher Ideas Press, 1990.

Blass, Rosanne J. and Jurenka, Nancy E. Allen. *Responding to Literature.* Englewood, CO: Teacher Ideas Press, 1991.

Burchby, Marcia. "Literature and Whole Language," in *The New Advocate,* vol. 1, no. 2, Spring, 1988, pp. 114-123.

Calkins, Lucy McCormick. *Living Between the Lines.* Portsmouth, NH: Heinemann, 1991.

Carbo, Marie; Dunn, Rita; and Dunn, Kenneth. *Teaching Students to Read Through Their Individual Learning Styles.* Englewood Cliffs, NJ: Prentice-Hall. 1986.

Clayton, Lucille R. *Explorations: Educational Activities for Young Children.* Englewood, CO: Teacher Ideas Press, 1991.

Cullinan Bernice E., editor. *Children's Literature in the Reading Program.* Newark, DE: International Reading Association, 1987.

Draper, Marcella X.; and Schwietert, Louise H. *A Practical Guide to Individualized Reading* revised and edited by May Lazar, publication # 40, New York City Board of Education, Bureau of Educational Research, October, 1960.

Eldredge, J. Lloyd; and Butterfield, Dennie. "Alternatives to Traditional Reading Instruction," *The Reading Teacher,* Vol. 40, no. 1 October, 1986, pp 32-38.

Fredericks, Anthony D. *The Integrated Curriculum: Books for Reluctant Readers. Grades 2-5.* Englewood, CO: Teacher Ideas Press, 1992.

Fredericks, Anthony D. *Social Studies through Children's Literature.* Englewood, CO: Teacher Ideas Press, 1991.

Goodman, Ken. "Look What They've Done to Judy Blume!: The 'Basalization' of Children's Literature" in *The New Advocate,* vol. 1, no. 1, 1988, pp 29-41.

Goodman, Ken. *What's Whole in Whole Language?* Portsmouth, NH. Heinemann, 1986.

Goodman, Kenneth S., Shannon, Patrick, Freeman, Yvonne S., and Murphy, Sharon. *Report Card on Basal Readers.* New York: Richard C. Owen, Publishers, Inc., 1988.

Goodman, Yetta M., Hood, Wendy J. and Goodman, Kenneth S. *Organizing for Whole Language.* Portsmouth, NH: and Heinemann, Toronto, Canada: Irwin, 1991.

Graves, Donald. *Writing: Teachers and Children at Work.* Portsmouth, NH: Heinemann, 1983.

Green, Judith

Griffiths, Rachel and Clyne, Margaret. *Books You Can Count On: Linking Mathematics and Literature.* Portsmouth, NH: Heinemann, 1991.

Hansen, Jane. *When Writers Read.* Portsmouth, NH: Heinemann, 1987.

Hornsby, David and Sukarna, Deborah. *Read On: A Conference Approach To Reading.* Portsmouth, NH: Heinemann, 1988.

Huck, Charlotte S., Hepler, Susan, and Hickman, Janet. *Children's Literature in the Elementary School,* 5th ed. Holt, Rinehart & Winston, 1993.

Jacobs, Leland, et al. *Individualizing Reading Practices.* Edited by Alice Miel. Teachers College Press, 1974.

Jenkins, Christine and Freeman, Sally. *Novel Experiences: Literature Units.* Englewood, CO: Teacher Ideas Press, 1991.

Kelly, Joanne. *The Battle of Books.* Englewood, CO: Teacher Ideas Press, 1990.

Kinghorn, Harriett R. and Pelton, Mary Helen. *Every Child a Storyteller: A Handbook of Ideas.* Englewood, CO: Teacher Ideas Press, 1991.

Kinghorn, Harriet R. and Smith, Fay Hill. *At Day's End: Book-Related Activities for Small Groups.* Englewood, CO: Libraries Unlimited, Inc., 1991.

Kruise, Carol Sue. *Those Blooming Books: A Handbook for Extending Thinking Skills.* Littleton, CO: Libraries Unlimited, Inc., 1987.

Kruise, Carol Sue. *Learning Through Literature.* Englewood, C0: Teacher Ideas Press, 1990.

Lee, Barbara, and Rudman, Masha Kabakow. *Leading to Reading.* New York, NY: Berkley, 1984.

McElmeel, Sharron L. *Adventure with Social Studies through Literature.* Englewood, C0: Teacher Ideas Press, 1991.

Mohr, Carolyn, Nixon, Dorothy and Vickers, Shirley. *Books That Heal: A Whole Language Approach.* Englewood, C0: Teacher Ideas Press, 1991.

Mohr, Carolyn, Nixon Dorothy and Vickers, Shirley. *Thinking Activities For Books Children Love.* Englewood, C0: Teacher Ideas Press, 1988.

Moore, Terry Jeffers and Hampton, Anita Brent. *Book Bridges: Story-Inspired Activities for Children Three through Eight.* Englewood, C0: Teacher Ideas Press, 1991.

Neamen, Mimi and Strong, Mary. *Literature Circles: Cooperative Learning for Grades 3-8.* Englewood, CO: Teacher Ideas Press, 1992.

Newman, Judith D. *Whole Language: Theory In Use.* Portsmouth, NH: Heinemann, 1985.

Norton, Donna E. *Through the Eyes of a Child.* 3rd edition, Columbus, OH: Merrill, 1991.

Olsen, Mary Lou. *Creative Connections: Literature and the Reading Program.* Littleton, CO: Libraries Unlimited, Inc., 1987.

Pappas, Christine C., Kiefer, Barbara Z. and Levstik, Linda S. *An Integrated Language Perspective in the Elementary School.* White Plains, NY: Longman, 1990.

Polkingham, Anne T. and Toohey, Catherine. *More Creative Encounters: Activities to Expand Children's Responses to Literature.* Englewood, CO: Libraries Unlimited, Inc., 1988.

Routman, Regie. *Transitions: From Literature to Literacy.* Portsmouth, NH: Heinemann, 1988.

Rudman, Masha Kabakow. *Children's Literature: An Issues Approach.* 3rd edition, White Plains, NY: Longman, 1993.

Rudman, Masha Kabakow, and Pearce, Anna Markus. *For Love of Reading.* Yonkers, NY: Consumer Reports Books, 1988.

Shanahan, Timothy. *Reading and Writing Together: New Perspectives For the Classroom.* Norwood, MA: Christopher-Gordon Publishers, 1990.

Smith, Frank. *Reading Without Nonsense.* 2nd edition, New York, NY: Teachers College Press, 1985.

Strippling, Barbara K. and Pitts, Judy M. *Brainstorms and Blueprints: Teaching Library Research as a Thinking Process.* Englewood, CO: Libraries Unlimited, Inc., 1988.

Thomas, Jane Resh. "Books in the Classroom: Unweaving the Rainbow" in *The Horn Book,* November/December, 1987.

Trelease, Jim. *The New Read-Aloud Handbook.* New York: Viking, 1989.

Turner, Rebecca. "How the Basals Stack Up," in *Learning,* Vol, No. April. 1988.

Tway, Eileen. (ed), *Reading Ladders for Human Relations.* 6th edition, Urbana, IL: National Council of Teachers of English, 1983.

Veatch, Jeanette. *How to Teach Reading with Children's Books.* 2nd edition. New York: Richard C. Owen Publishers, Inc., 1968.

Veatch, Jeanette. *Individualized Reading: For Success in Classrooms.* New York: Appleton Century Croft, 1954.

Veatch, Jeanette. *Reading in the Elementary School.* 2nd edition. New York: Richard C. Owen Publishers, Inc., 1976.

Watson, Dorothy. *Ideas and Insights.* Urbana, IL: National Council of Teachers of English, 1987.

Weaver, Constance. *Understanding Whole Language: From Principles to Practice.* Portsmouth, NH: Heinemann, 1990.

Children's Books Mentioned in this Chapter

Brown, Margaret Wise. The Runaway Bunny. New York: Harper & Row, 1977.

Carle, Eric. *The Very Hungry Caterpillar. New* York: Philomel, 1969.

Cooney, Barbara. *Miss Rumphius.* New York: Penquin, 1985.

Hall, Donald. *Ox-Cart Man.* Illustrated by Barbara Cooney. New York: Viking, 1979.

Kerr, Judith. *When Hitler Stole Pink Rabbit.* New York: Coward-McCann, 1972.

Lester, Julius. *This Strange New Feeling.* New York: Scholastic, 1985.

Levoy, Myron. *Alan and Naomi.* New York: Harper & Row, 1987.

Lobel, Arnold. *Frog and Toad Are Friends.* New York: Harper & Row, 1985.

Louie, Ai Ling. *Yeh Shen,* with illustrations by Ed Young. New York: Putnam, 1982.

Taylor, Mildred. *Song of the Trees,* New York: Bantam, 1975.

Taylor, Mildred. *Roll of Thunder. Hear My Cry.* New York: Dial, 1976.

Taylor, Mildred. *Let the Circle Be Unbroken.* New York: Dial, 1981.

White, E.B. *Charlotte's Web.* New York: Harper & Row, 1952.

Wordless Books

Ahlberg, Allan and Janet. *Each Peach Pear Plum.* New York: Puffin, 1986.

Alexander, Martha. *Out! Out! Out!* New York: Dial, 1968.

Anno, Mitsumasa. *Anno's Alphabet.* Illustrated by the author. New York: Crowell, 1975.

Anno's Animals. New York: Putnam, 1979.

Anno's Britain. Illustrated by the author. New York: Putnam. 1985.

Anno's Counting Book. Illustrated by the author. New York: Crowell, 1975.

Anno's Journey. Illustrated by the author. New York: Putnam, 1981.

Dr. Anno's Magical Midnight Circus. New York: Weatherhill, 1972.

Topsy-Turvies: Pictures to Stretch the Imagination. New York: Weatherhill, 1970.

Upside-Downers: More Pictures to Stretch the Imagination. New York: Weatherhill, 1971.

Arnosky, Jim. *Mouse Numbers and Letters.* Saddle Brook, NJ: Harcourt Brace Jovanovich, 1982.

Mouse Writing. Saddle Brook NJ: Harcourt Brace Jovanovich, 1983.

Aruego, Jose. *Look What I Can Do.* New York: Macmillan, 1988.

Barton, Byron. *Where's Al?* Boston: Houghton Mifflin, 1972.

Briggs, Raymond. *Father Christmas.* New York: Putnam, 1973.

Father Christmas Goes On Holiday. New York: Penguin, 1977.

The Snowman. Illustrated by the author. New York: Random House, 1986.

Carle, Eric. *Do You Want to be My Friend?* New York: Putnam, 1988.

I See a Song. Saxonville: Picture Book Studio, 1989.

One, Two, Three to the Zoo. New York: Putnam, 1990.

Charlot, Martin, *Sunnyside Up.* Honolulu: Island Heritage, 1972.

Corbett, Grahame. *Who is Next?* New York: Dial, 1982.

Crews, Donald. *Truck.* New York: Penguin, 1985.

Cristini, Ermanno, and Puricelli, Luigi. *In My Garden.* Saxonville: Picture Book Studio, 1985.

In the Pond. Saxonville: Picture Book Studio, 1985.

Daughtry, Duanne. *What's Inside?* New York: Knopf, 1984.

de Paola, Tomie. *The Hunter and the Animals: A Wordless Picture Book.* New York: Holiday House, 1981.

Pancakes for Breakfast. Saddle Brook, NJ: Harcourt Brace Jovanovich, 1978.

Sing, Pierrot, Sing. Saddle Brook, NJ: Harcourt Brace Jovanovich, 1988.

Degen, Bruce. *Aunt Possum and the Pumpkin Man.* New York: Harper & Row. 1977.

Emberley, Ed. *Ed Emberley's Big Green Drawing Book.* Boston: Little, Brown, and Co, 1979.

Fujikawa, Gyo. *Millie's Secret.* New York: Putnam, 1978.

My Favorite Thing. New York: Putnam, 1978.

Goodall, John S. *The Adventures of Paddy Pork.* Saddle Brook, NJ: Harcourt Brace Jovanovich, 1968.

The Ballooning Adventures of Paddy Pork. Saddle Brook, NJ: Harcourt Brace Jovanovich, 1969.

Creepy Castle. New York: Atheneum, 1975.

Jacko. Saddle Brook, NJ: Harcourt Brace Jovanovich, 1972.

Paddy Goes Travelling. New York: Macmillan, 1982.

Paddy Under Water. New York: Macmillan, 1984.

Shrewbettina 's Birthday. Saddle Brook, NJ: Harcourt Brace Jovanovich, 1983.

The Story of an English Village. New York: Macmillan, 1979.

The Surprise Picnic. New York: Macmillan, 1977.

Gorey, Edward. *The Tunnel Calamity.* New York: Putnam, 1984.

Greeley, Valerie. *Farm Animals.* New York: Bedrick Books, 1984.

Field Animals. New York: Bedrick Books, 1984.

Pets. New York: Bedrick Books, 1984.

Zoo Animals. New York: Bedrick Books, 1984.

Hauptmann, Tatjana. *A Day in the Life of Petronella Pig.* New York: Smith Publications, 1980.

Hill, Eric. *At Home.* New York: Random House, 1983.

Hoban, Tana. *Big Ones, Little Ones.* New York: Greenwillow, 1976.

Circles, Triangles, and Squares. New York: Macmillan, 1974.

Dig, Drill, Dump, Fill. New York: Greenwillow, 1975.

Is it Larger? Is it Smaller? New York: Greenwillow, 1985.

Is it Red? Is it Yellow? Is it Blue? New York: Greenwillow, 1978.

Is it Rough? Is it Smooth? Is it Shiny? New York: Greenwillow, 1984.

Look Again. New York: Macmillan, 1971.

One, Two, Three. New York: Greenwillow, 1985.

Round and Round and Round. New York: Greenwillow, 1983.

Shapes Shapes Shapes. New York: Greenwillow, 1986.

Take Another Look. New York: Greenwillow, 1981.

What Is it? New York: Greenwillow, 1985.

Where is it? New York: Macmillan, 1974.

Hughes, Shirley. *Up and Up.* New York: Lothrop Lee & Shepard, 1986.

Hutchins, Pat. *Changes, Changes.* New York: Macmillan, 1971.

Keats, Ezra Jack. *Clemintina's Cactus.* New York: Viking, 1982.

Kitten for a Day. New York: Macmillan, 1974.

Krahn, Fernando. *Arthur's Adventure in the Abandoned House.* New York: Dutton, 1981.

How Santa Claus had a Long and Difficult Journey Delivering His Presents. New York: Dell, 1988.

A Little Love Story. New York: Harper & Row, 1976.

The Mystery of the Giant Footprints. New York: Dutton, 1977.

Robot-Bot-Bot. New York: Dutton, 1979.

The Secret in the Dungeon. Boston: Houghton Mifflin, 1983.

Sleep Tight, Alex Pumpernickel. Boston: Little, Brown and Company, 1982.

Lemke, Horst. *Places and Faces.* Merrick: Scroll, 1978.

Lionni, Leo. *What?* New York: Pantheon, 1983.

When? New York: Pantheon, 1983.

Where? New York: Pantheon, 1983.

Who? New York: Pantheon, 1983.

McCully, Emily Arnold. *Picnic.* New York: Harper & Row, 1984.

Marol, Jean-Claude. *Vagabul and His Shadow.* Mankato, MN: Creative Education, 1982.

Vagabul Escapes. Mankato, MN: Creative Education, 1982.

Vagabul in the Clouds. Mankato, MN: Creative Education, 1982.

Vagabul Skis. Mankato, MN: Creative Education, 1982.

Mayer, Mercer. *Ah-Choo.* New York: Dial, 1976.

A Boy, A Dog, and A Frog. New York: Dial, 1979.

Bubble Bubble. New York: Macmillan, 1980.

Frog Goes to Dinner. New York: Dial, 1977.

Frog on His Own. New York: Dial, 1980.

Frog, Where are You? New York: Dial, 1980.

Hiccup. New York: Dial, 1976.

Mayer, Mercer, and Mayer, Marianna. *One Frog Too Many.* New York: Dial, 1977.

Mendoza, George. *And I Must Hurry for the Sea is Coming In.* Englewood-Cliffs, NJ: Prentice-Hall, 1971.

Morris, Terry Nell. *Good Night, Dear Monster!* New York: Knopf, 1980.

Ormerod, Jan. *Moonlight.* New York: Penguin, 1984.

Sunshine. New York: Penguin, 1984.

Oxenbury, Helen. *Beach Day.* New York: Dial, 1990.

Dressing. New York: Simon & Schuster, 1981.

Mother's Helper. New York: Dial, 1982.

Playing. New York: Simon & Schuster, 1981.

Working. New York: Simon & Schuster, 1981.

Piers, Helen. *Peekaboo series (Peekaboo Kitten, Peekaboo Mouse* and *Peekaboo Rabbit).* San Diego: Harcourt Brace Jovanovich, 1986.

Roennfeldt, Robert. *A Day on the Avenue.* New York: Viking, 1984.

Rojankovsky, Feodor. *Animals on the Farm.* New York: Knopf, 1967.

Sasaki, Isao. *Snow.* New York: Viking, 1982.

Spier, Peter. *Noah's Ark.* New York: Doubleday, 1981.

    Peter Spier's Rain. New York: Doubleday, 1987.

Tafuri, Nancy. *Early Morning in the Barn.* New York: Penguin, 1986.

Turkle, Brinton. *Deep in the Forest.* New York: Dutton, 1987.

Ueno, Noriko. *Elephant's Buttons.* New York: Harper & Row, 1973.

Van Allsburg, Chris. *The Mysteries of Harris Burdick.* Boston: Houghton Mifflin, 1984.

Ward, Lynd. *The Silver Pony: A Story in Pictures.* Boston: Houghton Mifflin, 1973.

Weisner, David. *Tuesday.* New York: Clarion, 1991.

Winter, Paula. *The Bear and the Fly: A Story.* New York: Crown, 1976.

Young, Ed. *The Other Bone.* New York: Harper & Row, 1984.

    Up a Tree. New York: Harper & Row, 1983.

Poetry — Practically

Lee Bennett Hopkins

Introduction

In the introduction to my collection, *Side by Side* (1988), I told about a letter I received from a child saying how much she loved poetry. The letter ended with a P.S.: "A poem refreshed the world."

I read that P.S. over and over again, and it has stuck in my brain.

I, and so many others, have written endlessly about the merits of using poetry with children in homes, classrooms, and libraries; countless definitions of poetry have been penned; yet one child—one voice—says it all, in a mere five words.

Scholars can talk about the magic poetry brings into children's lives. They can shout the message repeatedly. It will not be heard or listened to however, unless you yourself experience the impact that only poetry can convey.

At the end of this chapter I emphatically urge you to give children poetry and watch the magic take over.

Bring on the Books

If we want to bring children and poetry together, we must immerse them in verse while involving them.

An effective method is to have students classify four basic types of poetry volumes: Single Collections, General Anthologies, Specific Anthologies, and Poetry Picture Books.

After sharing several books in each category and pointing out the differences, girls and boys can sort and place them in a poetry library corner under appropriate headings.

Single Collections

A book of poems written by an individual poet comprise single collections of poetry.

General Collections

General collections are books put together by an anthologist to highlight a variety of topics. Books of this nature are usually divided into sections, offering a wide array of themes and a diversity of poets' work. A representative volume is *Talking Like the Rain* (1992), selected by X. J. and Dorothy Kennedy, a bountiful collection of more than 120 poems grouped into nine sections featuring topics as "Families," "Wind and Weather," and "Calendars and Clocks." The poets range from past masters (Edward Lear and Robert Louis Stevenson) to contemporary authors (Nikki Giovanni and William Stafford).

Specific Collections

Specific collections, compiled by an anthologist, focus on one specific theme, bringing it together by using a variety of works by different poets. Representative volumes include *If the Owl Calls Again* (1990), selected by Myra Cohn Livington, and *Extra Innings* (1993), selected by Lee Bennett Hopkins.

Livingston's volume, divided into five sections, portrays the birds from many perspectives: "Owls in Flight," "Owls of Night," and "Owls to Fright." The broad range of readings includes work from the Elizabethan era to contemporary selections by Tony Johnston, Deborah Chandra, and others.

Hopkins' selection of nineteen poems about baseball contains work from the past such as "Casey at the Bat" by Ernest Lawrence Thayer to contemporary writings by J. Patrick Lewis, Isabel Joshlin Glaser, and others.

Poetry Picture Books

Poetry Picture Books feature one poem by an individual poet, illustrated throughout by an artist who chose the work. Representative volumes include *Color* (1992) by Christina G. Rossetti and *A Road Might Lead to Anywhere* (1990) by Rachel Field.

Rossetti's familiar verse asking what is pink, red, blue, and white, etc. is illustrated in full-color etchings by Mary Teichman.

Field's verse is interpreted via full-color paper collages by Giles Laroche .

As readers dip in and out of poetry volumes they will become familiar with various poets. They might find a favorite work from a single collection appearing in one or several anthologies. In cases where the anthologies are illustrated, they can compare the different interpretations artists have rendered to depict the poems.

Anthologies can lead children to single collections. If they enjoy a particular poem they can seek out books by the same poet in school or public libraries. Using the acknowledgments that appear in anthologies can serve as both a guideline for selection and a learning experience for young researchers.

Children might also be encouraged to create their own mini-anthologies centered around a specific topic. These can be illustrated and added to the classroom library.

From Light Verse to Pure Poetry

In 1974, a new revolution of light verse stormed throughout the country via Shel Silverstein's *Where the Sidewalk Ends.* Six years later when *A Light in the Attic* (1981) was published, children of all ages continued to embrace his deft, sometimes irreverent rhymes with a passion. They continue to do so.

If Edward Lear was Lord of the Limerick of the nineteenth century, surely Silverstein is the most lauded purveyor of light verse of the twentieth.

Some children may not know of past or present day heroes or heroines but they *do* know Sarah Cynthia Stout, who refuses to take the garbage out; Geraldine, who shakes a cow to make a milk shake; and Jimmy Jet, who turned into a TV set.

Myra Cohn Livingston states:

> Silverstein's magnetism is not surprising to anyone in touch with children's feelings and their penchant for wild invention and hyperbole... behind the *seemingly* silly verses camouflaged in part by amusing pictures, breathes a twentieth-century moralist and didacticist... children, who normally shun didacticism in any form, accept it enthusiastically from Silverstein![1]

The work of Jack Prelutsky, another writer of light verse, remains popular fare in elementary classrooms. Although books by the prolific author appeared prior to Silverstein's, it was not until 1984, when *The New Kid on the Block* was published, that his name was linked to funny rhymes. The success of the volume was followed by *Something BIG Has Been Here* (1990).

Light verse is a good start to get children excited over rhythm and rhyme, but when the new kid on the block travels to where the sidewalk ends, it should be the start of new beginning, leading them to the wider world of poetry—pure poetry.

The Poets

Whereas light verse gets children to chuckle, laugh or guffaw, poetry by master writers helps them to see, hear, smell, touch, and feel the beauty of words strung together via forms unavailable anywhere else in our language.

By sharing works by the poets listed below you will bring the best poetry into readers lives.

The following represents poets whose work has appeared during the past two decades.[2] Nine of the poets have received the National Council of Teachers of English Excellence in Children's Poetry Award, established in 1977 to honor living American poets for their aggregate body of work. Initially the award was given annually. As of 1982, it has been presented every three years. Recipients include David McCord (1977), Aileen Fisher (1978), Karla Kuskin (1979), Myra Cohn Livingston (1980), Eve Merriam (1981), John Ciardi (1982), Lilian Moore (1985), Arnold Adoff (1988), and Valerie Worth (1991).

In addition to the above, other poets to introduce to readers of all ages include Ashley Bryan, Deborah Chandra, Barbara Juster Esbensen, Nikki Giovanni, Eloise Greenfield, Mary Ann Hoberman, X. J. Kennedy, and J. Patrick Lewis.

Arnold Adoff

From *black is brown is tan* (1973) to *In for Winter, Out for Spring* (1991), Adoff has offered his distinctive touch to the world of poetry. *black is brown is tan* is the first picture book of verse to depict an interracial family; *In for Winter, Out for Spring* celebrates family life via the cycle of the four seasons.

More whimsical are his *Eats* (1979) and *Chocolate Dreams* (1989), attesting his love of food.

Ashley Bryan

Alhough known for his picture books and collections of African American folktales and spirituals, Bryan's first book of poetry, *Sing to the Sun*, appeared in 1992. Words come alive via his tender, heartfelt text and glorious full-color illustrations. This collection marks the first book of poetry for children by an African-American male since Langston Hughes' The Dream Keeper appeared in 1932—a sixty-year span.

Deborah Chandra

Work by Chandra, an exciting talent to emerge in the 1990s, can be found in *Balloons* (1990), and *Rich Lizard* (1993). Tautly written poems reveal subjects as "Balloons... swollen creatures, / Holding their breath," and "Fog," which "...seeps in and presses / On trees and rocks and mud; / This old cold-blooded creature / Who wants its wet back rubbed."

John Ciardi
The work of Ciardi, who died in 1986, has been chanted and sung for decades. What child could resist "Mummy Slept Late and Daddy Fixed Breakfast" in *You Read to Me, I'll Read to You* (1962) or the many other wondrous rhymes he had created during his lifetime? In 1993, a welcome new edition of *Someone Could Win a Polar Bear* was reissued.

Barbara Juster Esbensen
The diversity of Esbensen's talent can be seen in *Cold Stars and Fireflies* (1984) and *Who Shrank My Grandmother's House?* (1992). *Cold Stars and Fireflies* takes readers on a poetry journey through the four seasons of the year. *Who Shrank My Grandmother's House?* features twenty-three selections about childhood discoveries—"Clouds," "Doors," and "Geode." Her free verse, "Pencils," where "noisy words yell for attention/and quiet words wait their turn..., is a must read for all would-be poetry writers.

Aileen Fisher
Fisher has been delighting readers with her ingenious verse for more than six decades. *Always Wondering* (1991) is a selection of her most requested poems from earlier works dating back to 1933.

Nikki Giovanni
In *Spin A Soft Black Song* (1985). the poet reflects life as experienced by an African-American child. *Vacation Time* (1980) contains nineteen selections on a variety of subjects in both rhyme and free verse.

Eloise Greenfield
Greenfield, one of the few African-American poets writing today, has created such favorite books as *Honey, I Love* (1972), sixteen poems of life's joys seen through the eyes of a child; *Under the Sunday Tree* (1988), portraits of life in the Bahamas; and *Night on Neighborhood Street* (1991), seventeen verses reflecting life in the city.

Mary Ann Hoberman
Fathers, Mothers, Sisters, Brothers (1991) is a collection of poems about different kinds of families. In addition to traditional family relationships, verses relate the pros and cons of being "An Only Child" and feelings about adoption and separation.

X. J. Kennedy

Kennedy is a poet who pens zany light verse, as seen in *Brats* (1986) and *Fresh Brats* (1989), as well as touching, sensitive poetry as in *The Beasts of Bethlehem* (1992).

The "Brats" books feature horrible children who wreak havoc on themselves and others. There is Sheila, who squirts a blob of Superglue into her Dad's right shoe; Liz Meyer, who flung her brothers into the dryer at the laundromat; and Brent, who substituted fresh cement in his mother's mudpack.

In *The Beasts of Bethlehem*, the poet offers nineteen sterling verses imagining what creatures at the manger on Christmas Eve might have said about the birth of Jesus Christ. Readers will look at the "Worm," "Ox," "Donkey," and "Mosquito" in a new light after reading and looking at this beautifully designed volume.

Karla Kuskin

Dogs & Dragons Trees & Dreams (1980) is a wondrous way to introduce Kuskin to readers. In addition to her terse verse, the notes preceding various selections tell how and why she came to write them.

Younger readers can sample her work in two "I Can Read" books— *Something Sleeping in the Hall* (1985) and *Soap Soup* (1992) .

J. Patrick Lewis

Lewis, another new exciting talent, has created works as *A Hippopotamusn't* (1990), *Two-Legged, Four-Legged, No-Legged Rhymes* (1991), both featuring poems about animals and insects, and *Earth Verses and Water Rhymes* (1991). celebrating the natural world. *Booklist* (May 1, 1990) stated: "If wordplay were an Olympic event, Lewis could go for the gold."

Myra Cohn Livingston

One of the most prolific poets writing today, Livingston has created a wide body of work over the past four decades since her first book, *Whispers*, appeared in 1958. Titles such as *There Was A Place* (1988), poems poignantly reflecting contemporary children dealing with social problems of our times, and *I Never Told* (1992), verses offering keen observations of a variety of things—"Statue of Liberty," "September Garden," "Rocky Mountains: Colorado"—show the poet's wide range of the use of form, style, and consumate talent.

David McCord

Another master of wordplay, McCord has been entertaining children since 1952 when his first book, *Far and Few* appeared. *One at a Time*

(1977), a 494-page treasury, contains works from seven earlier titles. In 1992, *All Day Long,* a collection of fifty rhymes that first appeared in 1965, made its first appearance in paperback. He has stated:

> ...poetry for children should keep reminding them without any feeling on their part that they are being reminded, that the English language is a most marvelous and availing instrument.[3]

David McCord plays it well.

Eve Merriam

A bonanza of eighty verses, consisting of over fifty out-of-print pieces and twelve new works penned before her death in 1992, appear in *The Singing Green* (1992), a lasting legacy from one of America's most beloved poets.

Lilian Moore

Although the verses in *Adam Mouse's Book of Poems* (1992) stem from her poetic-prose novels, *I'll Meet You at the Cucumbers* (1988) and *Don't Be Afraid, Amanda* (1992), the work stands on its own. A wide sampling of Moore's poetry appears in *Something New Begins* (1982), a timeless collection of contrasts between city and country life.

Valerie Worth

Worth's trademark is the creation of small poems—sharp, solid, eloquent evocations of ordinary objects to help readers see the everyday world in fresh ways. *All the Small Poems* (1987), a paperback volume, contains ninety-nine verses ranging in topics from an acorn to a zinnia.

Departing from her small poems, the collection *At Christmastime* (1992) presents a holiday cycle from early December to early spring, when a crumpled strand of tinsel glints by a muddy path.

The Professional Shelf

Three professional books offer practical ideas for rounding out poetry programs in classrooms.

In print for over two decades, *Pass the Poetry, Please!* by Lee Bennett Hopkins (1987) offers scores of ideas for bringing children and poetry together. In addition to twenty biographical sketches and interviews with poets, chapters focus on sparking children to write poetry and how to bring the world of verse into the classroom "as naturally as breathing."

"Like a song, poetry is meant to be heard," states Nancy Larrick in *Let's Do A Poem!* (1991). The subtitle of the volume says it all: "Introducing Poetry to Children Through Listening, Singing, Chanting, Impromptu Choral Reading, Body Movement, Dance, and Dramatization." Included throughout the text are ninety-eight songs and poems to illustrate each idea. Larrick, a distinguished reading expert and a well-known anthologist, offers suggestions appropriate from preschool through junior high school students.

Although Myra Cohn Livingston's *Poem-Making* (1991) is published as a book for middle- to upper-grade students, teachers will uncover a wealth of information to spark children to begin the poetry writing process. Throughout the book Livingston uses examples from a bevy of poets to underscore various ways to approach the creation of poetry.

End Note

Every day is a great day for poetry. We must lead children into the genre—ignite the spark for them to appreciate it, love it, and make it a part of their lives. This is one of the greatest gifts we can give to our students. There is a place for poetry—every day, everywhere—all of the time. Give children poetry. It is a gift to last them forever and ever.

References

1. Livingston, Myra Cohn. *Climb Into the Bell Tower: Essays on Poetry*. New York: HarperCollins, 1990, pp. 94-95.
2. For "A Chronology of American Poets for Children—1920-1990" see "American Poetry for Children—The Twentieth Century," by Lee Bennett Hopkins in *Fanfare* (Christopher-Gordon Publishers, Inc., 1992).
3. Hopkins, Lee Bennett. *Pass the Poetry, Please!* (revised edition). New York: HarperCollins, 1987, p. 104.

Books Cited in This Chapter

Adoff, Arnold. *black is brown is tan.* Illustrated by Emily Arnold McCully. New York: HarperCollins, 1973.

Chocolate Dreams Illustrated by Ture MacCombie. New York: Lothrop, 1989.

Eats: Poems. Illustrated by Susan Russo. New York: Lothrop, 1979.

In for Winter, Out for Spring. Illustrated by Jerry Pinkney. San Diego, CA: HBJ, 1991.

Bryan, Ashley. *Sing to the Sun.* New York: HarperCollins, 1992.

Chandra, Deborah. *Balloons and Other Poems.* Illustrated by Leslie Bowman. New York: Farrar, Straus & Giroux, 1990.

Rich Lizard and Other Poems. Illustrated by Leslie Bowman. New York: Farrar, Straus & Giroux, 1993.

Ciardi, John. *You Read to Me, I'll Read to You.* Illustrated by Edward
Gorey. New York: HarperCollins, 1962.

Someone Could Win A Polar Bear (reissue). Illustrated by Edward
Gorey. Honesdale, PA: Boyds Mill Press, 1993.

Esbensen, Barbara Juster. *Cold Stars and Fireflies: Poems of the Four
Seasons.* Illustrated by Susan Bonners . New York: HarperCollins,
1984.

Who Shrank My Grandmother's House? Poems of Discovery. Illustrated
by Eric Beddows. New York: HarperCollins, 1992.

Field, Rachel. *A Road Might Lead to Anywhere.* Illustrated by Giles
Laroche. Boston, MA: Little, Brown, 1990.

Fisher, Aileen. *Always Wondering.* Illustrated by Joan Sandin. New
York: HarperCollins, 1991.

Giovanni, Nikki. *Spin A Soft Black Song* (reissue). Illustrated by George
Martins. New York: Farrar, Straus & Giroux, 1985.

Vacation Time. Illustrated by Marisabino Russo. New York: Morrow,
1980.

Greenfield, Eloise. *Honey, I Love and Other Poems.* Illustrated by Leo
and Diane Dillon. New York: HarperCollins, 1972.

Night on Neighborhood Street. Illustrated by Jan Spivey Gilchrist.
New York: Dial, 1992.

Under the Sunday Tree. Illustrated by Mr. Amos Ferguson. New
York: HarperCollins, 1988.

Hoberman, Mary Ann. *Fathers. Mothers, Sisters. Brothers: A Collection of
Family Poems.* Illustrated by Marilyn Hafner. Boston, MA: Little,
Brown, 1991.

Hopkins, Lee Bennett, selector. *Extra Innings: Baseball Poems.* Illustrated by Scott Medlock. San Diego, CA: HBJ, 1993. *Pass the
Poetry, Please!* (revised edition). New York: HarperCollins, 1987.

Hughes, Langston. *The Dream Keeper and Other Poems.* Illustrated by
Helen Sewall. New York: Knopf, 1932.

Kennedy, X. J. *The Beasts of Bethlehem.* Illustrated by Michael
McCurdy. New York: McElderry, 1992. *Brats.* Illustrated by James
Watts. New York: Atheneum, 1986. *Fresh Brats* Illustrated by
James Watts . New York: McElderry, 1989.

Kennedy, X. J. and Dorothy M. (selectors). *Talking Like the Rain: A First
Book of Poems.* Boston, MA: Little, Brown, 1992.

Kuskin, Karla. *Dogs & Dragons Trees & Dreams.* New York:
HarperCollins, 1980.

Soap Soup and Other Verses. New York: HarperCollins, 1992.

Something Sleeping in the Hall. New York: HarperCollins, 1985.

Larrick, Nancy. *Let's Do A Poem!: Introducing Poetry to Children Through Listening, Singing, Chanting, Impromptu Choral Reading, Body Movement, Dance, and Dramatization.* New York: Delacorte, 1991.

Lewis, J. Patrick. *A Hippopotamusn't.* Illustrated by Victoria Chess. New York: Dial, 1990.

Earth Verses and Water Rhymes. Illustrated by Robert Sabuda. New York: Atheneum, 1991.

Two-Legged, Four-Legged, No-Legged Rhymes. Illustrated by Pamela Paparone. New York: Knopf, 1991.

Livingston, Myra Cohn (selector). *If the Owl Calls Again: A Collection of Owl Poems.* Illustrated by Antonio Frasconi. New York: McElderry, 1990.

I Never Told and Other Poems. New York: McElderry, 1992.

Poem-Making: Ways to Begin Writing Poetry. New York: HarperCollins, 1991.

There Was A Race and Other Poems. New York: McElderry, 1988.

Whispers And Other Poems. Illustrated by Jacqueline Chwast. New York: HBJ, 1958 (out of print).

McCord, David. *All Day Long: Fifty Rhymes of the Never Was and Always Is.* Illustrated by Henry B. Kane. Boston, MA: Little, Brown, 1965; paperback edition, 1992.

Far and Few: Rhymes of the Never Was and Always Is. Illustrated by Henry B. Kane. Boston: MA: Little, Brown, 1952.

One At A Time: His Collected Poems for the Young. Illustrated by Henry B. Kane. Boston, MA: Little, Brown, 1977.

Merriam, Eve. *The Singing Green: New and Selected Poems for All Seasons.* Illustrated by Kathleen Collins Howell. New York: Morrow, 1992.

Moore, Lilian. *Adam Mouse's Book of Poems.* Illustrated by Kathleen Garry McCord. New York: Atheneum, 1992.

Don't Be Afraid, Amanda. Illustrated by Kathleen Garry McCord. New York: Atheneum, 1992.

I'll Meet You at the Cucumbers. Illustrated by Sharon Wooding. New York: Atheneum, 1988.

Something New Begins. Illustrated by Mary Jane Dunton. New York: Atheneum, 1982.

Prelutsky, Jack. *The New Kid on the Block.* Illustrated by James Stevenson. New York: Greenwillow, 1984.

Something BIG Has Been Here. Illustrated by James Stevenson. New York: Greenwillow, 1990.

Rossetti, Christina. *Color.* Illustrated by Mary Teichman. New York: HarperCollins, 1992.

Silverstein, Shel. *A Light in the Attic.* New York: HarperCollins, 1981. *Where the Sidewalk Ends.* New York: HarperCollins, 1974.

Worth, Valerie. *All the Small Poems.* Illustrated by Natalie Babbitt. New York: Farrar, Straus & Giroux, 1987, paperback.

At Christmastime. Illustrated by Antonio Frasconi. New York: HarperCollins, 1992.

10

Global Education and Children's Literature

Jennifer Ladd

Social studies is the inquiry into how humans have lived together in the past, how we get along and deal with our challenges in the present, and how we think about and create our futures. It is the study of human interaction throughout time and all the factors that have affected that interaction.

Social studies has traditionally encompassed a long list of fields, which includes anthropology, sociology, geography, history, economics, political science, and civics. In today's complex world and in the interdisciplinary, busy realm of the classroom, themes from these various fields overlap and intermingle. As a result of the need to identify certain essential concepts, skills, and attitudes for living in the twenty-first century, educators have developed the new field of global education based in and drawn from the academic disciplines.

Teachers face questions about how to help children understand the issues of the world and how to deal with them creatively and effectively in the future. These issues include global warming, deforestization, the use of fossil fuels, overpopulation, hunger and sickness, human rights abuses, poverty, and the threat and presence of war among ethnic and religious groups and classes. These times and pressing issues demand that we equip our children to be competent and informed problem solvers, group members, and visionaries.

Teachers need to help children deal with their fears and strengthen their self-esteem based on their own inner inclinations. Children need to feel validated in their desires and interests and see the value in listening to and working with other children. Children also need to see adults addressing these global issues both at the macro and micro level. Global education is an approach shared by both adults and children that assists in making sense of the world and equips people to live together as a community on the planet. Much of this task has traditionally come from the academic field of social studies.

Global Education

In 1976 Robert G. Hanvey wrote a relatively short piece called "Attaining a Global Perspective." This modest publication has become the cornerstone for educators everywhere who are interested in bringing an international perspective and practice to their classrooms. Hanvey has outlined five perspectives that he thinks are key in developing an operative consciousness for the twenty-first century. These include an awareness of perspective, of global systems, a sense of planetary health, an appreciation of cultural diversity, and a self-awareness of one's own attitudes and actions and their impact on the world.

Parallel with the multicultural movement that grew out of the civil rights struggles of the fifties and sixties, the impulse for global education (at that time international education) grew out of a perception by the United States State Department that U.S. citizens needed to know something about the rest of the world if the United States was going to play an influential role. As early as the turn of the century programs were funded, first for a college level, eventually for the K-12 grades with the aim of educating students in language, geography, political science, and history of other countries. This impulse has grown and been joined by an increasing awareness of the need to work cooperatively with other nations to ensure a safe world for our nation and others.

During the 1980s there developed an intense debate about the place of traditional American values in education, values that have been carried and upheld primarily by white, Anglo-Saxon, Protestant, middle and upper class Americans. Some people feared that developing a global perspective meant devaluing the ideas they believed to be the foundation ideas of U.S. society. Though this debate is ongoing, the outcome so far has yielded a soul searching dialogue about who and what is the United States and an accompanying debate about the difference between education and advocacy.

David Selby and Graham Pike, in their book *Global Learner, Global Teacher,* acknowledge that educational process is as important as content. Skills in cooperative learning, group dynamics, visualization, and conflict resolution are essential elements of a global perspective and global education. Selby and Pike argue that children should be as able to look at the future as they are at the past, and to be as aware of global dynamics as they are of their own interpersonal dynamics.

Many authors have written about what should be included in Global Education. Sonia Nieto in her book *Affirming Diversity: The Sociopolitical Context of Multicultural Education* and Christine Bennett, author of *Comprehensive Multicultural Education,* both emphasize the need for American young people to combat racism, prejudice, discrimination, and inequity. They argue that it is not enough to understand the differences in the world; we must also be committed to and capable of fighting injustice and creating a more inclusive society.

Barbara Benham Tye and Kenneth A. Tye, authors of *Global Education: A Study of School Change,* have researched and written about the need for global education to be integrated into the "deep structure" of a school. They argue that a global perspective suggests a whole approach to education that touches and is touched by all aspects of a school's operation.

What, then, is the intersection between children's literature, social studies, and a global perspective? What does a child's life have to do with such a grand concept as the globe? What do the events of the world have to do with the daily life of a child at school? What is the role of an adult in making these connections with children? How can one teach young people a global perspective through story?

The role of literature here is to help teachers and their students to envision clearly the world they wish to create. It also helps them participate in bringing that vision into the present. Literature enlists the help of the imagination in understanding how humans have played out the dramas of the past from several points of view. It helps personalize and bring closer the lives of those far away geographically. It can bring life to maps, statistics, the words in a social studies text, and the black and white footage of a documentary. Literature also can help students travel into a totally different way of seeing the world and constructing reality through the weaving of a myth or fairy tale.

Children's literature can be used very effectively in the social studies to develop a global perspective. According to the National Council for the Social Studies Task Force on Scope and Sequence (1989) the following themes are suggested for each grade. Teachers can look for children's books that will correspond to these themes.

First Grade: The Individual in Primary and Social Groups: Understanding School and Family Life

Second Grade: Meeting Basic Needs in Nearby Social Groups: The Neighborhood

Third Grade: Sharing Earth Space with Others: The Community

Fourth Grade: Human Life in Varied Environments: The Regions

Fifth Grade: People of the Americas: The United States and Its
                      Close Neighbors

Sixth Grade: Peoples and Cultures: Representative World Re-
                      gions

Seventh Grade: A Changing World of Many Nations: A Global View

Eighth Grade: Building a Strong and Free Nation: The United
                      States

A global perspective has been integrated into this traditional perspective. Included in the above categories are themes such as commonalities across cultures, immigration experiences, cross-cultural skills and attitudes, global issues such as war, and global systems such as the environment.

As one begins the search for appropriate books it may be useful to keep some broad questions in mind:

- To whom is the book directed?
- What is the author's knowledge and experience?
- What are the values that come through?
- What words are used to describe those values?
- Is there a tone of respect throughout the book?
- Does the author have a basic respect for all characters?
- Do the illustrations create caricatures or seem genuinely representative?
- What information and experience is left out of the book?
- Is the plot realistic? According to whose reality?
- Whose voice is not heard?

These questions can be asked of any of the themes that follow.

1. TEACHING THROUGH THEMES COMMON TO ALL HUMANS

Choosing a common theme can be one of the best ways to examine the diversity within the unity of the human species. By the same token, one can find what is common to all of us among our many differences.

Only the emphasis is different.

The major challenge is to maintain a balance between the similarities and the differences so that one does not negate the other. One of the advantages of following a common theme around the world is that similarities and differences can be explored as close to or as far from home as a teacher and the children might desire.

Teachers may use a theme such as "hats," starting with *Hats Hats,* by Ann Morris. This a book on the simplest level that exposes children to the common theme of "hat" reflected in the photographs of hats on heads of people in different capacities all over the world. There are pictures of hats used in working, playing, keeping warm, and keeping cool. There are images of men, women, and children from all over the world wearing hats. The text is very simple and accessible to first graders. In reading this book a child might think, "Though you look different from me and you live far away you still need a hat, you still need to eat, you still share some aspect of what it means to be a human. I see how we are similar and now you are less strange to me, less scary and perhaps even friendly."

Other books present different themes but have a comparable intent to demonstrate the similarities shared by humans around the globe. *Everybody Cooks Rice* by Norah Dooley, as the title suggests, shows how people the world over eat and cook rice. *Nine O'Clock Lullaby* by Marilyn Singer is a series of detailed illustrations of people doing daily life activities starting at 9:00 p.m. in New York, moving on to Puerto Rico, England, Zaire, Moscow, India, and on, heading east, and then, after twenty-four hours, ending back in Brooklyn.

This is the Way We Go to School is an illustrated book about all the different forms of transportation children take to get to school. This one needs some discussion: there are examples such as getting to school on skis or horseback that may have been more true at one time than now. The main purpose of a book like this is for young children to begin to get the idea of different ways of accomplishing the same task: this case, getting to school. There is a map in the back showing the location that each illustration depicts.

It is important to be conscious of the timing and the audience. For instance, in a teacher workshop discussing Ann Morris's book, *Loving,* one teacher—a white, female American—found the book to be very moving in its straightforward message that people share love with one another all over the world. The other teacher—a black, male South African—said that because of the degree of active hatred being experienced in his country at this time, children in his school would react with cynicism to this book. They would disbelieve it and, in fact, feel angered by it because their own experience is so counter to the basic theme. To go into depth with a particular universal concept or theme one might choose a more complex concept, idea, or topic such as families.

Teachers and children can collect stories about families, siblings, relationships with relatives, roles, and expectations that are based in this country. There are stories about all kinds of families: single parent, extended families, gay or lesbian families, and traditional families. Many stories reflect the reality of the multitudes of ethnic, religious, and class groups in this country. Masha Kabakow Rudman's book *Children's Literature: An Issues Approach* is a useful resource for suggestions of books about families, siblings, divorce, and other related topics and ideas about ways of using these books.

After having looked at the variety of families in this country one can extend beyond the borders of the United States and find out about families in other countries and cultures. Both fiction and non-fiction are available. Some guidelines to consider before embarking on such a project might be:

- Study families within the context of the country and culture of which they are a part. Explore the economics, belief systems, politics, and social structures whenever possible.
- Ensure that stereotypes are avoided by providing several examples of different families.
- Prepare to help children learn to respectfully respond to customs and practices.
- Design strategies that help children learn more about their own culture and country as they learn about the families in other countries and cultures.
- Help children make sense of the concept of family and even be able to make sense of how their own families operate in contrast to how others do.

The important thing is to get children thinking about what is similar, what is different, and why to help them develop a perspective consciousness of other ways than their own to meet similar needs.

There is a multitude of books about families based in other countries and cultures. Lyn Miller-Lachmann has written and excellent resource for teachers, *Our Family, Our Friends, Our World: An Annotated Guide to Significant Multicultural Books for Children and Teenagers*. Teachers can find titles to many wonderful books about different cultures and countries. At the end of the book there is a listing of publishers, some of which have been included here. Franklin Watts has a series called *Families Around the World*, mostly for fourth through sixth grade students. Lerner also has a very extensive series covering thirty countries titled *Families the World Over,* also geared towards fourth through sixth graders but they can be read aloud to younger children. Gareth Stevens has a series called *Children of the World* looking at about forty countries.

A series of photograph books—*The Family of Man,* by Edward Steichen, *The World's Family* by Ken Heyman, and *The Family of Woman,* edited by Jerry Mason—illustrates the stages of human life reflected throughout the world from birth to death. These books have few words but offer a moving and compassionate look at human beings all around the world. Two other books that depict family life are *All Kinds of Families* by Norma Simon and *My Friends Live in Many Places* by Dorka Raynor. The first is an illustrated book that emphasizes the love, caring, and story telling that families share. The only drawback is in its effort to show how caring very different families can be it does not mention or show the struggles that also accompany family life. Some children who come from difficult homes may not feel included in this book even if their ethnicity is. The second book is simply a series of photographs of children in different countries. There is no text, just images of children who share aspects of youth in common.

All of these books are non-fiction. To the degree that they are one author's perspective about families in a complex society such as a country, they represent one person's description of reality. For example, *A Family in Mexico* by Tom Moran is primarily about a wealthy family in the region of Oaxaca. It may accurately depict the life of that family but children reading it here would be misled by the title to think the description is typical of many Mexican families. In addition to the above book it would be important to read a number of other stories about Mexican families, perhaps some that describe crossing the border, such as *Lupita Manana* by Patricia Beatty. This is the story of a thirteen-year-old Mexican girl and her brother who cross the U.S.-Mexico border illegally to find extended family and work so they can send money home to their family, which has become impoverished since their father's accidental death. Although this book is fiction it tells a story that is true for too many children.

It is always beneficial to get a number of books about one culture or country even if one is looking at families from around the world. A teacher could challenge students with the question of what a book called *A Family in the United States* might look like. Then the students could know how difficult it is to do justice to the wide variety of living conditions, family lifestyles, and heritages in this country and see how challenging it would be to write one book about all families of another country.

First person accounts are interesting forms of non-fiction for they are clearly written from the viewpoint of a particular person and they are making observations about a real place. There are two accounts of Americans who traveled to Russia, for example. In *Georgia to Georgia: Making Friends in the USSR* by Laurie Dolphin is about a young boy from Georgia, U.S.A. who travels to the state of Georgia in what was the USSR at the time. He delivers letters from his home town to children in Tiblisi and describes his experience there. Another book to complement this one is *Friendship Across Arctic Waters: Alaskan Cub Scouts Visit Their Soviet Neighbors* by Clare Rudolf Murphy. This is about the experience of a group of cub scouts who visit the Young Pioneers in a town only 200 miles away.

When teaching about families that live in other countries and other cultures there are a number of further questions to keep in mind:

- Is the family portrayed within the context of the larger society?
- Is it clear that this family is not necessarily representative of all families within that country?
- What is the author's attitude towards that family? Are there any words that indicate judgment?
- During which historical time is the story based. How have families changed or stayed the same since that time?

Nadia the Willful by Sue Alexander is a book about a young girl in a Bedouin family. The story is about the grief of losing a loved family member and how the family and larger community heals itself; it is about emotions shared the world over, but it is grounded in a very specific society.

My Uncle Nikos by Judy Delton is based in a small village in Greece where there is no running water or electricity. A young girl visits her uncle, who lives contentedly. They buy food for dinner at the market and go home, where he cooks on a fire while she sets the table and picks flowers from his thriving garden. They leave the dishes by the outside water pump, inspect the garden, and then she goes to bed by the light of a burning candle. This story could be useful in exploring what makes life satisfactory and lead to discussions about what it is like not to have "modern" amenities in this country.

Another book, *Lily and the Lost Boy* by Paula Fox, is about an American family on sabbatical on a small island in Greece. Although the story is told from the American viewpoint the reader learns much about Greek history and daily life on the island. This book can complement the first book about Greece and stimulate a comparison between an American and Greek family.

Some stories about difficult family situations such as war or separation are in books for older children such as *White Peak Farm* by Berlie Doherty, for seventh through ninth graders. This story about a poor family living on a farm in England focuses on the struggle for the teens to choose between pulls of urban life and commitment to their difficult family situation in the country.

Teachers should be aware of their own opinions of how others go about family life because these opinions will come across to the children. Books about families who live under apartheid or other forms of repression require that a teacher take the time to discuss the context of these books and be willing to address contemporary controversial issues in whatever way is appropriate.

The Middle of Somewhere: A Story of South Africa by Sheila Gordon, for fourth to sixth graders, is a portrait of black family life in South Africa. It is a realistic story about the horrors of living under apartheid with the threat of relocation and the trauma of a parent being jailed for speaking out.

Another book that describes the difficulty of family life for black South Africans is *Journey to Jo'burg* by Beverly Naidoo. This is the story of a sister and brother who leave their home in a "homeland" to fetch their mother, a domestic in Johannesburg, because their youngest sister is very ill. It is the story of their physical journey and of their journey into awareness of apartheid and what it may take to change it.

For younger children *At the Crossroads* by Rachel Isadora is a book about children who live in a shanty town of tin shacks. They are waiting for their fathers to return from the mines after ten months of absence. As they wait they talk, make instruments, sing, and dance and others from the community join in. Thus the children find a way to lighten a long-term, difficult situation.

In the social studies curriculum the key is to encourage children to discuss their questions, thoughts, and feelings that arise from reading the book. The power of a particular book is in the kind of response stimulated in children, The teacher needs to provide space for children to explore their reactions and to make the links with understanding their own lives.

2. TEACHING ABOUT IMMIGRATION EXPERIENCES: CROSS-CULTURAL SKILLS AND ATTITUDES.

Immigration is a concept that can be expanded to include the notion of transition and the idea of journeys. There isn't a community on earth that has not had some relationship to these concepts. This is one of the topics from which children can learn about change in their lives, how to sustain themselves in times of adversity, and how to know themselves.

One can learn a lot about the skills needed to communicate cross-culturally through reading immigration stories. They tell how people who have moved have kept the important aspects of their cultures alive and how both the newcomers and host groups are changed by one another. These stories can describe a process of negotiating similarities and differences in values, beliefs, and practices. Although it is true that only some children have had the experience of drastically shifting from one culture to another, all children have had to learn how to enter groups different from their own cultures, whether it was simply going to a friend's house that had different rules of conduct or attending a new school.

Immigration stories tell of American history from the multiplicity of perspectives of those who have moved. Of course, not all people have written stories of their transitions. For instance, African Americans in this country do not have, for the most part, written accounts of their excruciating passage. The history has been passed down through the oral tradition and through song. Teachers may want to look into music and storytelling to fill out their libraries on accounts of people's journeys both to this country and to others. *In Their Own Words: A History of the American Negro, 1619-1865,* edited by Milton Meltzer, does have some accounts by African Americans. *Follow the Drinking Gourd* by Jeanette Winter doesn't tell the story of the middle passage but it is one of a number of books that tell of the journey out of slavery and is a book for younger readers.

People have immigrated for a wide variety of reasons and with a wide variety of experiences. The term "immigrant" suggests thousands of years of different kinds of circumstances and motivations for movement. When children choose books on immigration they might be encouraged to ask the following kinds of questions in addition to the generic ones previously listed:

- Why are the children/family immigrating? Is there choice? Are they being forced? Are they coming because of war, environmental disaster, hopes of economic improvement, threat due to religious or political beliefs? Are they taken as slaves or prisoners? Are they being drawn by family that have already emigrated or the promise of a better life?
- What kind of status did they have in their country before leaving? What kind of status did they have when they arrived in their new home?

- How did they feel about leaving their home and going to their new home? How far away was it both geographically and culturally? How did they get there? What was the journey like?
- How different was the place they came to from their old home? What did they have to give up? What were they able or did they choose to keep? Language? Food? Customs? Clothes? Religion?
- What kind of support was or wasn't there when they arrived in their new home? What kind of treatment did they receive from the host nationals? Which groups welcomed their coming and which were hostile and why?
- What personal qualities seem to help or hinder the newcomer in surviving in the new home emotionally and physically?

These questions reflect the wide variety of circumstances for people's moves from one place to another. There are some wonderful books for children about immigration and they are on the increase. The best ones are those that convey the struggles and difficulties and the qualities of strength, fortitude, and community that it takes to face those challenges.

There are a variety of examples of stories that have come from the tales of recent immigrants—*Wilfredo: The Story of a Boy from El Salvador* by Teachers' Committee on Central America and *Aekyung's Dream* by Min Paek. *Wilfredo* is a bilingual book written in the first person by a young boy from El Salvador who has come to live in Los Angeles. He describes his life at school and talks about missing his home and family. He mentions the war that is the cause of his move.

Aekyung's Dream is another story (fictional) about the difficulty in adapting to another culture, encountering the stereotypes held of one by the host culture, and the process of finding strength in oneself and the symbols of one's culture to grow through such a transition. This is one of the few books from a Korean perspective and highlights the propensity of some North Americans to group all Asians together.

Stories about children who have had to leave a war-torn area have much in common. Though Central America and Southeast Asia are far apart children face some of the same traumas and some of the same skills are needed to cope.

Journey of the Sparrows by Fran Leeper and Daisy Cubias describes the trials of escaping and crossing the borders coming from El Salvador. *Lupita Manana* by Patricia Beatty is about the same difficulty of crossing into the United States, but the protagonists are from Mexico where they struggle with poverty, not death squads. Another book about the fortitude needed to undergo trying times is *The Clay Marble* by Minfong Ho. This is the story of a young girl who has fled Cambodia and is now in a refugee camp in Thailand. The child discovers that the strength required to survive in such conditions comes from within and not from objects outside herself. This story reflects the author's life; she has since returned to live in Cambodia.

Some stories are based on the real life of particular children and thereby give an authenticity to the story that can not be argued with, only supplemented and complemented in one's other choices of books. Two such books are *Children of the River* by Linda Crew and *Dimitry: A Young Soviet Immigrant* by Joanne E. Bernstein, photographs by Michael J., Bernstein.

The first story is about a Cambodian girl's experience in a high school in Oregon. She had to leave her family and boyfriend in Cambodia and now finds herself being pulled between the traditional ways of interacting with the opposite sex in her own culture and her attraction to an American young man who grew up with a different set of ways. The book is written by a woman who lives in Oregon and has heard the stories of Cambodian refugees who are now farm workers.

Dmitry: A Young Soviet Immigrant is the true story of a boy from the Soviet Union who has moved to the United States with his parents. It chronicles the trials and tribulations that his family and he face as they seek work and make themselves a place in this new society. The book is told by a teacher who had Soviet students in her class and wanted to educate the class about what this transition is like.

We Came From Vietnam by Muriel Stanek is about the documented life of a Vietnamese family in Chicago. The title is misleading in that the reader expects the story to be told by the Nguyen family. It is slightly disconcerting to be told about the life and opinions of the Nguyens without hearing their voices, even if only in translation. One feels a slight distance that could reinforce a we-they kind of thinking though certainly that family's life is told with respect.

Another book that can be misleading is *How Many Days to America: A Thanksgiving Story* by Eve Bunting. This book has gorgeous pastel illustrations and tells the story of a group of people from some unspecified Caribbean island making a long and difficult sea journey due to war in their home country. The people on other islands will not accept them, but when the travelers reach the shores of the United States they are welcomed with open arms and it happens to be Thanksgiving.

No doubt this story has been the experience of peoples from certain islands with a particular political relationship to the United States. There are other people however, such as Haitians, who have been turned away and sent back to their unstable countries. Children would be misled to think that the United States has a totally open door immigration policy. Another book that links immigration and Thanksgiving is

Molly's Pilgrim by Barbara Cohen. It is about a Jewish girl whose family escaped the pogroms in Russia. When told to make a Pilgrim woman doll, Molly's mother makes a doll of herself, drawing the connection between Pilgrims and Russian Jews who both journeyed to gain religious freedom. Neither book acknowledges the impact of this journeying on the Indian cultures they met.

New Kids in Town by Janet Bode is an excellent book of first person accounts by young people who have recently come from countries such as Lebanon, Nicaragua, and the Soviet Union. The entries are long enough to get a feel for the experience of the speaker but short enough to hold the attention of the reader. Reading this book can be an effective way of bringing children from different cultures into one's classroom.

Then there are those stories of immigrants who have come to the United States earlier in history, such as the following. *The Keeping Quilt*, by Patricia Polacco is a book that describes keeping the past and the culture of Europe alive in the pieces of cloth that have been used in special family rituals and celebrations over the years. This book follows generations through, demonstrating that the integrity of a family can be kept alive through craft and care. *The Long Way Westward* by Joan Sandin is an I Can Read book that tells the story of a family from Sweden that immigrates to the midwest during 1868-69. It begins in Sweden and describes the journey that the family takes, illustrating the challenges and the way the family faces them. Another I Can Read Book, *Chang's Paper Pony* by Eleanor Coerr, is the story of a young boy and his grandfather who have recently come from China at the time of the gold rush.

Some books talk about the exploitation that families have encountered here in the United States when they arrived. *Immigrant Girl: Becky of Eldridge St.* by Brett Harvey is the story of a Jewish Russian girl who comes to New York City in 1910. The story describes daily life, which includes grueling work in the shirtwaist factory and the workers decision to strike, and also going to school, selling newspapers, picnicking and spending time together performing the rituals and practices that keep the wisdom of the old world alive.

Other books describe the anxiety of moving from one's own language and culture to another while still maintaining some sense of self. *I Hate English* by Ellen Levine is a book about a Chinese girl from Hong Kong who refuses to learn English for fear of losing her sense of herself. She does not know herself in English. Her teacher is of great assistance, patient, compassionate and eventually helpful to Mei Mei.

Teachers may find that they have questions about whether or not to use certain books. For instance the book, *The Little Weaver of Thai Yen Village* is about a girl in Vietnam whose family is killed by a bomb. Her throat is badly cut, she gets taken to the hospital, and then is shipped out to the United States. This is a difficult story to hear for young American children, especially if they have not encountered much violence. However, there may be children who have themselves been through some similar kind of trauma both in and outside of this country. For them this book might be of great solace.

3. TEACHING ABOUT ANOTHER COUNTRY

Whatever authority I have rests solely on knowing how little I know—
Socrates.

This is a useful quote to keep in mind while studying another country or culture. The aim is not just to know the facts and figures of a country, which are often changing, but also to know the complexity of a people. If children can generate more questions about what else they would like to know at the end of a unit about a particular country the teacher is doing well. Continual inquiry is the goal. One might start by asking the following questions:

- Why are we studying this country?
- How did I/we choose this country?
- What relevance is there for the students in the class?
- What do we know about this country? Where have we gotten our information? How do I know the information is true?
- What are my feelings about this country? What are they based on?
- What do I want the children to go away with after we have learned about and from the people in this country?
- How long am I willing to spend learning about this country?
- How can I ensure a multiplicity of perspectives that reflect the variety of peoples in the culture?

Why is it that children learn about other countries? What is a country? These days this is a very relevant question as borders and governments change and as groups of countries begin working in confederation as a region. How are the countries of study chosen? Who decides and how is it decided which country merits attention in school?

Children's literature can be of great assistance in bringing the people and land of other countries closer. Very often social studies curricula rely on non-fiction books to inform children. Fiction that is based in that country or region can bring a feeling tone and a richness of daily detail to a study that might otherwise be dry and distant.

One needs to be conscious of what historical time period one is teaching so as not to mislead children with images and information that may have been true two centuries ago but is not valid now. One must select wisely not to alienate children and introduce a whole new array of stereotypes that fail to provide a complete picture.

Because other countries tend to be far away and out of reach of one's students there is an imperative, as there is in the study of an historical period, to get a broad range of perspectives from that country so as to ensure a complex and rich understanding.

Being aware of one's own and student attitudes about a particular country is important, as these attitudes will shape how the learners interpret what they learn. For instance, not too long ago many teachers might not have chosen to teach about the Soviet Union because it was an "enemy" of the United States. A teacher and his or her students might not have striven to understand the people of the Soviet Union as much as to bolster already existing perceptions about the area. Now conditions have changed and U.S. teachers are much more willing and interested in teaching about Russia sympathetically. By not learning about the people in the Soviet Union before this thaw, teachers contributed to children's concept of enemy. All societies are in a process of evolving. The more teachers can introduce the concept of change, of culture as dynamic, not static, the more equipped children will be to deal with the changes in their own families and the wider world.

There is a series by Lerner that discusses the changes in Latvia, Russia, and Estonia since the dissolution of the USSR. Each book covers Land and People, History, Making a Living, and What is Next. Another series of books about changing societies is the Vanishing Cultures series that tell the stories of cultures that are in danger of disappearing. *Himalaya: Vanishing Cultures* by Jan Reynolds is a photography book that tells the story of Tibetans who live in what is now China. The author introduces the reader to a family he encountered on his travels and talks about how the old life is blending with the new.

The purpose in learning about other countries and cultures is to better understand ourselves as humans. It is important that the humanity be found within even and especially those countries with whom the United States is having difficulty. What are different people's lives like in Iraq, South Africa, China, Nicaragua, and Japan? How can children be helped to understand all the complex factors that contribute to how people live and treat one another. Most often teachers will rely on non-fiction children's books that have the daunting task of explaining the complexities of dynamic human organization that stretches over time in such a way that a child of eight, nine, or ten can understand.

There are a number of nonficition series listed by Lyn Miller-

Lachman that are available for students doing research: *Countries* by Silver Burdett; *Take a Trip, Countries of the World,* and *Living Here* by Franklin Watts, *Discovering Our Heritage* by Dillon, *Enchantment of the World* by Children's Press; *Let's Visit Places and Peoples of the World* by Chelsea House; and *Visual Geography Series* by Lerner. Although the quality of these books may not be consistent, they could be useful for teachers to use as a stepping off point from which to begin discussions, questioning, and further research.

Some of the best books about other countries are those that are about one person, and through the experience of that one individual the reader gains a sense of place. An example would be *Rehema's Journey: A Visit in Tanzania* by Barbara Margolies, the story of a nine-year-old girl who leaves her rural mountain home for the first time to travel with her father. She meets others who live in her country. The book has wonderful photographs of people and the countryside.The book *Family Pictures/ Cuadros de Familia* by Carmen Lomas Garza is a book of lively paintings of the author's life in Mexico. Text describing holidays, cooking, and family life accompany the colorful and descriptive pictures. This is an excellent example of non-fiction that reads and feels as magical as fiction can. *Ntombi's Song* by Jenny Seed, who lives in Africa, is a fictional story for young children about a girl in South Africa who goes for sugar for her mother. The story is about the courage it takes to make the trip on her own, and it depicts, through excellent illustrations, life along the road and in small towns. It does not address apartheid but does give the feel of what an afternoon errand might be like for a girl of six.

Other books that help one get a feel for a country and get to know its underlying beliefs are legends, myths, tales, and religious parables. It is imperative that teachers be prepared to acknowledge different belief systems that often are the foundation of other cultures and sometimes countries. To avoid this issue is to prevent children from knowing that people all over the world grapple with the great human questions of life, death, the unknown, and meaning in the world. One must be clear that in teaching about other religious beliefs one is neither criticizing nor proselytizing but instead informing and equipping children with the language of meaning making the world over.

Some examples might be *The Mountains of Tibet* by Mordicai Gerstein. This is a story that draws on the philosophy of the *Tibetan Book of the Dead.* A boy travels, ages, dies, and reincarnates as a girl to see what that is like. *Power of Light* by I.B. Singer offers stories that illuminate beliefs of the Jewish faith. Often books about children and holidays provide an understanding of underlying beliefs of a culture. *Seasons of Splendor: Tales, Myths, and Legends of India* by Mahdur Jaffrey tells about the Hindu holidays of India through stories that teach about basic cultural beliefs. *Tonight is Carnaval* by Arthur Dorros is a story about a young Peruvian boy preparing for Carnaval. It is illustrated with *apilleras*, quilted tapestries especially made in South America, that give the reader the flavor of the culture.

For young children the issues of the world can often be found in a micro level in the classroom. There are lots of ways that teachers work with children around the concepts of interconnection, different points of view, ecological awareness, learning to live with the ambiguity of change, and taking responsibility for oneself and one's part in a larger group. Literature can support these efforts by using books that emphasize cooperation, self-esteem, and curiosity about others. These concepts can also be found in myths and stories from other cultures which introduce these concepts and expose children to differences as well.

In a recent workshop teachers talked about their own experience with children's literature when they were young. One of the functions children's literature played was to provide adventure and a chance to look beyond their own worlds. The challenge for a teacher is to be able to encourage that sense of adventure as the child encounters what is different in another culture and also to find the places of connection so that "they" can also be experienced as "we."

4. TEACHING ABOUT ISSUES: PEACE/WAR

Often when one is teaching about another country one comes across the issue of war. Why teach it? To teach children that war is a costly solution and questionable at that. We are capable of finding other ways of solving our differences, we are capable of living for more, of creating more, of engaging in activities that can call forth as much from us as war does without the cost of cruelty and inhumanity. As with other topics one might begin by asking oneself the following questions:

- Why am I teaching about war/peace?
- What do I want children to go away with?
- What questions do the children have about this conflict?
- What are my feelings about this particular war involving this particular country or countries?
- What is my relationship to this war?
- What are the underlying issues in this war and are there any manifestations of those same underlying issues in our classroom or our community?
- How can I integrate a variety of perspectives?
- How do all the parties involved in this war justify their actions?

- When I think about it, is there anything I would be willing to kill for? What are my justifications for war?
- What does it take to have peace?
- What is my definition of peace?
- Do I believe peace is possible?

Teachers can deal with issues of war with young children by examining instances of conflict within the classroom and the family. Reading books on conflict resolution, mediation, cooperation, competition with self and engaging in other kinds of challenges are all activities that can be done at an early age.

At what point can children deal with the realities of war? Children originally from Vietnam, Cambodia, El Salvador, Guatemala, Lebanon, and South Africa have already had to deal with war. Other children may very well live in war zones here in the United States; places where guns, murder, death, gang warfare are the norm. Both these groups of children may need to hear some discussion of war. They may need models of children who have lived in such circumstances and been able to love, connect, act courageously, deal with feelings of fear, sorrow, and anger. They may need models of adults who have done their best to face war situations and worked to bring peace and humanity back into daily life and national conduct.

Some children who have not been exposed to the ugliness and horror of war do not need to have their exposure come out of context. For them the discussion may be an extension of their understanding of something happening in their communities, classroom, family, neighborhood or region. Two books geared towards younger children are *The Wall* and *Terrible Things: An Allegory of the Holocaust,* both by Eve Bunting.

The Wall is about a father and son who visit the Vietnam Memorial looking for and remembering the boy's grandfather. The illustrations are soft, the text gentle, and it may well be within many children's experience. *Terrible Things* is a very powerful and possibly scary book about animals in the forest who do not protect and defend one another thinking that nothing will ever happen to them but it does.

If war is going on, adults need to be prepared to answer children's questions as directly as possible and have as many materials on hand that will help children make sense of the nonsensical. During the Gulf War many teachers chose to follow up on their students' questions responding to deeply felt fears and worries. Children's literature can be useful in exposing children to the reality of war and to the variety of ways that people have dealt with it and participated in it. Children need to understand the concept of perspective and of differing interests. What are the human qualities that have led to war as a way of coping with problems between people? What have those problems been in the past? What are they today? How can we learn to hear one another's concerns and express our own without turning to war? Children can and are asking these questions of themselves as they deal with conflict in their lives and examine conflict between groups of which they are a part.

What do we mean by peace? Are we simply speaking of an absence of war? Or are we talking about all the creative capacities of the human spirit? What else calls us to be as noble, as heroic and as clear as war? *Peace Begins with You* by Katherine Sholes is a non-fiction book that talks about ways children can make peace in their daily lives.

What is the attraction of war? The idea that might makes right, the temptation and relief of a simplistic view of good and bad guys? Does it remind us of the value of human life even as it is devalued by mass slaughter?

War calls us to be outside of ourselves whether we are in support of the cause or opposed to it. Children in this country can learn about fortitude and perseverance from children who are coping with war in other countries. Books such as *The Clay Marble, The Little Weaver of Thai-Yen Village* and *Journey of the Sparrows* referred to in the family and immigration sections can be useful in looking at issues of war and peace. *Sami and the Time of the Troubles* by Florence Parry Heide and Judith Heide Gilliland is a story for young readers about the life a family under siege in Lebanon. Everyone stays inside until there is a break in the fighting, then normal bustling outdoor life goes on until, once again, the family must return to safety in a shelter they had decorated with special belongings.

Sadako and the Thousand Paper Cranes by Eleanor Coerr is about a young Japanese girl who is dying of leukemia due to radiation of the atom bomb. The story of others who came to support her in her last efforts to promote peace is told. Then there is always the *Diary of a Young Girl* by Anne Frank, a classic that illustrates how one can maintain a sense of wonder in and curiosity about life and love despite the worst conditions.

Looking at issues of war can invite looking at our interconnections through our similarities. War is something that we as humans hold in common but it is often due to our differences that we are at war and due to our narrow sense of community. The more expanded our definition of self interest, the more likely we are to treat others as part of our community and arrive at peaceful solutions to our conflicts.

5. GLOBAL ENVIRONMENTAL ISSUES: THE GLOBAL COMMONS: AIR, WATER, SPECIES, FORESTS

How does teaching about the environment fit into a global

perspective? The study of the environment provides one of the clearest avenues for conveying the concept of interconnection and interdependence. A study of the environment also reveals much about the value of diversity in the midst of unity. Change is certainly a constant throughout the natural world, and every human being is in a position to make choices about his or her relationship to that world. Here are a few suggested guidelines:

- Be clear about why you are teaching about a particular issue.
- Think about what exactly you want children to go away with.
- Examine your own feelings about this issue.
- Assess what you know and how you know it.
- Assess what the children know, how they know it, and what resources are available for them to learn more.
- Be aware of the contradictions, the vying interests and needs involved in the issue.
- Examine how your actions or inactions might be part of the issue.
- Be aware of what your vision of the future is.
- Think about what your students can do to affect the situation.

The Pacific Ocean laps at the coast of numerous countries and the fish that swim there know no boundaries. The air is filled with the carbon monoxide of all our vehicle exhaust, and, though the air in Los Angeles and Mexico City may be particularly thick, global weather patterns have been altered and therefore affect the growing of food the world over.

Teachers can use children's literature to demonstrate how shared problems are seen and dealt with in different countries. Books can help children better understand the complicated interrelationship of factors that contribute to both the problems and their solutions. Teachers can also begin to discuss the concept of "sustainable development," an approach that, "...meets the needs of the present without compromising the ability of the future generations to meet their own needs." According to Global Learning, Inc. this is a concept that forms a triangle, the three sides being:

1. The needs of the environment;
2. The needs of humans for development; and
3. The need for equity among humans in sharing of access and use of resources.

One could explore the relationship among these three needs by choosing a topic such as fishing. *Shark Beneath the Reef,* by Jean Craighead George (Harper Collins 1989) is about a boy who loves fishing, and school. In the course of fishing with his family and trying to catch a hammerhead shark he encounters the politicians of his village in the Baja who are trying to push fisherman out of business to develop the town for tourist trade. The book deals with environmental issues associated with marine life and deep sea fishing. Some readers may feel that some characters verge on being stereotypic: the uncle who has turned to drinking after losing his job as a deep sea diver, is one example. The story looks at a town that is moving from a more traditional to more "modern" way of life. George addresses some of the losses and gains associated with that transition and questions who benefits from these changes.

Another book about the ocean and its inhabitants is *A Thousand Pails of Water*, illustrated by Vo-Dinh Mai and written by Ronald Roy (Knopf 1978). This is the story of a boy who lives in a Japanese fishing village whose inhabitants make their living by whaling. A little boy does not understand why this has to be and does his best to save a whale that gets washed up on the shore. Eventually villagers help him in his effort to keep the whale alive and send it back out to sea. Though this book illustrates kindness as expressed by the boy and the villagers who helped him, it does not help the reader better understand how the villagers can continue to be kind to whales and rely on them for their livelihood simultaneously.

There is a danger of North American authors writing books about peoples and issues in Third World countries of writing in a simplistic manner that makes the environment the protagonist and the people the exploiters. Issues of deforestization, overpopulation, and air pollution are complex. By not fully fleshing out the difficult choices that particularly poor people have to make between short-term survival and long-term ecological balance, authors run the risk of blaming the victim.

Some people have the power to make changes in their daily lives that will decrease environmental degradation, and often there are governmental policies, and corporate behavior that need to be challenged. In so many cases there appears to be a contradiction between the needs of the environment to sustain itself (and therefore humans) over the long run and the immediate survival needs of humans. Children's books are doing a service if they can help children begin to understand the complexities and not just think in terms of who is good or bad.

Books that demonstrate a sustainable interrelationship between humans and the natural world help children imagine how humans can live on the earth healthily.

My Grandpa and the Sea by Katherine Orr is a book about the possibility of a healthy, respectful relationship with nature. A young girl who lives on the island of St. Lucia learns about loving the natural world, herself, and others from her grandfather. He loves the sea; it is where he feels most alive and in touch with his sense of God. Unfortunately his fishing business is destroyed by the entry of bigger boats and more expensive technology. He is almost broken by separation from what he loves but then uses his imagination and finds another way to make a living by working with his ingenuity and the fruits of the sea.

The Gift of the Willows by Helena C. Pittman is a story based in Japan of a potter who diligently cares for a willow growing on the river bank. After many years there is a flood; the willow falls and by doing so provides a bridge that saves their lives. The willow then sprouts again and the circle of life starts over. This is a gentle book with lovely illustrations demonstrating the interdependent relationship between humans and the natural world.

Where the Forest Meets the Sea by Jeannie Baker is about Australia and rainforests. This book illustrates the beauty of the rainforest through collages and also hints at the dangers to the environment and humans themselves if they continue on as they have. This book is good for preschool through third graders. Miriam Schlein's *The Year of the Panda* is a story based in the People's Republic of China that follows the interest a young boy has in a small panda he found that is migrating due to the lack of bamboo. The story combines a caring for an endangered species while understanding human needs. The book illustrates the transition that a small rural village in China is making while exploring the impact of these changes on the environment and the governments attempt to deal with it.

In terms of global education, environmental issues that stress humanity's sharing of the global commons will help children understand themselves as a species among others regardless of national boundaries that have no meaning to the planet itself. Indigenous cultures all over the world have often held an attitude toward the earth that has enabled them to live on and with it. There are an increasing number of children's books written by people who have a philosophy of stewardship rather than ownership of the earth.

Finally, there are many books being written and published that help children take action. There are many non-fiction books that describe and explain about the variety of environmental problems facing humans and are a growing number of books that are practical how-to books designed to assist children in making a change in and individuals' communities' lifestyles now. The titles include *Fifty Simple Things Kids Can Do to Save the Earth* by Earthworks Group, *Save the Earth: An Action Handbook for Kids* by Betty Miles, and *Going Green: A Kids Handbook for Saving the Planet* by John Elkington et al. In addition, there are a number of annotated booklists that can be useful guides to teachers and librarians.

One in particular is *E for Environment: An Annotated Bibliography of Children's Books with Environmental Themes* by Patti Sinclair.

CONCLUSION

Children's literature has the capacity to link students with people from other lands and times. Each book is one story, one truth, and one author's interpretation of a culture, country, issue, or system. A combination of good books can bring the reader into a new world, a different time, a broader understanding of a problem that may have plagued humankind. As in all literature, it is important that students develop their own critical capacities and their own voices so they empathize with others' perspectives and know what it is to write from one's own viewpoint.

As teachers we have the responsibility and the privilege of exposing children to the larger world and the complexities of their very own world and to help them make the connections between these dimensions. As Selby and Pike point out, the curriculum can enable a student's consciousness to travel out to a global perspective and into a very personal perspective. It can peer into the past, journey through the present, and voyage on into imagining the possible futures that might be created. Children's literature is the vehicle for this travel. With each book we can make a stop, stroll around and get the feel of a place or time as described by that person.

Also as teachers we have the responsibility and challenge of making sure many voices are heard. It is difficult to acquire new books that might bring forward the voices of previously disregarded people. At one time, the shelves held few books that were by and about people and children who were not European American, middle class, or from a Judeo-Christian background. Due to much work on the part of many people, this is changing. There is an increasing number of books that tell the stories of people from a wide array of backgrounds in many areas of the United States and the world. In fact, this is an exciting time to be reading. As children are encouraged to write their own stories and share them with one another they will understand the concept of voice, they will see that you have your story and I have mine and that we do touch each other's lives and share a human story together.

Bibliography

Younger

Alexander, Sue. *Nadia the Willful.* Illustrated by Lloyd Bloom. New York: Pantheon. 1983.

Baer, Edith. *This is the Way We Go to School: A Book About Children Around the World.* Illustrated by Steve Bjorkman. New York: Scholastic, Inc. 1990.

Baker, Jeannie. *Where the Forest Meets the Sea.* Illustrated by the author. New York: Greenwillow Books. 1987.

Bunting, Eve. *How Many Days to America: A Thanksgiving Story.* Illustrated by Beth Peck. New York: Clarion Books. 1988.

Bunting, Eve. *Terrible Things: An Allegory of the Holocaust.* illustrated by Stephen Gammell. Philadelphia: Jewish Publication Society. 1989.

Bunting, Eve. *The Wall.* Illustrated by Ronald Himler. New York: Clarion Books. 1990.

Coerr, Eleanor. *Chang's Paper Pony.* Illustrated by Deborah K. Ray. New York: Harper & Row, Publishers. 1988.

Cohen, Barbara. *Molly's Pilgrim.* Illustrated by Michael J. Deraney. New York: Lothrop, Lee & Shepard Books. 1983.

Delton, Julie. *My Uncle Nikos.* Illustrated by Marc Simont. New York: Thomas Y. Crowell. 1983.

Dooley, Norah. *Everybody Cooks Rice.* Illustrated by Peter J. Thorton, Minneapolis: Carolrhoda. 1991.

Dorros, Arthur. *Tonight is Carnaval.* New York: Dutton Child Books. 1991.

Garza, Carmen L. *Family Pictures/Cuadros de Familia.* Illustrated by author. San Francisco: Children's Book Press. 1990.

Gerstein, Mordicai. *Mountains of Tibet.* Illustrations by author. New York: HarperCollins. 1987.

Harvey, Brett. *Immigrant Girl: Becky of Eldridge St.* Illustrations by Deborah Kogan Ray. New York: Holiday House. 1987.

Heide, Florence P. & Gilliland, Judith H. *Sami and the Time of the Troubles.* Illustrated by Ted Lewin. New York: Clarion. 1992.

Heyman, Ken. *The World's Family.* New York: Pound Press Books. 1983.

Isadora, Rachel. *At the Crossroads.* New York: Greenwillow Books. 1991.

Levine, Ellen. *I Hate English.* Illustrated by Steve Bjorkman. New York: Scholastic, Inc. 1989.

Moran, Tom. *A Family in Mexico*. Minneapolis: Lerner Publications. 1987.

Morris, Ann. *Hats Hats*. Photográghs by Ken Heyman. New York: Scholastic, Inc. 1989.

Morris, Ann. *Loving*. Photographs by Ken Heyman. New York: Lothrop, Lee & Shepard Books. 1990.

Orr, Katherine. *My Grandpa and the Sea*. Illustrations by the author. Minneapolis: Lerner/Carolrhoda. 1990.

Paek, Min. *Aekyung's Dream*. Illustrated and translated by author. San Francisco: Children's Book Press. 1988.

Pittman, Helena C. *The Gift of the Willows*. Illustrated by the author. Minneapolis: Lerner/Carolrhoda, 1988.

Polacco, Patricia. *The Keeping Quilt*. Illustrated by author. New York: Sinon and Schuster. 1988.

Reynolds, Jan. *Himalaya: Vanishing Cultures*. Photographs by author. San Diego: Harcourt Brace Jovanovich. 1991.

Roy, Ronald. *A Thousand Pails of Water*. Illustrated by Vo-Dinh Mai. New York: Knopf. 1978.

Sandin, Joan. *The Long Way Westward*. Illustrated by author. New York: Harper and Row. 1989.

Seed, Jenny. *Ntombi's Song*. Illustrated by Anno Berry. Boston: Beacon Press Books. 1987.

Sholes, Katherine. *Peace Begins with You*. Illustrated by Robert Ingpen. Boston: Little Brown & C. 1991.

Singer, Marilyn. *Nine O'Clock Lullaby*. Illustrated by Fran Lessac. New York: HarperCollins. 1991.

Stanek, Muriel. *We Came From Vietnam*. Photographs by Wm. Franklin McMahon. Niles, Illinois: Albert Whitman & Company. 1985.

Steichen, Edward (Ed.). *Family of Man*. S&S Trade. 1987.

Teacher's Committee on Central America. *Wilfredo: The Story of a Boy from El Salvador*. Illustrated by Alberto Oropeda. Los Angeles: Los Angeles Teachers' Committee on Central America. 1986.

Tran-Khanh-Tuyet. *The Little Weaver of Thai-Yen Village*. Illustrated by Nancy Hom. Translated by Christopher N. H. Jenkins & Tran-Khanh-Tuyet. San Francisco: Children's Book Press. 1977.

Winter, Jeanette. *Follow the Drinking Gourd*. Illustrated by author. New York: 1988.

Older

Beatty, Patricia. *Lupita Manana.* New York: Beech Tree Books. 1981.

Bernstein, Joanne E. *Dmitry: A Young Soviet Immigrant.* Photographs by Michael J. Bernstein. New York: Clarion Books. 1981.

Bode, Janet. *New Kids in Town: Oral Histories of Immigrant Teens.* New York: Scholastic. 1991.

Coerr, Eleanor. *Sadako, and the Thousand Paper Cranes.* Illustrated by Ronald Himler. New York: Putnam. 1977.

Crew, Linda. *Children of the River.* New York: Delacorte Press. 1989.

Doherty, Berlie. *White Peak Farm.* New York: Orchard. 1990.

Dolphin, Laurie. *Georgia to Georgia: Making Friends in the USSR.* New York: Clarion Books. 1981.

Earthworks Project Staff. *Fifty Simple Things Kids Can Do to Save the Earth.* Kansas City: Andrew and McMeel. 1990.

Elkington, John et al. *Going Green: A Kids Handbook for Saving the Planet.* Illustrated by Tony Ross. New York: Puffin Books. 1990.

Fox, Paula. *Lily and the Lost Boy.* New York: Orchard. 1987.

Frank, Anne. *The Diary of a Young Girl.* Translated by B.M. Mooyart. New York: Doubleday. 1967.

George, Jean Craighead. *Shark Beneath the Reef.* New York: Harper Collins. 1989

Gordon, Sheila. *The Middle of Somewhere: A Story of South Africa.* New York: Orchard, 1990

Ho, Minfong. *The Clay Marble.* New York: Farrar Straus Giroux. 1991.

Jaffrey, Madhur. *Seasons of Splendour: Tales, Myths, and Legends of India.* Illustrated by Michael Foreman. New York: Puffin Books.

Leeper, Fran & Cubias, Daisy. *Journey of the Sparrows.* New York; Dutton. 1991.

Margolies, Barbara. *Rehema's Journey: A Visit in Tanzania.* New York: Scholastic, Inc. 1990

Mason, Jerry (Ed.). *The Family of Woman.* New York: Grosset & Dunlap. 1979.

Meltzer, Milton (Ed.). *In Their Own Words: A History of the American Negro, 1619-1865.* New York: Thomas Y. Crowell. 1964.

Miles, Betty. *Save the Earth: An Action Handbook for Kids.* Drawings and photos by Nelle Davis. New York: Knopf. 1991.

Murphy, Clare R. *Friendship Across Arctic Waters: Alaskan Cub Scouts Visit Their Soviet Neighbors.* New York: Dutton Child Books. 1991.

Naidoo, Beverly. *Journey to Jo'burg.* Illustrated by Eric Velasquez. New York: Harpercollins. 1986.

Schlein, Miriam. *The Year of the Panda.* Illustrated by Kam Mak. New York: HarperCollins. 1990.

Singer, Isaac B. *Power of Light.* New York: Avon. 1982.

Staples, Suzanne F. *Shabanu, Daughter of the Wind.* New York: Knopf. 1989.

Series

Carolrhoda. *The World's Children.*

Chelsea House. *Let's Visit Places and Peoples of the World.*

Children's Press. *Enchantment of the World, New True Books.*

Dillon. *Discovering Our Heritage.*

Franklin Watts. *Take a Trip, Countries of the World, Living Here, Families Around the World, Inside, Passport to...*

Gareth Stevens. *Children of the World.*

Lerner. *Visual Geography Series, Families the World Over, Count Your Ways Books, Latvia, Russia, Estonia: Then and Now.*

Silver Burdett. *Countries, People and Places.*

Teacher Books and Publications:

Bennett, Christine I. *Comprehensive Multicultural Education: Theory and Practice.* Second Edition. Boston: Allyn and Bacon. 1990.

Global Learning, Inc. *A Sustainable Development Curriculum Framework for World History and Cultures.* New Jersey. 1991.

Hanvey, Robert. *An Attainable Global Perspective.* New York: American Forum. 1976.

Kruse, Ginny M. & Horning, Kathleen T. *Multicultural Literature for Children and Young Adults: A Selected Listing of Books 1980-1990 By and About People of Color.* Third Edition. Madison: Wisconsin Department of Public Instruction. 1991.

Miller-Lachmann, Lyn. *Our Family, Our Friends, Our World: An Annotated Guide to Significant Multicultural Books for Children and Teenagers.* New Providence, New Jersey: RR Bowker. 1992.

Nieto, Sonia. *Affirming Diversity: The Sociopolitical Context of Multicultural Education.* New York: Longman. 1992.

Pytowska, Ewa, I. & Willett, Gail P. *Theme Centered Bibliography of Children's Literature: Books with Themes of Personal, Cultural, and Social Empowerment.* Cambridge, MA: Intercultural Training Resource Center and Savanna Books Company. 1987.

Rudman, Masha K. *Children's Literature: An Issues Approach.* Third Edition. New York: Longman. 1993.

Sinclair, Patti. *E for Environment: An Annotated Bibliography of Children's Books with Environmental Themes.* New Providence, NJ: R.R.Bowker. 1992.

Selby, David & Pike, Graham. *Global Learner, Global Teacher.* London: Hodder and Stoughton. 1988.

Publications

Access: Information on global, international, & foreign language education. New York: American Forum.

Book Links: Connecting Books, Libraries, and Classrooms. Chicago: Booklist Publications.

Rethinking Schools: An Urban Educational Journal. Milwaukee, WI

The New Advocate; For Those Involved With Young People and Their Literature. Boston: Christopher-Gordon Publishers, Inc.

11

The Family-School Partnership and Literature

Nancy Larrick

Let me tell you about Rosie, and then about Jonathan.

At fifteen months of age both children were enrolled by Gordon Wells of Bristol, England, as part of a longitudinal study of their language development through elementary school. Wells taped the oral language of thirty-two children at home with their parents and siblings and later at school with teachers and classmates. As writing skills were developed at school, children's stories were collected.

Samples of the children's written and oral language, along with informal commentary of observers, make a highly readable report, now published by Heinemann under the title *The Meaning Makers: Children Learning Language and Using Language to Learn* (1986).

By comparing the children's home experience with subsequent progress at school, Gordon Wells concludes that "it is growing up in a literate family environment in which reading and writing are natural occurring daily activities that gives children the particular advantage when they start formal education.[1]"

Rosie did not have such an environment.[2] She had never had a story read to her before entering school. Through elementary school, Rosie had increasing problems with oral language, reading and writing. At age two her language skills placed her slightly above average in the group. Within a year and a half Rosie had dropped to near the bottom. At age seven she was the poorest reader in the group. At age ten, she was at the very bottom in oral language, writing, reading, and overall achievement.

Mr. Wells reports:

> As far as we could tell, there was no deficiency in Rosie herself; what she lacked were the experiences necessary to nourish her intellectual and linguistic development. Perhaps the most serious deficiency in Rosie's experience, at least with respect to her subsequent progress at school, was the complete lack of stories.

Jonathan's record was very different.[3] On entering school he had had close to 6,000 book and story experiences. At age ten, Jonathan ranked number one in the group in oral language, reading, writing, and overall achievement. He spoke easily and well, wrote with unusual skill and humor, and read continuously.

As the only child of literate parents, Jonathan had enjoyed hundreds of read-aloud sessions where he was often the reader as well as an eager participant in book-related conversation. In contrast, Rosie said of her home life: "There's nothing to do when we're at home . . . only just sit . . . staring at the telly . . . or help mum wash up . . . and that's all, I think."[4]

Rosie and Jonathan are not unique. Almost every class includes at least one Jonathan and one Rosie, with the experience of the other children ranging between these extremes. Numerous research studies make it clear that each child's in-school progress in oral language, writing, and reading reflects his or her language experiences at home.

One of the great challenges, and great opportunities, that a teacher faces is to encourage the strong support of parents in providing home experiences that will enable children's language skills to flourish. Parents can do wonders that are often beyond the range of the teacher's influence.

Usually parents have the dominant role during a child's early years, sometimes called the "peak language learning years." So parents have the opportunity to lay the groundwork, to set the pattern for listening and talking, observing, and questioning. They are with the child for longer periods of time than any teacher and thus have the opportunity to know the child more intimately. Through the years, family activities can easily and naturally contribute to rich language experiences for the child.

Yet, as I meet with parents, I find few who realize the importance of their influence on their child's interest in reading and progress in reading at school. Many parents would like to help but do not know how. Others assume that reading is for the teacher to take care of and leave it at that.

There are hundreds of ways in which parents can give positive support to their children's reading in the warm, informal atmosphere of parent-child activities. As I talk to parents, I try to focus on three big areas of activity within the reach of almost any family:

1. Encourage the child's facility with oral language.
2. Read aloud to the child each day.
3. Provide rich experiences to broaden the child's vocabulary and understanding.

Facility with Oral Language

This comes first because it should begin in infancy when the baby hears songs, stories, and conversation directed to him even before he can participate with words himself. Hearing oral language, echoing repeated lines, then initiating words and phrases are the ideal preparation for meeting language in print later on.

The words a child hears again and again are the ones he picks up to use on his own. If he has heard lullabies and nursery rhymes and is encouraged to chime in on repeated lines and phrases, he knows such words as *hush-a-by, treetop, cradle, kittens, mittens, London Bridge, falling down, spider, pail of water, up a hill, king's horsemen, hot cross buns,* and more. The words he hears and uses are the ones he finds easy to recognize and read later on.

It is said that a child with this kind of oral language experience may have a vocabulary of 32,000 words on entering school. Sitting next to him or her may be a child of the same age who knows only 4,000 words. As reading lessons begin, the high-vocabulary child is eager and ready to face words in print because he or she knows many of them by ear. Soon he or she can read and talk about the ideas they convey.

The low-vocabulary child cannot keep up unless he or she has extra help. Indeed, the gap between the two children may widen as they move through the grades. This is what happened with Rosie and Jonathan: Rosie's rank in the group went down, down, down, while Jonathan's went up.

The positive effect of a child's facility with oral language has been convincingly documented through many research studies. One of the most impressive is the Verbal Interaction Project, which has been underway for more than twenty years in Nassau County, New York, under the direction of Dr. Phyllis Levenstein.[5] In this project, now referred to as the "Mother-Child Home Program," selected two-year-olds and one parent of each are enrolled for twice-a-week home visits by trained teacher-demonstrators. On each visit the demonstrator shows the parent how to involve the child in play and conversation in a natural and interesting fashion.

Children who have had this language experience for two years have made an average gain of seventeen IQ points. Later they have adjusted well and have maintained a positive place in school. When a second child in the same family is enrolled in the program, his or her IQ gains an average of eight points greater than the first.

As we read the transcript of the conversation of a program-trained mother with her small child, we realize that she is giving a remarkable amount of information about the toy or book before them. She is encouraging the child to think imaginatively and to raise questions. As a result, her child does a great deal of the talking, thinking, and questioning.

The inexperienced mother seems to grope for words. Her comments lack the sparkle and curiosity of the program-trained mother. Not surprisingly, her child has little to say, raises few questions, and ventures few ideas. One can easily predict that this child, who has such limited facility with oral language, is likely to have difficulties at school unless his experience with oral language is broadened dramatically.

Parent's Check-List for Successful
Conversation with Preschoolers

1. Name the object (animal, person, food, flower, toy) that is the center of attention. "Here is a banana for our lunch."
2. Give the color, size, shape, or other distinguishing feature. "This is a yellow banana with brown spots."
3. Tell of action or movement. "Let's peel the banana and break off a small piece."
4. Raise questions requiring more than a yes-or-no answer. "Where did we get this banana?"
5. Suggest an imaginative use of the object. "Let's pretend to feed the banana to the teddy bear."
6. With words, smiles, gestures, give warm praise for the child's responses.
7. Reply to the child's vocalization, whether a question or not, *within three seconds.*

(Adapted from Check-List of the Verbal Interaction Project)

Although the Verbal Interaction Project focuses on preschool children, it documents a need that continues long after the toddler stage. Children who have met new words and meanings are eager for more. A five-year-old is proud to drop his baby word "doggie" and refer to his "golden retriever: ' By seven or eight, many a child speaks knowingly of *cholesterol, the wind chill factor, homogenized milk, a music synthesizer,* or *the Gaza strip.* He does, that is, if he has met the word or phrase and has made it his own in a meaningful situation.

Children who are frequently part of a stimulating conversation are ready to cope with provocative questions that demand more than yes-and-no answers. In time, they will learn to use the dictionary or encyclopedia for verification and possibly further information. They lap up the warm, approving comments of a partner in conversation. These are the children who become good readers.

What about the foreign-language family: the mother who speaks English haltingly? The grandmother who speaks only Spanish? Can they help? Of course, for as they sing their folk songs and tell their stories, they are introducing the children to the sounds and significance of language. When they join in singing the Puerto Rican folk song that begins *Dos y dos son cuatro,* they are learning about words and the meaning they have in combination. Eventually they can relate this experience to the same words in print and their equivalent in English. When the grandmother tells a folk tale from her childhood, she communicates the sequence of story that prevails in every language. Intellectually stimulating oral language helps to keep children thinking and questioning no matter what language is used.

Experiences of this kind lead directly and positively to success in reading. Every teacher provides some of this, but parents can do more because they have more time with the child, and their one-to-one relationship can be more nurturing.

Reading Aloud to the Child Each Day

If you grew up in a family where read-loud time was a part of every day's schedule, you can count yourself lucky. I certainly do, for some of my happiest memories of childhood relate to the time when my mother or father read to me. My father's specialty was the Brer Rabbit stories, which have lots of conversation among the animals whose sly wit and wisdom go straight to a child's heart.

I will always remember the sound effects created for the frogs' conversation.

"Jug-er-rum-kum-dum!" from one frog.

"Knee-deep! Knee-deep!" from another.

And finally, "Don't-you-ber-lieve-im! Don't-you-ber-lieve-im!" from old Brer Bull-Frog.

No one could read those bull-frog lines like my father, but again and again he brought me in to help out with the "Knee-deep!" or "Don't you ber-lieve-im!" My pride in accomplishment was boundless.

I am sure that part of my pleasure in the story of Brer Bull-Frog and his cronies came from my participation in reading the story. Nursery rhymes, old folk tales, and many modern stories and poems have lovely repetition that is perfect for two-part reading. Children participate eagerly.

One of the kindergarten favorites is "Henny Penny," the story of the little hen who sets out to tell the king that the sky is falling. On the way she meets Cocky-Locky, who asks to join her, then Ducky-Daddles and Goosey-Poosey and all the rest. Each time a new member is added, the ridiculous list of names is repeated. Children ask for this story again and again and are soon chanting the tongue-twisting roster with delight.

Or they may want to chime in on the words of story characters: the three little pigs with frightened squeaky voices and the grumbling wolf who is out to get them.

Those who have participated in two-part reading at this early level seem to be prepared later on to raise questions about the stories they hear and read: why characters speak and act as they do, what would have happened if something else had been said, how we might have behaved in that situation. These are questions with no right-or-wrong answers; questions to ponder, to enrich with experience. They are puzzle questions that stimulate thinking.

As children become independent readers, they still need the read-aloud sessions and enjoy taking their turn at reading, perhaps selecting a favorite poem to read or the chapter in a story too good to miss.

Eight and nine-year-olds make good bedtime readers for the two or three-year-olds. Fathers and grandfathers always seem to bring something special when they choose their favorites for family reading aloud.

One thing we have to remember is that today's children are accustomed to the trained voices of television. They welcome the sound-effect words and can often out-squeak or out-growl any adult reader. They like dramatic variation in the reader's tone of voice as the mood of the story changes. They welcome the gravelly voice of the ancient sea captain and the snarl of the Halloween witch sending shivers down their spines.

Like the rest of us, children become creatures of habit so it is important to establish a regular time for reading aloud. With preschoolers just before naptime may be the most convenient. With older children bedtime seems the perfect time to wind down, relax, and let story and poetry take over.

In many households, this may take a little planning to avoid the interruptions of television, telephone and queries that can be postponed. Children who have experienced the undivided attention of an adult recognize the delight of reading together and then talking about the ideas the story or poems suggest. It becomes a private time for questioning and pondering, time to become involved in the experiences and thinking of storybook characters. This is the kind of reading that leads to more reading.

Parents' Check-List for Successful Read-Aloud Times at Home

1. Start singing, storytelling, and reading aloud in cradle and playpen days.
2. Read aloud at least fifteen minutes each day. Read with feeling and enthusiasm so that the story or poem seems to come alive. Allow time for fun as well as more thoughtful talk.
3. As often as possible, bring the child in as a participant: echoing repeated lines, retelling part of the story, talking about the story and the illustrations, and, later on, reading a section aloud to the parent.
4. Provide appealing reading materials: books borrowed from the public library or purchased at the bookstore, book club membership in the child's name, children's magazines, books for Christmas and birthday presents. For help in finding the most appropriate books, consult the child's teacher, the school librarian, and the public librarian.
5. Visit the public library for book borrowing and special programs for children. Help the child get a library card in his own name.
6. Take time to talk about stories that have been read and information found in reference books, newspapers, and magazines.
7. Set an example as a reader. When the child sees you reading and learns of your pleasure in reading, he is apt to follow your example.

Providing Rich Experiences

Parents must recognize that reading is a two-way process with the reader bringing his or her experience to extend the meaning of the printed page. As Dr. Dolores Durkin puts it: "The more we know before we read, the more we know after we read."

On a very simple level, the child who has played in the snow brings that experience to the pictures and story of *The Snowy Day* (1962) by Ezra Jack Keats. He knows the feel of snow and how it looks on the branches of a tree. Experience makes it his story as well as Peter's. His background of information enriches text and pictures for him.

The three-year-old who has looked at the moon night after night and noted its changing shape is quick to follow the moon through her favorite picture book *Goodnight Moon* (1947) by Margaret Wise Brown.

Older children who have had a train ride or who have watched fishermen unload the day's catch on the dock have experiences that will give meaning to stories they hear or read. It is through the family that children can have the greatest opportunity to build the background of information that can someday enrich their reading.

As a beginning, it is important to help sharpen a child's powers of observation. Note the raindrops running down the window pane. Listen to the sound of rain on the roof and the splashing of cars as they dash through the puddles. Take time to go outside on a clear night and locate the Big Dipper or the Evening Star.

Neighborhood excursions offer a wealth of information provided there is time for questions, comparisons, and speculation: the super-market with exotic foods from all over the world, the florist shop and greenhouse with new plants to meet and know, the animal shelter with its appealing residents, the auto repair shop, the airport, the junkyard. Think of the conversation those scenes can generate! The new words! New places to find on the map! New distances to measure!

All contribute to the skills and habits of the good reader.

Making the Parent-Teacher Connection

For some families, the activities I have described may seem routine. But family patterns are changing. There are more one-parent homes today, more working mothers, more and more hours devoted to television by both children and adults. Often home reading is crowded out unless the teacher makes a direct personal connection to explain and encourage parent support for the child's reading.

I do not think this can be accomplished by an occasional mimeographed note from the teacher to the parent. The subject is too important, the need too great.

A face-to-face conference between parent and teacher may be difficult to arrange in some situations, but it is surely the most effective strategy. My first years of teaching were in a community where teachers were required to make at least one visit in the home of each child in the class. It was a tough assignment for this beginning teacher, I can assure you, but it proved very rewarding.

I soon learned that my role must be that of the diplomat asking for help, not the dictator giving orders. My purpose must be to establish a warm, friendly relationship.

As a starter, I often took out a snapshot of the child at work or play in the classroom. Sometimes I would bring a picture or story the child had created. I think every mother was pleased to have these gifts.

To strengthen my case for a daily read-aloud time at home, I usually brought a favorite library book the child had met at school and suggested that parent and child read it together some evening at home. Talking about read-aloud time often centered on that book—how to help the child search for picture details in a simple picturebook, how to draw him into echoing repeated lines or chorus, how he can change his voice tone for different storybook characters, and so on.

For some parents, the parent-teacher conference is a bit threatening when it takes place at school so they arrive feeling out of place and on the defensive. I found they began to relax if given a tour of the classroom to see projects underway, meet classroom pets, and sample library books on display. In some schools each child is invited to come with his parent so he can serve as guide, pointing out favorite books, his artwork or construction project, and perhaps pointing out the reference books he is learning to use.

Foreign-language parents welcome an interpreter—either the child, if his language skills are equal to it, or someone from the school staff trained as an interpreter. One elementary school in Toronto with a large Hispanic enrollment has interpreters on hand at every parent open house or PTA meeting.

The public schools of Alexandria, Virginia, have established a Parent Resources Center to help parents of children who are not performing well. The center will teach parents how to help their children improve reading and communication skills. Two parent coordinators visit in the homes of children who seem to need help, encouraging parental support. Activities, newsletters, and announcements from the Center are in English and Spanish.

In some communities the Chapter One parent workshops have become so popular that they have been extended to all parents. Being part of a group seems to give courage to the shy parents and comfort to those who find others have similar questions and frustrations.

Since 1971 the Public Library of Orlando, Florida, has offered workshops in "Sharing Literature with Children."[6] By this time over 30,000 adults and teenagers have participated, learning how to select books for children, how to read aloud to them, how to explore pictures with children, and how to bring the child in as an active participant.

Knowing that many parents are uncomfortable in the formal setting of the central library, the project director offers to come with books and materials to any location that workshop participants select. "Get together six people who are interested," she says, "and we will meet you at the place of your choice." So workshops have been held in church basements and firehalls as well as crowded project apartments.

In 1981 I spent two weeks in Singapore meeting with teachers, librarians, publishers, booksellers, reading specialists, and some parents. On several occasions I spoke of the importance of recruiting parents as partners in children's reading and told of the Orlando Public Library Project among others But the Singaporeans were sure such programs would not work for them. Too many parents had limited facility with English or were too busy to read to their children. Children had too much homework. I felt my message was not heard.

But the next year Singapore set aside September as National Reading Month with the advertised theme: "Read with your child." The Singapore Teachers Union and the National Library organized workshops on storytelling and book selection. The Women's Section of the National Trade Unions Congress sponsored workshops at several of the day-care centers.

From Orlando, Florida, to Singapore, there is a great outreach to recruit parents as partners in children's reading.

Parent education projects show tremendous variation and range. One teacher may set up a workshop for half a dozen parents of children in her class, or there might be a schoolwide, even citywide, drive to bring parents into workshops that will contribute to their children's love of reading.

I have been with many groups of these parents, and I can report that their enthusiasm is contagious. They are meeting exciting children's books for the first time, books that they enjoy almost as much as the children. They see how happily the children respond to storytelling and read-aloud sessions.

They see that reading can become a vibrant experience for the child, an experience that parents can contribute to and enjoy as well.

I am convinced that parents are ready and children are ready whenever we are willing to make the imaginative outreach to bring them together for the joys of reading.

References

1. Wells, Gordon. *The Meaning Makers: Children Learning Language and Using Language to Learn.* Portsmouth, NH: Heinemann Educational Books, Inc., 1986, p. 194.
2. *Ibid.* Chart, p. 167; pp. 169-171
3. *Ibid.* Chart, p. 167; pp. 181-185.
4. *Ibid.* p. 171.
5. Levenstein, Phyllis. Messages from Home: *The Mother-Child Home* Program and the Prevention of School Disadvantage. Columbus, OH: Ohio State University Press, 1988.
6. Children's Department, Orlando Public Library, Ten North Rosalind, Orlando, Florida 32801.

Prospects and Perils:
A Final Word

The Good, the True,
and the Beautiful

Julius Lester

In 1978 novelist John Gardner published a small book called *On Moral Fiction.* It was met with a few tepid reviews, and for good reason. Gardner set forth a view of literature that is quite unfashionable.

He demonstrates much courage by daring to use the word "moral" for he risks the danger of guilt-by-association with reactionary forces in the country that are banning books from libraries and seeking to legislate personal behavior. However, not to use the word risks the even greater danger of allowing the vision of what it means to be human to be removed from our lives.

To talk about the moral is not to present a list of do's and don'ts but refers to the spirit we bring to our living and, by implication, to literature. If, in the presence of a person or a book, we feel ourselves mysteriously but unmistakably confirmed as human beings and we sense that life itself is being celebrated in this book or person, despite the threats of ecological disasters and nuclear annihilation, then we are in the presence of the moral.

John Gardner puts it this way:

> We recognize true art by its careful, thoroughly honest search for and analysis of values. It is not didactic because, instead of teaching by authority and force, it explores, open-mindedly, to learn what it should teach. It clarifies and confirms . . . moral art tests values and rouses trustworthy feelings about the better and the worse in human action.

Perhaps the key phrases are "thoroughly honest search" and "explores open-mindedly." But we are not accustomed to conceiving of the moral either as searching or exploring open-mindedly. This is not surprising because we do not encounter often human beings who search with care and thoroughness for values, who explore with open minds to learn what they should teach (even when walking along a street, we are teaching something about how to be in the world).

Let me explain more by talking briefly about my own career as a writer. Because I have published fiction for adults and children, poetry for adults and children, as well as essays and books ranging from politics to literature to history and religion, reviewers do not know how to classify me. Thus, the books written for young adult readers are reviewed as adult books or as children's books, with the reviewer protesting that if he found the book so meaningful, it proves that "special books for young readers [are] unnecessary." So wrote the reviewer of *To Be A Slave* (1986) and *Long Journey Home* (1972) in *The New York Review of Books*.

This seems to imply that a book meaningful to an adult is too good for children, which tells us something about the attitude of the literary establishment toward children's literature. It considers children's books somewhat lesser than, not as good as, "real literature" and if a children's book is as good, then it cannot be considered children's literature.

Children's literature is condescended to by the literati and deemed noteworthy only when a member of the literati writes a children's book. When that happens the book is praised, because it demonstrates the writer's versatility, showing that he or she can *even* write for children. However, professionals in children's literature almost invariably recognize that such books are simply lousy books. The only other occasions when children's books are recognized outside the field of children's literature are (1) when something seems to be controversial (e.g., the work of Judy Blume); and (2) when a book is deemed to be art (e.g., the work of Maurice Sendak).

The literary establishment never recognizes, however, that children's literature has its own *raison d'etre*. Just as the literary establishment does not quite know what to do with children's literature, the society does not quite know what to do with children. As my oldest daughter once asked me: "Is childhood just a preparation for being an adult?" By the same token, the prevailing view of the literary establishment is that people who write children's books do so to get practice to write a "real" book, or we tried to write a "real" book, failed, and took up children's books.

The truth is far simpler. We are in children's literature because we have some dim moral vision of what it means to be human that includes children, and that means the child within ourselves also.

That reviewer for *The New York Review of Books* who found two of my books so edifying that he resented their being written for children not only dishonors children but fails to recognize that children's literature offers a kind of moral space absent from "real literature."

Some years ago I had a book of short stories rejected by an editor because she preferred fiction that put extraordinary people into extraordinary situations to see what would happen.

We had an irreconcilable conflict. I like to put ordinary people into ordinary situations and watch what happens, because that is who we are—ordinary people living in the ordinary situations of family, school, work, and leisure. When my step-daughter came home from school once and said that her best friend would not speak to her any longer because she had a new best friend, that was an ordinary situation. However, because it was so ordinary a situation, it was not to be devalued or ignored; it was a situation so ordinary that it demanded my full attention.

This is why my own work in children's literature focuses on the lives of the ordinary people who are the bedrock of black history instead of the extraordinary ones historical writing has singled out. In 1964 when I went to Mississippi for the first time, it was to stand alone in a field and try to know what my slave foreparents felt standing there 150 years before. That was the genesis of *To Be A Slave, Long Journey Home,* and *This Strange New Feeling* (1985).

My confrontation with the editor mentioned before has led me to wonder if the only place I can publish fiction is children's literature, because it is the only literature that gives full attention to the ordinary. For that reason, it is moral.

The literature praised and beloved by the establishment, be it John Updike or Norman Mailer, almost invariably leaves me with a vision of humanity in which people do not endure "the slings and arrows" of a fortune becoming increasingly outrageous, that people do not muddle through the problems of love and family. Yet, most of us do muddle through with a battered and bent heroism, and, sometimes, we are even triumphant. Contemporary literature is immoral precisely because alienation, despair, and defeat are the norms. It is immoral precisely because it debases the ordinary.

John Gardner writes: "To worship the unique, the unaccountable and freaky, is—if we're consistent—to give up the right to say to our children, 'Be good.' "

We live in a time, however, when the unique, unaccountable, and freaky are worshipped. Witness the popularity of such a television show as "That's Incredible," which should be renamed "That's Stupid!" The real measure of the extent to which our society worships the unique, unaccountable, and freaky is the popularity of the *Guinness Book of*

World Records. It is as if we have become so disdainful and contemptuous of the ordinary that only through the outlandish do we experience ourselves as alive. There is something current in our culture compelling us to do anything, anything at all, so that we can stand above the ordinary for a single moment. The values represented by the *Guinness Book of World Records* and "That's Incredible" are far more immoral than anything The Moral Majority has denounced.

I wonder if we are coming to worship the unusual and freaky because we no longer know how to say to our children, "Be good," because we are losing all recognition of what good might be. If we adults lose all knowledge of and faith in the good, we lose the power to imbue our children with awe of the good, leaving them with no alternative but to seek a place in the *Guinness Book of World Records* instead of their place amidst what John Gardner, quoting Henry James, calls life's "buzzing, blooming confusion."

John Gardner writes:

> For the most part our artists do not struggle—as artists have traditionally struggled—toward a vision of how things ought to be or what has gone wrong; they do not provide us with the flicker of lightning that shows us where we are .... The good of humanity is left in the hands of politicians.

And if you really consider that the good of humanity is being left to the likes of George Bush, you may never sleep again.

Children's literature represents a particular kind of hope, because its audience—children—are not susceptible to literary tricks and sleights-of-hand. Children don't read reviews and therefore cannot be conned into believing that a bad book is a good one. Writing for children is especially demanding because as writers we must communicate the essence of whatever we are writing about. Children are not that concerned with nor get that excited about a well-turned phrase or a stunning metaphor. These must be present in the writing, but not as things-in-themselves to be acclaimed. All the tricks-of-the-trade we as writers must know must be used in the service of essence, that is, the truth of whatever experience we are conveying. In other words, children demand that the tale be moral.

"The true artist," Gardner writes, "is the one who can distinguish between conventional morality and that morality which tends to work for all people through the ages." One of the more dismal facts of our time may be that education has become a process that takes children away from "that morality which tends to work for all people through the ages" and substitutes a conventional and arid morality that governs and restricts behavior while stultifying all awareness and love of life's "buzzing and blooming confusion."

I make this assertion on the basis of what is acknowledged as the universal children's literature—folktales. Folktales know no national boundaries or cultural constraints., They represent the timeless morality that works throughout the ages. The ultimate irony is that while our society places folktales into the category of children's literature, in traditional societies (i.e., those societies which created the tales), the tales are not children's literature at all. They represent the literature of the society itself. It is the literature in which the people find what they need to know to be human. It is precisely this kind of literature the Updikes and Mailers and Styrons do not provide.

Children's literature has done this in the past, though I wonder if it is not developing its own literary ethos now that it has discovered that contemporary problems like divorce, homosexuality, drugs, and the like, are proper for children's literature.

Maybe over time, however, this will break down the artificial barrier between children's literature and adult literature, and we will recognize what traditional societies already know—there is only literature, and the concern of that literature is to discover and rediscover in each generation "what is necessary to humanness," as John Gardner phrased it.

Having talked so much about moral fiction, it is only fair if I close with an example of it. I would like to share with you an African tale that my wife and I have rewritten. It is a tale from the Baila people of Zambia which they call "The Child and the Eagle." My wife and I have renamed it "The Man Who Knew Too Much."

And the Old Man began . . .
"A woman had a child."

He stopped and looked at the boys sitting on the ground in a semicircle before him. "A woman had a child," he repeated and smiled. "The simple events are not simple. The rising and setting of the sun. The wind. The rain. The beating of our hearts and the breath in our bodies. A woman had a child. A woman carried life within her and at the appointed time, it came forth. Creation was renewed."

His words were a mystery to the boys, which was as he wanted it. Living could not be found in the realm of understanding alone.

"One day the woman went to work in the fields. She carried her child in a sling on her breasts. As she began hoeing, the child awoke and started to cry. The woman stopped, sat down in the shade of a nearby tree, and nursed it. The child was soon asleep and the woman laid it in the shade and returned to her work.

"She had scarcely resumed working when the child awoke and started crying. The woman was annoyed. She had a lot of work to do and how could she work if the child wouldn't sleep. She sighed, put down the hoe, and started toward the child."

"Suddenly, a large eagle came out of the sky. The flapping of its wings was like the sound of distant thunder as the eagle flew toward the child and landed on it. The mother watched, and her heart swelled and hurt with terror."

"The eagles of our land are mighty birds. They are so strong they easily kill and eat monkeys, jackals, and small antelope. The woman looked at the bird sitting with its sharp talons on her child, the eagle's wings moving slowly up and down like storm clouds gathering during rainy season. The baby made no sound now, and the woman knew that the eagle had torn out its heart already. Terror was so great within her that her body became hard with strength, and grabbing her hoe, she ran toward the eagle, her heart pounding like the feet of elephants in stampede. The eagle lifted its wings and flew away."

"But when the woman reached the child and looked at him, he was sleeping peacefully, and though the woman looked closely, she found no scratches on his body."

"She stood slowly, looking at the sky into which it seemed the eagle had vanished. She didn't know what to think. Had she scared the eagle away before it could kill her baby? But the eagle's talons should have left deep cuts on the child's chest. Yet, there were none and her baby slept where before he had cried."

"'It's a marvel!' she whispered."

"For the rest of the day the child slept peacefully, and she got much work done. That evening she returned to the village and her home, eager to tell her husband of the marvel she'd witnessed that day. But she said nothing. How could she tell her husband that an eagle had comforted their child? He would think she had stayed in the sun too long."

"She needed time to be alone with the wonder of what she had seen. Sometimes, we must guard what is within us, refusing to share it even with our best friend. There are those things which are ours alone, and it is as much love not to share as it is to share."

The Old Man smiled to himself, knowing the boys understood this. How many of them had secret lives in which eagles stopped their sobbing and lions spread their manes as pillows to sleep on?

"The next morning," the Old Man continued, "the woman returned to the fields with her son. The same thing occurred. She lay the child in the shade of the tree. It awoke, crying. The woman waited, and yes, the eagle came, alighted on the child, and moving its wings up and down slowly, comforted the child until it was soon asleep. When the woman went to examine the child, the eagle flew away, leaving the child unscratched."

" 'What a wondrous thing!' the woman exclaimed. 'I must tell my husband.' And she picked up the baby and ran to the village."

"When she told her husband what had happened, he was scornful: 'Have you been in the sun too long, woman? Either that, or you've gone crazy. I've seen eagles kill antelope big enough to feed us for a week. You've gone crazy!' "

"'I know what I saw,' the woman insisted."

"The husband laughed. 'Maybe you fell asleep with the baby and saw this eagle with your night-eyes.' "

"The woman was angry now and told her husband to come to the field and see for himself."

The Old Man sighed. "The woman should have known that sometimes we are privileged to witness great wonders, and it is natural to want to share them with those we love. But if they reject what we say, sharing is impossible. If that happens, we should feel sorry for our loved ones who know so much that they kill wonder. A wonder can never be proved. It is there, alive as the fire in the sun, for those who know what they don't know. The woman, however, challenged her husband to come to the field with her and then they would see who was a liar. Although the husband did not believe in this eagle, he picked up his bow and arrows and followed her and on reaching the field, hid in some bushes at its edge."

"The child, awake and crying now, was laid beneath the tree by his mother and as soon as she was in the field hoeing, the eagle came out of the sky and alighted on the child. The man saw in horror and remembered how he had seen the spear-like talons of eagles rip flesh from jackals, how their beaks, like knives, tore the throats of antelope, causing the blood to gush forth hot like sand. And seeing the eagle sitting on his son, he strung his bow with an arrow and pulling the bow with all his strength, he let the arrow go. And as he watched its swift, silent flight, he saw the eagle fly up at the last instant and the arrow sank with a soft sound into the body of his son, killing him."

"The eagle, seeing what had happened, flew at the man, cursing him, saying:

'Now is kindness among people at an end, because you killed your child. Beginning now and forevermore, people shall kill each other.' "

"And that is how murder came into the world. The man knew too much, because he thought he knew what he had never seen and never experienced. Remember this, you who are about to become men. Remember this."

Literature should provide us with that "flicker of lightning that shows us where we are" while at the same time helping us struggle "toward a vision of how things ought to be."

This is the function of literature, if it is to be worthy of the good, the true and the beautiful within us.

(This was originally presented as a talk to the Perspectives in Children's Literature Conference at the University of Massachusetts in Spring, 1982.)

Index of Authors, Illustrators, and Titles